ROYAL HISTORICAL SOCIETY

STUDIES IN HISTORY

New Series

THE LOCAL CHURCH
AND GENERATIONAL CHANGE
IN BIRMINGHAM
1945–2000

THE LOCAL CHURCH
AND GENERATIONAL CHANGE
IN BIRMINGHAM
1945–2000

Ian Jones

THE ROYAL HISTORICAL SOCIETY
THE BOYDELL PRESS

First published 2012

A Royal Historical Society publication
Published by The Boydell Press
an imprint of Boydell & Brewer Ltd
PO Box 9, Woodbridge, Suffolk IP12 3DF, UK
and of Boydell & Brewer Inc.
668 Mt Hope Avenue, Rochester, NY 14620–2731, USA
website: www.boydellandbrewer.com

ISBN 978–0–86193–317–4

ISSN 0269–2244

A CIP catalogue record for this book is available
from the British Library

The publisher has no responsibility for the continued existence or accuracy of
URLs for external or third-party internet websites referred to in this book,
and does not guarantee that any content on such websites is,
or will remain, accurate or appropriate.

Papers used by Boydell & Brewer Ltd are natural, recyclable products
made from wood grown in sustainable forests

Printed and bound in Great Britain by
CPI Group (UK) Ltd, Croydon, CR0 4YY

Contents

List of Figures and Tables

Acknowledgements

This book has been a long time in the making. Its origins lie in a gap year spent as a volunteer youth and children's worker with a group of churches in the north of England in 1994–5. The unfamiliarity of the church and city context, and my general lack of life experience, made the year a steep learning curve. Most challenging of all was the clash of aspirations that I found between the group of teenagers with whom I worked – wanting to belong to the church but uncomfortable with its assumptions about youth and with many of its cultural forms – and older, long-standing church members who desperately wanted to welcome teenagers to church but felt frustrated at their reluctance to embrace cherished patterns of worship and church life. How and why had such different expectations of church and attitudes to wider culture developed? Listening more closely, I began to consider whether the kinds of assumptions and life experiences developed in youth and young adulthood were critical to these different perspectives. As a history graduate, I looked for historical studies which might help to contextualise these individual life experiences. I read several fine studies, but each one concentrated heavily on national movements, bishops, academic theologians, councils and synods, to the almost complete exclusion of changes in local congregational life. Several questions about the changing character of local congregational life, the experiences of successive generations of churchgoers, and their attitudes to wider social change therefore remained unanswered. Attempting to reconstruct the recent history of Christianity 'from below' eventually led me into research into popular postwar Christianity. For a while, the question of generational change which inspired me to start reading disappeared from view as I sought to get to grips with defining a research topic and reviewing the relevant literature. However, amidst a series of oral history interviews with members of seven case study congregations across the city, themes of age and generation began to emerge once again. That I began to pursue these questions more intentionally is in no small part due to Professor Hugh McLeod, who encouraged me to take such questions seriously and to pursue their relevance to wider debates over secularisation and religious change. Whether I have achieved this adequately in the present book is left to the reader to judge, but it seems right here to record my debt of gratitude for Hugh's wise support throughout the research for this book, and on many occasions since.

The book itself has been eleven years in the making (a fact for which I feel somewhat apologetic), having largely been written in such gaps as work and family circumstances have allowed. As well as thanking those who have finally helped it come to fruition, I also want to reiterate my thanks to the people who were there at the beginning. First, I continue to be grateful to the people of the seven churches across the city of Birmingham who allowed me to spend time with each of them, observing and participating in church life and hearing their life stories. I still count some of those occasions as amongst the most meaningfully human moments of my life, and I am grateful for the trust that I was shown in being allowed to listen. I sincerely hope that this book has been faithful to their testimony. I would like to thank the British Academy for the postgraduate studentship which made the initial research possible, and to members of the University of Birmingham's history of religion seminar who offered such a stimulating and hospitable scholarly community during that time. I would like to thank the staff of Birmingham City Archives (where a substantial part of the primary documentary research was undertaken), and also staff at the Birmingham Archdiocesan Archives, the Church of England Records Centre in Bermondsey and the Special Collections at the John Rylands University Library, Manchester. I am also grateful to the Lincoln Theological Institute for the Study of Religion and Society, University of Manchester, for my one brief period of dedicated week-day writing time on this book during 2005–6.

I am also grateful to friends and colleagues who have discussed aspects of the book with me over the last ten years, or commented on material in it. Amongst these I must particularly thank Hugh McLeod, Peter Webster and Robert Jones for reading draft chapters. The collaborative research on church music that Peter and I have undertaken over several years has been not only immensely enjoyable but also a significant influence on some of the ideas presented in this book. My thanks also go to Martin Stringer, Gordon Lynch, Clive Field, Stephen Parker, Leslie Francis and Jeremy Gregory for conversations on themes in this book. Alana Harris and Andrew Perry were kind enough to share their recent unpublished theses with me. I particularly wish to thank Arthur Burns for his patience and wisdom as my consultative editor on behalf of the Royal Historical Society. As a result of the robust yet fair feedback that he offered, this is undoubtedly a better – and more streamlined – book than it would otherwise have been. Errors and omissions of course remain my own. My thanks also go to Christine Linehan for her patience and dedication in the copy-editing stages and to Rohais Haughton. I am grateful to Catherine d'Alton for the splendid map, and to Wulf Forrester-Barker for proof-reading the manuscript. I would like to thank my Mum and Dad, Pam and Martin Jones, for supporting me in so many ways. Above all, this book is dedicated to my wife, Alison, for her love, support and encouragement throughout the writing process, and to our children Ben and Noah – two of the next generation whose story is only just beginning.

Ian Jones,
January 2012

Abbreviations

BAA	Birmingham Archdiocesan Archives
AC	*Ad clerum* letters
AP	Archbishops' papers
DP	Diocesan papers
BCA	Birmingham City Archives
BCL	Birmingham City Library
CERC	Church of England Records Centre, Bermondsey
GBC	Grenfell Baptist Church
JRUL	John Rylands University Library, Manchester
QC	Questionnaire for Congregations
SCH	Studies in Church History
UBISWRA	University of Birmingham Institute for the Study of Worship and Religious Architecture
URC	United Reformed Church
ASR	*American Sociological Review*
BDL	*Birmingham diocesan leaflet*
BJS	*British Journal of Sociology*
BP	*Birmingham Post*
CLJ	*Carrs Lane Journal*
GBCN	*Grenfell Baptist Church Newsletter*
HJ	*Historical Journal*
HSBCN	*Heneage Street Baptist Church Newsletter*
JBS	*Journal of British Studies*
JEH	*Journal of Ecclesiastical History*
JHI	*Journal of the History of Ideas*
JRH	*Journal of Religious History*
JSSR	*Journal for the Scientific Study of Religion*
KNPM	*Kings Norton Parish Magazine*
OCD	*Official Catholic directory of the archdiocese of Birmingham*
OH	*Oral History*
P&P	*Past and Present*
SACPM	*St Agnes Cotteridge Parish Magazine*
SBBPM	*St Bede's Brandwood Parish Magazine*
SGEPM	*St George's Edgbaston Parish Magazine*
TCBH	*Twentieth Century British History*
UKCH	P. Brierley and V. Hiscock (eds), *The UK Christian handbook, 1994/5*, London 1993
WMBAY	*West Midlands Baptist Association Yearbook, 1946*

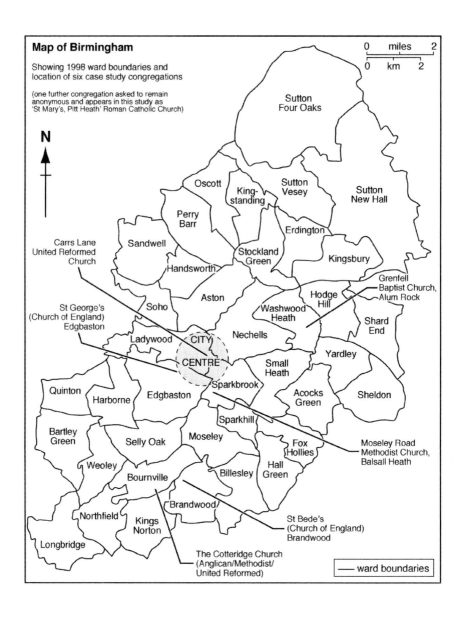

Map of Birmingham

Showing 1998 ward boundaries and
location of six case study congregations

(one further congregation asked to remain
anonymous and appears in this study as
'St Mary's, Pitt Heath' Roman Catholic Church)

N

0   miles   2
0   km   2

Sutton
Four Oaks

Oscott

King-
standing

Sutton
Vesey

Sutton
New Hall

Perry
Barr

Erdington

Carrs Lane
United Reformed
Church

Sandwell

Stockland
Green

Kingsbury

Handsworth

Grenfell
Baptist Church,
Alum Rock

Aston

Hodge
Hill

St George's
(Church of England)
Edgbaston

Soho

Washwood
Heath

Shard
End

Ladywood

CITY
CENTRE

Nechells

Yardley

Small
Heath

Sparkbrook

Quinton

Harborne

Edgbaston

Acocks
Green

Sheldon

Sparkhill

Bartley
Green

Selly Oak

Moseley

Moseley Road
Methodist Church,
Balsall Heath

Fox
Hollies

Weoley

Billesley

Hall
Green

Bournville

Brandwood

Northfield

Kings
Norton

St Bede's
(Church of England)
Brandwood

Longbridge

The Cotteridge Church
(Anglican/Methodist/
United Reformed)

—— ward boundaries

Introduction

In January 1968 the bishop of Birmingham, Leonard Wilson, wrote in his diocesan newsletter of the fresh ideas sweeping English society in the preceding years. Discernment was crucial, he argued, but a wholesale rejection of change risked quenching the Spirit of God at work in the world. Special wisdom was needed regarding relations between young and old:

> The problems of communication between the different generations ... which exercise the minds of thoughtful people today, will always remain.... When we want to understand the people of other countries we know we must learn their language, and between the generations there is also a different language. We may not like that new language, but if we are to understand people we must be ready and even eager to learn it.[1]

The bishop's words were powerfully emblematic of the way in which, by the 1960s, relations between young and old had become a hotly-debated social question. Youth was frequently identified with new social and political agendas that gave short shrift to authorities and institutions – including organised religion. The assertive self-confidence of youth – expressed in myriad ways from student protests to gang violence – was widely discussed in politics, the arts and media. 'Teenagers' (a comparatively recent coinage[2]) were increasingly conspicuous as consumers and the fashions and tastes that they adopted were often consciously distinct from those of their parents. For themselves, adult observers often spoke of a 'generation gap' and anxiously discussed its causes. Was teenage rebellion a praiseworthy revolt against convention, or a lamentable symptom of national decline? If the latter, were young people themselves to blame, or did responsibility lie with older adults for failing to provide appropriate guidance to the rising generation? Such debates also occurred within the Christian Churches. When formal religious adherence began to fall sharply in the late 1950s, there was particular evidence of decline amongst the young. Young people also numbered heavily amongst those within the Churches insisting that 'the church should move with the times'. For some commentators, such patterns were but the most obvious manifestations of a wider 'generational shift' in the religious life of the nation.[3]

---

[1] *BDL* (Mar. 1968).
[2] 'Teenager' originates from the USA in the mid-1940s, 'generation gap' from the late 1950s, though first recorded in 1964: R. Williams, *Keywords: a vocabulary of culture and society*, London 1983 edn, 141; B. Osgerby, *Youth in Britain since 1945*, Oxford 1998, 33–5.
[3] The phrase 'generational shift' derives from G. Davie, *Religion in Britain since 1945*,

1

The question of how, why and how far such a 'generational shift' took place stands at the heart of this study of local church life in Birmingham after the Second World War. Drawing on oral history, documentary sources and social research methods, it explores the lived experience of active lay Christians and their clergy in a period synonymous with far-reaching cultural change. In the second half of the twentieth century, much of the contingent and the carefully-cultivated which had become cherished as Christian tradition was challenged by new ideas and cultural styles emerging both within and outside the Church. Some bishops and theologians asked grass-roots Christians to abandon existing conceptions of God; new styles of liturgy and music brought fresh and sometimes startling sounds into Sunday worship; numerical decline and the cultural marginalisation of Christianity prompted extensive, sometimes profound, reappraisal of existing patterns of congregational life and ministry and of the most appropriate ways to nurture faith amongst fresh generations.

Rather than exploring these changes through the eyes of church leaders, councils, synods and national religious movements, this book seeks to understand the history of postwar English Christianity 'from below', from the perspective of the men and women who comprised local congregations and those who led them. This constitutes one of the study's chief claims to originality: despite the welcome attentiveness to matters of self-identity, everyday life and leisure and popular culture in recent accounts of the period, there are as yet almost no historical studies of popular, church-based Christianity in postwar England. One honourable exception, Richard Sykes's study of the Black Country, ends in the 1960s.[4] As Simon Green has noted, the history of the Christian Churches has too often been ignored by historians (including some historians of religion) who have supposed that there is very little to write about.[5] However, far from being hermetically sealed enclaves, local churches were 'connected communities' (in Nancy Ammerman's phrase[6]), shaping and shaped by wider developments, often consciously reflecting upon them as they sought to discern their identity and calling within a society increasingly perceived to be hostile or indifferent to Christianity. Moreover, while important aspects of the interior lives of local congregations are considered, this book also explores churchgoers' perceptions of wider changes taking place within postwar English society. Even at the end of the twentieth century at least a tenth of English people attended church

Oxford 1994, 121–7, although a generation gap in religious practice was also identified by contemporary commentators.

[4] R. Sykes, 'Popular religion in decline: a study from the Black Country', *JEH* lvi (2005), 287–307.

[5] S. J. D. Green, *The passing of Protestant England: secularisation and social change* c. 1920–1960, Cambridge 2011, 5.

[6] N. T. Ammerman with A. E. Farnsley and others, *Congregation and community*, New Brunswick, NJ 1997, 360–2.

monthly or more frequently, constituting a diverse but significant proportion of the population whose lives and opinions offer rich evidence for the ways in which the changing landscape of postwar Britain was inhabited and interpreted. In Birmingham, local churchgoers saw slums cleared and vast new housing estates erected around the edges of the conurbation. They witnessed the birth of a multi-cultural society as migrants from the Caribbean, South Asia and Africa arrived in the city in their tens of thousands. They discussed the impact of television, pop music and changing sexual attitudes, their hopes and fears for their children, parents and grandchildren at a time when the apparent speed of social change created greatly different challenges and opportunities for successive generations.

This last theme constitutes the central thread of this book. The study of generations in history is by no means new but has received renewed attention from historians and sociologists in recent years – including from those seeking to understand secularisation and religious change.[7] However, whilst the 'generation gap' has long been part of the iconography of the 1960s, we still understand comparatively little about the shape and meaning of age-related and generational identity in specific cultural contexts and communities in the period. Here, the cultural and religious significance of age is explored within the specific, grass-roots experience of the Christian Churches, and through this, this study seeks to demonstrate the importance of the 'generation' as a conceptual tool for unlocking some key aspects of religious change in postwar Britain which would otherwise remain concealed. This is a bold claim, since many scholars have found the 'generation' too fuzzy a concept to be useful in historical analysis. Taking those difficulties seriously, this book nevertheless seeks to delineate precisely how the concept of generations is (and is not) to be deployed, arguing in particular for an understanding of the term which is dialectical, multi-layered, culturally-constructed rather than imagining pre-given 'generations' in history, and linked only in certain specific respects to birth cohort. First, however, it is important to set the scene, outlining some of the key religious contours of postwar English society, surveying the current state of scholarly debate about the nature of secularisation and religious change, and through this explaining why historians and sociologists of religion have found questions of age, generation and religion increasingly difficult to ignore.

Interpreting secularisation and cultural change

When assessing the religious temperature of postwar English society, many general historical accounts begin with secularisation. Many also end there, making occasional reference to marginal, deviant or declining forms of reli-

---

7 For some significant studies see nn. 48, 51–8 below.

gion but otherwise assuming its irrelevance for wider society.[8] However, several recent studies have suggested that religion remained more significant within English society – and for longer – than traditionally thought. To contextualise what follows, it is thus helpful to begin by considering to what extent postwar England was a 'secular' society (and in particular here, one shaped by Christian norms and values). Amongst many possible definitions of 'secularisation', one of the most sophisticated is offered by Hugh McLeod, who defines secularisation as a process whereby religion loses its significance in: (1.) individual belief; (2) the decline of formal religious practice; (3) public life; (4) public debate; (5) personal and collective identity; and (6) popular culture.[9] Most specialist historians and sociologists of religion agree that a measure of secularisation occurred in postwar English society, but that the extent of change differed (some say considerably) across the six areas that McLeod identifies. Moreover, the causes of secularisation and its inevitability – are hotly debated.

First, to consider individual belief and formal religious practice. Both the percentages of the population claiming belief in God and describing themselves as Christian declined only a little over the 1945–2000 period (the former hovering around two-thirds to three-quarters of the population[10]). However, formal indicators of religious adherence fell sharply, particularly in the last three decades of the twentieth century. Regarding Christianity in particular, perhaps a fifth to a quarter of the population attended church weekly at the beginning of the postwar period (precise figures are hard to come by), falling to 11.7 per cent by 1979 and 6.3 per cent by 2005.[11] Over the long term, patterns of churchgoing have been uneven: a period of strong growth in the late eighteenth/early nineteenth centuries was followed by a decline in the proportion of churchgoers within the total population from the 1880s. Nevertheless, certain indices of affiliation – such as the proportion of baptised Anglicans – continued to rise into the mid-twentieth century. In the early 1950s three-quarters of adults over thirty had attended Sunday school during their childhood, and at least a third of fourteen-year-olds still attended.[12] Even the decline in church attendance remained gradual and uneven until the late 1950s, only declining more sharply thereafter. Certain developments bucked the trend. Non-denominational Evangelical

[8] For a critique of such an approach see J. Cox, 'Master-narratives of long-term religious change', in H. McLeod and W. Ustorf (eds), *The decline of Christendom in western Europe, 1750–2000*, Cambridge 2003, 201–17 at p. 201.

[9] H. McLeod, *Secularisation in western Europe, 1850–1914*, Basingstoke 2000, 285–6.

[10] Mass Observation, *Puzzled people: a study in attitudes to religion, ethics, progress and politics in a London borough*, London 1947, 21; G. Davie, *Europe: the exceptional case: parameters of faith in the modern world*, London 2002, 7; Davie, *Religion in Britain*, 78; R. Gill, *The myth of the empty church*, London 1993, 202–3.

[11] P. W. Brierley, *Pulling out of the nosedive: a contemporary picture of churchgoing: what the 2005 English church census reveals*, London 2006, 12.

[12] C. G. Brown, *Religion and society in twentieth century Britain*, Harlow 2006, 279.

'house churches' grew rapidly from the 1960s onwards, accounting for more than 6 per cent of all attendances by 2005.[13] Numerical decline in Christian affiliation was also partially stemmed by migration from the Caribbean and subsequently elsewhere (notably Africa), boosting the historic Churches, importing new denominations and establishing new independent Churches. By the new millennium, almost one in six Christian worshippers in England was Black or Asian.[14]

Migration from South Asia, East Africa and beyond also brought large Muslim, Hindu and Sikh populations into British society. The combined effect of these new Christian and other faith communities was a higher level of religious practice in many urban areas than existed fifty years previously.[15] Significant growth also occurred in what Paul Heelas and Linda Woodhead have termed the 'holistic milieu'; an eclectic range of spiritual practices encompassing the 'new age', Celtic spirituality, alternative healing and therapies and various strands of mystic and pagan practice. Whilst the growth of alternatives to Christianity did not outweigh the decline in church participation[16] and the diversity of faith and practice made it difficult to speak of a 'faith constituency' in any homogenous sense, the actively devout and/or spiritual continued to constitute a significant minority of the population to the end of the century. Moreover, as this study seeks to demonstrate, far from merely surviving as a set of existing traditions and practices, Christianity remained (even in its weakened state) capable of generating a plethora of new ideas, movements and expressions; some in response to wider social change, others anticipating it.

Numerical strength does not, of course, necessarily signify cultural significance. The later twentieth century witnessed a general waning of religious influence in both public life and public debate (McLeod's third and fourth dimensions of secularisation), albeit that more recently historians have reassessed the timing and permanence of that development. Early secularisation theorists suggested that the Churches were already a spent force in public life by the turn of the twentieth century.[17] Certainly, as Frank Prochaska has noted, the century saw a greatly reduced role for Christian institutions in education, health and welfare.[18] The reduced public role of religion was also

---

[13] These figures are based on attendances at 'New Churches' in 2005. The true figure is probably higher since some fellowships may have placed themselves in the categories 'Independent' (6%), 'Pentecostal' (9%) or 'Others' (3%): P. W. Brierley (ed.), *Religious trends 6*, London 2006, 12.2.

[14] Idem, *Nosedive*, 90.

[15] G. Smith, 'The unsecular city: the revival of religion in East London', in M. Northcott (ed.), *Urban theology: a reader*, London 1998, 329–38.

[16] P. Heelas and L. Woodhead, *The spiritual revolution: why religion is giving way to spirituality*, Oxford 2005, 127.

[17] For example, A.D. Gilbert, *The making of post-Christian Britain*, London 1980.

[18] F. Prochaska, *Christianity and social service in modern Britain*, Oxford 2006, especially chapters ii, iii, v.

evident, for example, in the BBC's abdication of an earlier Reithian commitment to Christianity as the national religion. However, Simon Green has recently suggested that it was the middle third of the twentieth century which witnessed the decisive eclipse of Christianity as a public force; for example, in the evaporation of religion as a party-political issue, or in a series of legislative defeats for the Protestant conscience (for instance, the historic precedent set by the Sunday Entertainments Act of 1932).[19] Despite this, as Matthew Grimley has argued, the rhetoric of Christian nationhood if anything increased in currency during the 1940s and 1950s (partly as a cultural buffer against the ideologies of hostile powers), only being largely discarded when the notion of a cohesive 'national community' itself began to be challenged in the postwar period.[20] Public figures in the 1980s and 1990s rarely invoked God or religious ethics with the same ease as their forebears, and at the end of the twentieth century Christianity was but one possibility in a society variously described as 'pluralist' or 'multicultural'.[21] Yet the challenges of accommodating a variety of religious and cultural sensibilities in fact meant that by the 1980s, religion was once again becoming a live public and political issue. The decision of successive governments in the 1990s and early 2000s to court the faith communities as potential partners in public service delivery also served partially to reverse the marginalisation of religion and the Churches in public life. All of this suggests that the study of postwar Christianity has considerable relevance to wider debates concerning the nature of postwar consensus culture and politics, and the relationship between the marginalisation of Christianity and the rise of a pluralist society.

Christianity also remained more influential than historians have previously thought in shaping popular culture, personal and collective identities (McLeod's fifth and sixth dimensions of secularisation). With religious and voluntary organisations traditionally perceived to be in crisis by the late nineteenth century,[22] the Churches' role in urban communities in the twentieth century has often been overlooked. However, Sarah Williams has argued that, well into the twentieth century, Christianity and the Churches provided influential resources for the construction of meaning and identity in urban working-class communities in matters such as charity, rites of passage and the upbringing of children.[23] Nor did large-scale population movement necessarily lead to declining Christian influence in local neighbourhoods.

[19] Green, *Passing*, 34–60, 163–75.

[20] M. Grimley, *Citizenship, community and the Church of England: Liberal Anglican theories of the state between the wars*, Oxford 2004, 226.

[21] J. Wolffe, '"And there's another country …": religion, the state and British identities', in G. Parsons (ed.), *The growth of religious diversity: Britain from 1945*, II: *Issues*, London 1994, 85–121.

[22] S. Yeo, *Religious and voluntary organisations in crisis*, London 1976; J. Morris, *Religion and urban change: Croydon, 1840–1914*, Woodbridge 1992.

[23] S. C. Williams, *Religious belief and popular culture in Southwark, 1880–1939*, Oxford 1999.

Rex Walford's study of church-building in the new inter-war estates of north London notes that local churches could be the first institutions established in new residential areas, often becoming deeply embedded in neighbourhood life.[24] The continued influence of 'discursive Christianity' has been identified in contexts as diverse as wartime Birmingham, the Black Country of the 1950s, the North Yorkshire coast in the 1970s and post-industrial Kingswood, Humberside and Lincolnshire in the 1980s and 1990s – albeit often within a narrower constituency or in a more diffusive form.[25] Congregational life was particularly important for overseas Christians arriving in Britain from Ireland, the Caribbean and beyond in the postwar period, offering a 'zone of transition' between homeland and new country.[26] More widely, opinion surveys suggested that religious identity continued to exert discernible influence on voting behaviour, charitable giving and volunteering amongst the population as a whole.[27]

Nevertheless, the significance of organised religion in personal identity undoubtedly receded in the postwar period (save for a minority of committed subscribers), partly because a growing emphasis on individual autonomy, personal authenticity and personal identity challenged collective identities of all kinds.[28] For Hugh McLeod, the turn away from Christianity as a common cultural *lingua franca* was the most significant way in which secularisation occurred in the post-Second World War period.[29] In popular culture, both Christian and other faith institutions also found it increasingly difficult to influence, and compete with, a mass of alternative leisure opportunities. While religious language and imagery continued to be a rich resource in culture and the arts, ethical imperatives derived from religions were increasingly regarded as problematic rather than helpful. As a result, some have cast organised religion in the role of villain, as suppressive of personal liberation and self-expression.[30] Others suggest that the picture is

---

[24] R. Walford, *The growth of 'New London' in suburban Middlesex (1918–1945) and the response of the Church of England*, Lampeter 2007.

[25] S. Parker, *Faith on the home front: aspects of church life and popular religion in Birmingham, 1939–1945*, Bern–Oxford 2005; Sykes, 'Popular religion in decline'; D. Clark, *Between pulpit and pew: folk religion in a North Yorkshire fishing village*, Cambridge, 1982; P. G. Forster (ed.), *Contemporary mainstream religion: studies from Yorkshire and Humberside*, Aldershot 1995; T. Jenkins, *Religion in English everyday life: an ethnographical approach*, New York–Oxford 1999.

[26] J. Rex and R. Moore, *Race, community and conflict: a study of Sparkbrook*, London 1967; N. Toulis, *Believing identity: Pentecostalism and the mediation of Jamaican ethnicity and gender in England*, Oxford–New York 1997.

[27] R. Gill, *Moral communities*, Exeter 1992, 17–20.

[28] A. Giddens, *Modernity and self-identity: self and society in the late modern age*, Oxford 1991; C. Taylor, *The ethics of authenticity*, Cambridge, MA 1991. Specifically on the religious life of postwar Britain see also C. G. Brown, *The death of Christian Britain: understanding secularisation, 1800–2000*, London 2001, 115–44, 193–6.

[29] H. McLeod, *The religious crisis of the 1960s*, Oxford 2007, 264.

[30] For example J. Green, *All dressed up: the Sixties and the counter-culture*, London 1999.

more complex, and point to the variety of moral and ethical stances adopted within both Christianity and other faiths.[31] Most agree, however, that the revolutions in identity and behaviour seen in the postwar period were in part an attempt to deal with a legacy of norms and values owing a considerable debt to Christianity in one form or another.

Explaining the decline or persistence of Christian influence in postwar England thus becomes a pressing question, not just for church historians but for historians of culture, politics and society in general. For much of the twentieth century the dominant historical and sociological orthodoxy has been that the postwar period constituted the tail-end of a longer process of secularisation occurring as a result of long-term urbanisation, rationalisation and individualisation.[32] Though classical secularisation theory still has compelling advocates, its dominance has been increasingly questioned by sociologists who have asserted that the western experience is exceptional,[33] and by historians who have questioned the timing and causes of secularisation. Of the latter, arguably the most revolutionary recent hypothesis is put forward by Callum Brown, in his *The death of Christian Britain* (2001).[34] Rejecting the idea of a long, slow decline in religious influence, Brown has instead seen the nineteenth and early twentieth centuries as a period of religious vitality in which (regardless of fluctuations in church attendance), Christianity remained discursively dominant in English society, shaping beliefs, norms, values and language even for many non-churchgoers. Challenging long-standing preoccupations with modernisation, urbanisation and class, Brown argues that the crucial ingredient in the Churches' success was the fostering of a close identification between piety and femininity. Evangelical Christianity appealed widely amongst women and the centrality it gave to the 'godly home' helped to ensure high levels of religious participation not only amongst women themselves but also amongst their children.

For Brown, this connection functioned remarkably effectively until the late 1950s, when – with comparative suddenness – women began to discard Christianity as a source of personal identity, turning instead to alternative paradigms found in the workplace, films and the media, amongst others. As a result, the Churches not only lost the support of many women, but also lost contact with their children, who were no longer socialised into Christian belief and practice by their mothers and grandmothers. This, says Brown, dealt the fatal blow to a century and a half of Christianity's discursive domi-

---

[31] For example G. Parsons, 'Between law and licence: Christianity, morality and permissiveness', in Parsons, *Growth of religious diversity*, ii. 231–66, and G. I. T. Machin, *The Church and social issues in twentieth century Britain*, Oxford 1998.

[32] Gilbert, *Post-Christian Britain*, 78–9.

[33] Davie, *Exceptional case*.

[34] See also second edition (2009) with a new postscript, 'The mortality of Christian Britain reconsidered'.

nance and marked the beginning – rather than the end – of secularisation.[35] In a subsequent book Brown has suggested further factors in Christianity's erosion, notably the role of the media in disseminating competing world-views and rendering traditional evangelistic methods obsolete; alienation from Christianity caused by theological ferment (echoing earlier work by Gilbert and Norman[36]); and the Churches' obsession with criticising the sexual and leisure habits of the populace, particularly the young. However, Brown's central thesis – the loss of the 'central paradigm of religious behaviour, the respectable and sexually-abstinent single woman' – is reasserted, with greater emphasis on cultural permissiveness and the consequences of sexual liberation.[37]

Brown's work has attracted both praise and criticism: since *The death of Christian Britain* one can scarcely ignore either the 1960s as a critical period of religious change or gender as a significant religious variable. Nevertheless, some have suggested that Brown over-estimated both the influence of Evangelical piety on nineteenth-century women and the degree to which the subsequent 'de-feminisation of piety and de-pietisation of femininity' could have been caused by women's liberation or sexual revolution (which only really began to affect behaviour in the 1970s – after church attendance began its dramatic decline).[38] Others have suggested that Brown's thesis ignores other factors involved in the rise and decline of Christianity. For instance, Hugh McLeod and Gerald Parsons have noted how Christianity received vital support from the state and social institutions in the late nineteenth and early twentieth centuries, support which was increasingly withdrawn in the late twentieth.[39] Frank Prochaska has likewise highlighted the nationalisation of public services which historically bound the Churches to their local communities (notably healthcare, schooling and social welfare), narrowing the Churches' influence towards primarily 'devotional' activities.[40] Most recently Simon Green has argued that Brown has over-estimated both the degree to which inter-war Britain was discursively Christian, and the

---

[35] C. G. Brown, 'The secularisation decade: what the 1960s have done to the study of religious history', in McLeod and Ustorf, *Decline of Christendom*, 29–46.

[36] Gilbert, *Post-Christian Britain*, 120–30; E. Norman, *Church and society in England, 1770–1970: a historical study*, Oxford 1976, 416–74.

[37] Brown, *Religion and society in twentieth century Britain*, ch. vi.

[38] J. Morris, 'The strange death of Christian Britain: another look at the secularisation debate', *HJ* xlvi (2003), 963–76 at pp. 968ff; personal communication with Julie-Marie Strange.

[39] G. Parsons, 'How the times they were a-changing: exploring the context of religious transformation in Britain in the 1960s', in J. Wolffe (ed.), *Religion in history: conflict, conversion and co-existence*, Manchester 2004, 161–89; H. McLeod, 'The religious crisis of the 1960s', *Journal of Modern European History* iii (2005), 205–29, and 'The crisis of Christianity in the west: entering a post-Christian era?', in H. McLeod (ed.), *The Cambridge history of Christianity, IX: World Christianities*, Cambridge 2005, 323–47.

[40] Prochaska, *Christianity and social service*, 148–61.

significance of the brief upturn in religious affiliation in the decade immediately following the Second World War.[41]

The most comprehensive response to Brown's thesis thus far is contained in Hugh McLeod's *The religious crisis of the 1960s* (2007). McLeod accepts several of Brown's major contentions, but also emphasises further factors (some medium and long-term) which he believes that Brown has overlooked. Although attributing the emergence of 'post-Christendom' (a term preferred to 'post-Christian' or 'secular') to no single cause, McLeod particularly emphasises 'the weakening of collective identities that had been so important in the years before 1960s' and the corresponding rise of an ethic of personal authenticity and choice.[42] Whilst acknowledging the importance of the Sixties as a 'hinge-decade' in the emergence of post-Christendom, McLeod nevertheless reasserts the significance of longer-term trends, notably growing religious toleration since the seventeenth century, political emancipation and a mounting intellectual critique of Christian beliefs and ethics since the eighteenth, and an increased tendency for political and legal authorities to act in morally permissive and/or religiously agnostic ways. McLeod also notes the importance of postwar affluence, and to an extent agrees with Brown on the importance of changes in the role of women and in family and sexual relationships.[43] However, regarding Brown's thesis on sexual liberation, he finds 'little evidence that involvement in unapproved sexual activity was in itself a cause of alienation from the church or religious belief'.[44] Despite their differences, however, Brown and McLeod agree upon the significance of generational change – an idea which sits at the heart of this study.

Generational change and the emergence of post-Christendom

'Generational change' is a potentially a complex concept, fraught with interpretational difficulties. However, at this stage, by way of basic orientation, it should be made clear that 'generational change' does not simply equate to 'historical change' (i.e., that alterations occur over a passage of time), but more specifically relates to the changing attitudes and practices of particular population groups linked by a shared span of time, the changing interrelationships of those population groups with one another and the cultural variations between them, and the varying impact of wider historical change on those groups. Care is needed to discern which of these dimensions of 'generational change' is being explored at any particular point.[45] But here it is sufficient

---

[41] Green, *Passing*, 244–8, 256, 260.
[42] McLeod, *1960s*, 259.
[43] Ibid. 258.
[44] Ibid. 257.
[45] See pp. 21–2 below.

to say that historians and sociologists of religion have become increasingly interested in questions of historical change as they specifically relate to ageing, the life course, relationships between old and young and difference between population cohorts. For McLeod, whilst 'the great majority of those coming to maturity in the 1960s ... had received a Christian upbringing', younger cohorts growing up at the end of the twentieth century had 'so little exposure to the Bible or Christian language and ritual that all those things seemed strange and were not so much rejected as unconsidered'.[46] Brown suggests that 'whilst the anti-deferential revolt by young people in the 1960s was ... influential in their escape from the churches, the more fundamental aspect was a boredom amongst adults and young people with organised religion'.[47] For both Brown and McLeod, changing young people's attitudes to religion were crucial, but so were the attitudes of adults towards the religious socialisation of the young.

Academic researchers have been aware of the potential importance of age and generation in religious change since the 1970s. In 1973 the US sociologist Robert Wuthnow identified a strong cohort effect at work in surveys of American beliefs and practices.[48] In the British context, Currie, Gilbert and Horsley noted that 'negative growth' in church affiliation in the late nineteenth century was partly related to the Churches' failure to replenish their adult membership from amongst Sunday school and youth members.[49] Grace Davie's *Religion in Britain since 1945* (1994) implies a generational dimension to shifts in the postwar cultural mood and a breakdown in the transmission of faith between parents and children.[50] Research on the Cumbrian town of Kendal by Paul Heelas, Linda Woodhead and others in 2000–2 also indicated a generational pattern to both churchgoing and to the rising popularity of alternative/holistic spiritual practices.[51] Quantitative research by Alasdair Crockett and David Voas, using British Household Panel data, concurs that declining attachment to religious beliefs and practices has been 'overwhelmingly generational in nature' (although they regard it more as a 'gently accelerating' decline than the sharp turnaround for which Brown argues – perhaps a reflection of the different data sources that the authors use).[52]

---

[46] McLeod, *1960s*, 262.

[47] Brown, *Religion and society in twentieth century Britain*, 238.

[48] R. Wuthnow, 'Recent pattern of secularisation: a problem of generations?', *ASR* xli (1973), 850–67.

[49] R. Currie, A. D. Gilbert and L. Horsley, *Churches and churchgoers: patterns of church growth in the British Isles since 1700*, Oxford 1977, 87–9. See also J. Cox, *The English Churches in a secular society: Lambeth, 1870–1930*, Oxford 1982, 226–37.

[50] Davie, *Religion in Britain*, 29–43, 117–36.

[51] Heelas and Woodhead, *Spiritual revolution*, 119–10.

[52] A. Crockett and D. Voas, 'Generations of decline: religious change in 20th century Britain', *JSSR* xlv (2006), 567–84 at pp. 567, 573.

11

Besides questions of decline and renewal, an increasing number of studies has focused upon the distinctive cultural and religious characteristics exhibited by different age cohorts. Many, though not all, have employed generational labels originally developed by sociologists and marketing consultants interested in understanding the new youth cultures emerging in the 1950s and 1960s. Particular distinctions have been made between a 'world war generation' (born *c.* 1901–24), a 'builder generation' (born *c.* 1925–45), a 'baby-boomer generation' (born *c.* 1946–63) and a 'baby-buster generation', also called 'Generation X' (born *c.* 1964–81). More recently, the spotlight has turned upon 'Generation Y' (born early 1980s to late 1990s).[53] Much of such writing has emerged from the USA although British sociologists, practical theologians and missiologists have found resonances with the United Kingdom context.[54] Particular attention has been given to the spiritual lives of the baby-boomers and to Generation X. Regarding the former, Wade Clark Roof, a pioneer in the field, has identified baby-boomers as spiritual seekers; suspicious of *a priori* religious authorities, convinced that faith could and should be redefined according to their own terms, open to experimentation with a variety of religious possibilities yet (in the USA if not in Britain) frequently returning to Christian roots in later life.[55] Whilst the optimism of the 'baby-boomers' may partly have related to their coming of age during a period of unparalleled prosperity, 'Generation X' has by contrast been characterised as more cynical, more knowing and more sceptical with regard to truth claims and grand visions. Though sharing their parents' individualised approach to questions of truth and behaviour, X-ers have been presented as more ready to seek out communities of the like-minded, amidst which some meaning and consolation may be discovered in an otherwise senseless world.[56] For Gordon Lynch such cohort-based studies have been important in breaking new ground for sociologists of religion, yet at their crudest risk reducing the significance of age and generation to a series of attitudinal

[53] See, for example, S. Collins-Mayo, B. Mayo, S. Nash and C. Cocksworth, *The faith of Generation Y*, London 2010.

[54] Amongst the best are P. Richter and L. J. Francis, *Gone but not forgotten: church leaving and returning*, London 1998; D. Hilborn and M. Bird, *God and the generations: youth, age and the Church today*, Carlisle 2002; and G. Lynch, *After religion: 'Generation X' and the search for meaning*, London 2002.

[55] W. Clark Roof, *A generation of seekers: the spiritual journeys of the baby-boom generation*, San Francisco 1993; N. T. Ammerman and W. Clark Roof (eds), *Work, family and religion in contemporary society*, London–New York 1995; W. Clark Roof, J. W. Carroll and D. A. Roozen (eds), *The postwar generation and establishment religion: cross-cultural perspectives*, Boulder, Co 1995; J. W. Carroll and W. Clark Roof, *Bridging divided worlds: generational cultures in congregations*, San Francisco 2002.

[56] R. W. Flory and D. E. Miller (eds), *Gen X religion*, New York–London 2000; Lynch, *After religion*

generalisations whilst ignoring the possible significance of other dimensions.[57]

If the role of generational change in religious change is increasingly established in historical consensus, its precise nature and extent remain to be fully explored (particularly in historical perspective, and in its cultural rather than statistical manifestations). Whilst rejecting mono-causal explanations, this book ultimately concurs with Crockett and Voas's contention that 'the relationship between the religiosity of parents and children'[58] was of critical importance to the (non-) transmission of Christian belief, identity and practice in the postwar period. However, several questions remain to be addressed: first, what do we mean by 'generational change', and is it possible to arrive at a workable definition of a term that historians have traditionally found slippery? Second, in what sense can religious change be understood to be related to generational change in particular? Was the postwar turn from Christianity a sudden occurrence, related particularly to the experience of one 'generation', or a more gradual process? And was the progressive rejection of Christianity primarily a function of youth rebellion, or were adult attitudes equally significant? Third, if age and generational difference are significant, is this primarily because of discernible differences in attitude and experience between the different cohorts, or in some other way?

Local and congregational perspectives

In seeking to answer these questions, a key challenge remains the lack of in-depth research into late twentieth-century English Christianity, particularly at the more local level which could help to 'earth' more securely general claims about the nature of recent religious change. Here, a case study of local church life in Birmingham is offered in partial redress of this imbalance. Whilst Birmingham's size makes it highly atypical in certain respects, its recent history nevertheless reflects many significant postwar trends: its industries were amongst the chief beneficiaries of the postwar boom and also casualties of the subsequent slump. Birmingham's new outer-ring housing estates were championed as examples of cutting-edge town planning in the 1950s, and decried as archetypal 'sink' estates by the end of the century. In the 1970s and 1980s the suburbs of Handsworth and Lozells became national by-words for social dislocation, racial tension and political neglect. Birmingham's enormous social diversity encompassed multi-ethnic inner-city neighbourhoods such as Balsall Heath, the wealthy, tree-lined suburbs of Edgbaston and newer, mainly white, working-class estates such as Brandwood. All the major Christian and other faith groups were represented in the

[57] G. Lynch, '"Generation X" religion: a critical evaluation', in S. Collins-Mayo and P. Dandelion (eds), *Religion and youth*, Farnham 2010, 32–8.
[58] Crockett and Voas, 'Generations of decline', 582.

city. Birmingham thus offers a promising testing-ground for theories about Christianity and generational change, accepting that generalisations from this particular case require considerable care.

The concentration on local congregational life constitutes a distinctive feature of this study – indeed, at the time of writing it is virtually unique amongst historical accounts of the postwar period. Though shaped by social and cultural forces beyond their control, local churches were not therefore merely passive victims of social change. Decisions for or against organised Christianity depended on a variety of concrete local and personal inter-actions which were often more important in shaping identity than class or nationhood.[59] Local congregations could remain active agents in their own destinies, their choice of actions bringing vitality or stagnation even amidst a national decline in church attendance.[60] Such choices were not, as Alan Gilbert has argued,[61] straightforwardly between 'accommodation' with cultural trends and 'resistance' to them, but between resistance to certain wider trends and accommodation with others. Indeed, for Gerald Parsons, 'deciding how far you can go'[62] in adapting to cultural change became a particularly vexed question in postwar society as the boundaries between 'sacred' and 'secular' themselves shifted and hardened in the minds of many contemporaries. A local congregational study can contextualise discussions of those dilemmas more securely in the lives of grassroots Christians and their communities.

The congregations selected here come from the older, larger denomina-tions which historically constituted the 'mainstream' of English Christianity: two Anglican churches, one Roman Catholic, one Baptist, one Methodist, one United Reformed and one Anglican-Methodist-URC Local Ecumenical Project (i.e. a congregation formed through formal denominational partner-ship). These were located in a range of neighbourhoods: one in central Birmingham, two in the 'inner city', one in a wealthy suburb, one in a more modest residential surburb and two on interwar/postwar estates. The full variety of English Christianity is beyond the scope of a single book. One particular regret is that no large suburban Charismatic Evangelical church amongst those approached was willing to take part in the study. In the post-1960s period, such churches often bucked the trend towards decline and held particular appeal amongst younger cohorts.[63] As a result this study focuses slightly disproportionately on the perspectives of older adults. However, it

[59] J. Bourke, *Working class cultures in Britain, 1890–1960: gender, class and ethnicity*, London–New York 1994, 211.

[60] Ammerman, *Congregation and community*, 43–8.

[61] Gilbert, *Post-Christian Britain*, 102ff.

[62] G. Parsons, 'Introduction: deciding how far you can go', in Parsons, *Growth of religious diversity*, ii. 5–22.

[63] For a good sociological study of such a congregation (St Michael-le-Belfry in York) see M. Guest, *Evangelical identity and contemporary culture: a congregational study in innovation*, Carlisle 2007.

was decided not to make a larger, youthful Charismatic congregation the focus of a second research phase lest this skewed the generational contours emerging in the original study. Renewed Evangelical perspectives nevertheless feature here particularly in the stories of Grenfell Baptist and St Bede's. Altogether, the selection of congregations offers a series of bore holes (rather than anything more representative) into the diversity of English church life in the period.

A third feature of this study is the fusion of historical and social scientific research methods, made possible by the local congregational focus and the recent nature of the experiences discussed. Eighty-one original oral history interviews were conducted to complement archival research into local congregational records, notably church magazines. In addition, one month's participant observation took place within each of the seven churches, and a short questionnaire was distributed to a sample of churchgoers (covering personal faith journeys, church and community involvement and private religious practice), eliciting 228 responses. The two disciplinary approaches were mutually reinforcing: the questionnaire and observations enabled a richer contextualisation of the oral history, but, equally significantly, a historical approach to studying local churches added welcome longitudinal depth to the understanding of the congregational form. Originating largely in the USA but now increasingly influential in the UK, the emerging subdiscipline of 'congregational studies' (involving the application of insights from sociology, anthropology, practical theology and organisational studies to understanding congregational structure and power, culture and social function) has grown significantly in recent years.[64] However, many congregational studies remain largely contemporary in focus, occasionally resulting in a-historical interpretations of contemporary challenges, and a corresponding neglect of the power of story and the symbiosis between congregational memory and current experience.[65] This study in part seeks to redress that imbalance.

'Generations' in history

A fourth distinctive feature of the book is its focus on age and generational identity. Since this is comparatively unfamiliar territory even for many contemporary historians, it may be helpful to explain the concept further here. The study of generations in society and history is hardly new, featuring

---

[64] M. Guest, L. Woodhead and K. Tusting (eds), *Congregational studies in the UK: Christianity in a post-Christian age*, Aldershot 2004, chs i–ii; H. Cameron, P. Richter, D. Davies and F. Ward (eds), *Studying local churches: a handbook*, London 2005.
[65] J. F. Hopewell (ed. B. G. Wheeler), *Congregation: stories and structures*, Philadelphia 1987.

in the writings of Herodotus, Vico, Gibbon and Dilthey amongst others.[66] Yet contemporary scholars have until recently given little critical attention to the concept of generations, partly due to the difficulty of arriving at a definition which is both sufficiently coherent and sufficiently flexible. The modern social scientific exploration of generation originated with Karl Mannheim in the 1920s, but it was not until the 1960s that scholars returned to the phenomenon,[67] and not until the 1990s did Mannheim's observations experience a general rehabilitation. Cruder accounts of generation have overlooked important social and cultural differences (America's baby-boom occurred at a slightly different time and rate to Britain's, for example). However, even where care has been taken to apply terminology in a cultural appropriate way, theoretical rigour in discussing generations in history and society remains patchy, and in some cases the existence of 'generations' in history is accepted almost wholly uncritically. In particular, sociologists and practical theologians have tended to neglect the historical development of generational identity, whilst historians – with some notable exceptions[68] – have generally tended to leave generational identity as a footnote in history, or consider it a self-explanatory concept needing little further elaboration.[69]

Five particular problems present themselves. First, can one meaningfully talk about generations when there is 'one born every second'?[70] Even the most reasonable periodisations are human constructions, and history does not come ready-packaged along generational lines. Second, what level of affinity is needed to constitute a 'generation', what level of variety is permissible, and how far is this limited by birth date? In what sense are Prince Charles, Mick Jagger and my own parents part of the same 'generation'? A third question concerns how generational identity might develop: if older adulthood is correctly associated with greater 'conservatism' theoretically this could relate as much to formative experience in a more 'conservative' age as to more universal patterns of psychological development across the life course. Several factors require disentanglement. Fourth, if 'culturally distinctive cohorts' are discernible at particular points in history, do their

---

[66] K. Mannheim, 'The problem of generations', in his *Essays on the sociology of knowledge* (1927), London 1952 edn (ed. with intro. by P. Kecskemeti), 280–6; R. G. Collingwood, *The idea of history*, Oxford 1946, 21–31; H. Jaeger, 'Generations in history: reflections on a controversial concept', *History and Theory* xxiv (1985), 273–92.

[67] For example H. Butterfield, *Discontinuities between generations in history: their effect on the transmission of political experience*, Cambridge 1972.

[68] H. Moller, 'Youth as a force in the modern world', *Comparative Studies in Society and History* x (1967–8), 237–60; S. Brigden, 'Youth and the English Reformation', *P&P* xcv (1982), 37–67; Cox, *English Churches*; D. Rosman, *Evangelicals and culture*, London 1984; N. Jones, *The English Reformation: religion and cultural adaptation*, Oxford 2002.

[69] D.W. Bebbington, *Evangelicalism in modern Britain: a history from the 1730s to the 1980s*, London 1989, 75.

[70] A. B. Spitzer, 'The historical problem of generations', *American Historical Review* lxxviii (1973), 1353–85 at p. 1355.

contours change beyond recognition as a result of subsequent life experience? Finally, even if all these difficulties are overcome, are age and generation simply another new meta-narrative of religious change to rival earlier emphases on class or gender in this particular historical context?

Here let me offer some theoretical justifications and explain how the word 'generation' is to be used in this book. Many apparent methodological difficulties are quickly resolved if it is accepted that (like gender, class and ethnicity) age and generation are culturally constructed. Definitional problems only become insurmountable if we assume (as did Comte and Hume) that social generations are naturally-occurring entities whose existence in history only requires narrating.[71] A more discursive approach recognises the essential fluidity of the term and immediately steers us away from a concept of generations vainly reliant upon chronology and birth date alone for coherence. Similar scepticism should be exercised towards those accounts which assume that generational contours are fixed or pre-existing. As a result, though I have occasionally used the familiar 'boomer' and 'X-er' labels, I have preferred not to assume their relevance, but to allow generational identity to emerge (or not) from the specific sources considered.

Matters become still clearer if we disentangle the variety of meanings that 'generation' has accrued. Notably, we should distinguish between the anthropologist's 'generation' (denoting kinship, especially parent-child relations – hereinafter a 'familial generation'), the demographer's 'generation' (more properly and henceforth a 'cohort' – a population group defined by birth date or chronology with no necessary attitudinal affinity) and a wider 'social generation' in a historical or sociological sense, which David W. Thomson helpfully defines as:

> a birth cohort to which history has given a distinctive character and unity ... a group of people, linked by birth in a shared span of years, who as a consequence accumulate through life a common set of experiences that is peculiar to them and to no others born either earlier or later.[72]

Though these three usages are distinct, they may at times interrelate (for example, where the experiences of a particular birth cohort result in altered parent-child relationships, perhaps in turn creating new social generational identities). Though this book explores all three facets of 'generation', particular attention is given to the third. Strikingly, few researchers have recognised that the idea of a 'social generation' itself also has multiple layers and meanings. Honourable exceptions are David Hilborn and Matt Bird, who, by bringing contemporary generational definitions into critical conversation

---

71 Mannheim, 'Problem of generations', 278.
72 D. W. Thomson, 'A lifetime of privilege? Ageing and generations at century's end', in V. L. Bengtson and W. A. Achenbaum (eds), *The changing contract across generations*, New York 1993, 215–38 at p. 217.

with the biblical use of the term, have distinguished nine different meanings.[73]

Table 1
David Hilborn and Matt Bird's nine common meanings of 'generation'

Type	Relating to/Distinguished by	Example
1. Genealogical	Kinship	'Grandparent', 'parent', 'child', etc.
2. Natal	Birth-year or birth-year period	'The thirty-something generation'
3. Periodical	Time span lived through	'The sixties generation'
4. Epochal	Dominant 'ethos'/spirit of age lived through	'The boom generation'
5. Eventual	Key historical event experienced/ lived through	'The Vietnam generation'
6. Attitudinal	Defining spiritual, philosophical or ideological orientation	'The Beat generation'
7. Affectual	Dominant spiritual, emotional or psychological experience	'The wounded generation'
8. Behavioural	Dominant activity or behaviour	'The chemical generation'
9. Functional	Social, cultural and institutional significance	'Elders', 'senior citizens', etc.

Source: Hilborn and Bird, *God and the generations*, 36

These terms are best regarded as facets of a single idea rather than precision categorisations. For instance, a 'Sixties generation' may be 'periodical' (those who lived through the Sixties), 'eventual' (those for whom 'the Sixties' were culturally defining) or 'attitudinal' (those who adopted the dominant values associated with the decade). However, far from rendering 'generation' meaningless, such variety actually widens the scope for study. Whilst I have chosen only occasionally to employ Hilborn and Bird's terminology, their polyphonic approach to generations is accepted throughout.

Much can therefore be learned merely by viewing age and generation as 'nodes of discourse' and mapping their changing meanings. But how far do ascriptions of generational identity also relate to actual social groupings? Given that social attitudes vary across any given population, is it reasonable to speak of 'social generations' at all? Here the answer is 'yes', albeit with careful definition and acknowledgement that human experience inevitably eludes definitive categorisation. Just as it is possible to speak of social classes without being enchained to a reductive and homogenising theory of 'class', so it is legitimate to speak of 'generations' without expecting fixed or monolithic entities. A first step is to recognise that 'social generational' iden-

---

[73] Hilborn and Bird, *God and the generations*, 36.

tity is produced through the interaction between 'life history and historical moment' (in Erik H. Erikson's phrase[74]). A 'social generation' must at least share a particular span of years. In this sense, all those living between 1939 and 1945 could be considered part of a common 'periodical' generation, broadly defined, albeit not necessarily in an 'eventual' sense, since the war impacted upon individual lives to varying extents. Cultural and geographical proximity to events may be almost as essential as birthdate to this first layer of social generational identity, which Karl Mannheim describes as 'generation location'.[75]

At this basic level of affinity, notes Mannheim, shared experience need not imply a shared sense of identity, just as socio-economic strata may share common attitudes and experiences without automatically displaying class consciousness.[76] Indeed, the way a period or event is experienced and remembered may vary greatly depending upon the age of the participant. This is partly due to ongoing psychological development, partly since memory is influenced by subsequent experience, and partly since events experienced at certain stages of life appear to be more influential on subsequent outlook than others. On the first point, social psychologists have frequently noted the emergence of certain orientations or concerns at particular stages of life (for example, the importance of choosing beliefs and identity in adolescence, a hardening of attitudes and worldviews in mid-life, and a desire to review and assess life story and legacy in old age[77]). If such impulses are fairly universal, they are likely to shape the ways in which events or experiences are viewed at different points in the life course. Interpreting oral history thus demands particular care.[78]

Formative experiences in childhood, adolescence and young adulthood can also continue to influence later life identity. James W. Fowler suggests a marked upsurge of interest in the wider world and the beliefs of others from early adolescence into adulthood. At this 'conforming' or 'synthetic-conventional' stage, the imprint of dominant experiences, assumptions and social mores appears particularly strong.[79] Similarly, in one 1985 study of American citizens' memories of era-defining historical events, respondents typically prioritised occasions from their youth or young adulthood, the oldest remembering World War Two as their 'most significant event'

---

[74] E. H. Erikson, *Life history and the historical moment*, New York 1975.

[75] Mannheim, 'Problem of generations', 288–90.

[76] Ibid. 289.

[77] E. H. Erikson, *Identity and the life cycle* (1959), New York–London 1980, 178–9; J. W. Fowler, *Stages of faith: the psychology of human development and the quest for meaning*, San Francisco 1981, 181–2; J. Benson, *Prime time: a history of the middle-aged in twentieth century Britain*, London 1997, 129–33.

[78] See further S. Chandler, 'Oral history across generations: age, generational identity and interview testimony', OH xxxiii/2 (2005), 48–56.

[79] Fowler, *Stages of faith*, 71–6, 110–11.

and those in middle age remembering the Vietnam War.[80] June Edmunds and Bryan S. Turner have even suggested that traumatic events underpin cultural differences between cohorts, though it is not necessary to adopt a 'trauma theory' of generations to accept that formative experience can play a key role.[81] Indeed, as Michael Corsten has argued, generational affinity or identity can arise from the assumptions and choices (or 'semantic ordering') made in youth or young adulthood, as well as the events experienced.[82] As successive cohorts begin life at different chronological starting points, they will be exposed to contrasting formative experiences and potentially travel different paths as a result. Though choices and attitudes may subsequently change, formative experience is more difficult to escape, often leaving its 'imprint' in later life. The strength of this imprint will vary from person to person. Nevertheless, if we accept (with Maurice Halbwachs) that memory is ultimately social,[83] those sharing a common 'generation location' will arguably often remember in similar ways (and distinctively from other cohorts). When shared memories are widely and deliberately preserved within a cohort, more explicit generational self-consciousness may arise. Mannheim calls these more distinctive occurrences of shared cohort identity 'generations as actualities'.[84]

Although common generational consciousness may sometimes extend throughout a whole cohort (as perhaps for a 'war generation'), such affinity is usually mitigated by other social divisions. Even within one cohort, shared experience may be interpreted in different ways (for example, in the polarisation of opinion over the legacy of the 'permissive' 1960s). If this at first appears to undermine attempts to define generational identity coherently, one should remember that historians of class and gender also face similar challenges (for instance, 'working class consciousness' may exist across a population despite meaning very different things for women and men). Age cohorts sharing strong common generational consciousness may also divide into opposing 'camps'. Mannheim calls these 'generation units'[85] – though we need not adopt this optimistically precise language to recognise that individuals may share particular life experiences but derive different implications from them.

[80] H. Schuman and J. Scott, 'Generations and collective memories', ASR liv (1989), 366–7.
[81] J. Edmunds and B. S. Turner, *Generations, culture and society*, Buckingham 2002, 68 and passim.
[82] M. Corsten, 'The time of generations', *Time and Society* viii (1999), 249–72 at pp. 265–6.
[83] M. Halbwachs (ed. and trans. with intro. by L. Coser), *On collective memory*, Chicago 1992 (first publ. as *The social frameworks of memory*, Paris 1952), 22.
[84] Mannheim, 'Problem of generations', 302–4.
[85] Ibid. 304–12.

Just as social generational identity may be negotiated within cohorts, it also develops dialectically with other age groups.[86] E. P. Thompson's dictum that 'class is a relationship and not a thing'[87] could apply equally to age. Generational identity is neither totally self-ascribed nor completely derived from others. Nor is it fixed in content: whilst formative experience certainly seems influential in shaping cohort distinctiveness it is not determinative, being modified through new experience or interaction with other cohorts. The impact of 'fresh contact' (as Mannheim calls it) means that no individual or group moves through life with all their formative assumptions intact. Consequently, today's generational contours should not be read straightforwardly back into the past. Whilst this raises interpretational problems, these are not insurmountable. After all, historians are well used to discerning points of continuity and change. Indeed, an awareness of change over time makes it more (not less) important to study the ways in which generational identities develop, since generational identity always has an important retrospective dimension.

This begs the question of how far cultural and religious change can legitimately be described as 'generational'. This partly depends on what we mean. Jane Pilcher highlights the need to unravel three distinct but interrelated dimensions of age-related change over time. Change may variously be attributable to 'age' effects (the tendency for outlook and behaviour to change across the life course – either for social or psychological reasons), to 'period' effects (the impact of wider social change across all age groups) or to 'cohort' effects (variations in attitudes between different cohorts arising from their experiences of differing historical circumstances).[88] Thus changing levels of religiosity within a given society may be influenced by age effects (for example, if the young are 'naturally' less religious than the old), by cohort effects (for instance, if one cohort grows up to become less religious than their elders were at the same age) or by period effects (for example, if there is a general decline in churchgoing across the whole population).[89] Evidence for a general decline in attendance is indisputable, but recent studies have also suggested a strong 'cohort' dimension to late twentieth-century religious change.[90] Likewise, this study identifies some significant attitudinal differences between cohorts, but also argues that the significance of age and

---

[86] J. Garnett, A. Harris, M. Grimley, W. Whyte and S. Williams (eds), 'Transmission and transformation', in J. Garnett, A. Harris, M. Grimley, W. Whyte and S. Williams (eds), *Redefining Christian Britain: post-1945 perspectives*, London 2007, 115–26 at pp. 117–22.

[87] E. P. Thompson, *The making of the English working class*, London 1963, 10.

[88] J. Pilcher, *Age and generation in modern Britain*, Oxford 1995, 24.

[89] Crockett and Voas, 'Generations of decline', 567–8.

[90] Ibid; Davie, *Religion in Britain*; E. Barker, 'The postwar generation and establishment religion in England', in Clark Roof, Carroll and Roozen, *Post-war generation*, 1–26; Heelas and Woodhead, *Spiritual revolution*, 94–115; R. Hirst, 'Social networks and personal beliefs: an example from modern Britain', in G. Davie, P. Heelas and L. Woodhead (eds), *Predicting religion: Christian, secular and alternative futures*, Aldershot 2003, 86–94;

generational identity in popular postwar Christianity goes well beyond a simple identification of cohort distinctiveness.

Indeed, concentrating solely on cohorts in a purely demographic sense or 'social generations' in a Mannheimian sense also risks overlooking cultural shifts in the multiplicity of meanings of age and generational identity identified by Hilborn and Bird – not all of them easily reducible to carefully delineated social groupings. Some historians of Christianity have already noted the different ways in which religious change may have a generational dimension. At times, generational change may be 'periodical'. For example, Norman Jones has argued that the Protestant Reformation only really became embedded in English culture once patterns of late medieval devotion had passed out of living memory.[91] Generational change might also be 'attitudinal'. Thus Doreen Rosman notes how Evangelical nonconformity was transformed in the early nineteenth century by a second generation of leaders whose concerns were different from those of the Wesleys and their contemporaries.[92] Generational change might equally be 'genealogical' in the sense that a 'changing contract' between parents and children or elders and youth, might exemplify, or even contribute to, wider social change.[93] Indeed, this will become a significant part of this book's argument. Of course, historical change is never reducible to mono-causal explanations. The changing fortunes of church-based Christianity in postwar Britain must be understood with reference to a variety of causes and indices of identity. This book none the less argues that questions of age and generation are more relevant to this story than has sometimes been supposed.

The book proceeds as follows: chapter 1 surveys the recent history of Birmingham and its Churches, introducing the case-study congregations and arguing for the significance of age alongside other variables in postwar local church life. Chapter 2 revisits the familiar issue of declining church participation, noting significant statistical trends but also considering how local church members perceived and explained decline. It notes the increasing centrality of age and generation to interpretations of religious change, and the impact of decline on successive cohorts of the churchgoing population. Chapters 3 to 6 then explore progressively widening circles of meaning and belonging important in postwar church life – family, congregation, community and wider society.[94] Chapter 3 considers youth and family life in local congregational perspective, in some ways offering the core of the book's argu-

---

J. R. Tilley, 'Secularisation and ageing in Britain: does family formation cause greater religiosity?', JSSR xlii (2003), 269–78.

[91] Jones, English Reformation, 23–4.

[92] Rosman, Evangelicals and culture.

[93] V. L. Bengtson, 'Is the "contract across generations" changing? Effects of population ageing on obligations and expectations across different age groups', in Bengtson and Achenbaum, Changing contract, 3–24.

[94] This framework owes much to Joanna Bourke's Working class cultures.

ment. It charts the changing ways in which local congregations and clergy sought to relate to young people and their parents from the 1940s to the 1960s, as 'teenage' became a widely-recognised stage in the life course and 'the generation gap' became a matter of increasing concern. In particular, the chapter notes a significant renegotiation of relationships and expectations between elders and the young in postwar British society, with profound implications for both Church and society.

Chapter 4 places the congregation in the historical spotlight, considering how some key postwar developments in worship and congregational culture were received, enacted and understood at local church level, and the generational dimensions observed in debates over worship. Chapter 5 then explores the local church within its local community context during a period of considerable urban transformation, exploring key themes through the stories of particular congregations. Chapter 6 sets church participation within its wider social and cultural context, exploring attitudes to morality and public behaviour within a pluralist society in which the changing relationship between 'public' and 'private' spheres was crucial both to changes in societal views of morals and ethics and to the outlook of successive cohorts of church members. Finally, a conclusion reconsiders the usefulness of the concept of 'generational change' to historians of religion, secularisation and wider cultural change.

Overall, it is hoped that, as a result of this study, readers will take the local parish and congregational experience seriously as an integral part of the overall story of secularisation and religious change in the later twentieth century, and indeed to inspire further locally-based research in this area. It should also encourage a recognition that local churches were not entirely passive in the face of religious change, continuing to exercise genuine agency in their ability to attract or discourage participation, even within the overall context of the shrinking and progressive marginalisation of the actively Christian community. The congregational perspectives explored here aim to nuance and enrich the interpretations of religious change given in more general historical accounts, even suggesting some potentially significant new themes for further exploration (not least the importance of shifting norms of aesthetics and taste, personal responsibility, neighbourliness and everyday social interaction). In particular, this study aims to highlight the significance of age and generation to patterns of recent religious change; not only with regard to variations in attitude and behaviour between cohorts but also the changing relationships between generations and the implications that the recognition of such changes had for local church life. Whatever the reader's primary area of research, the concept of generations should be given due weight as a heuristic tool for historical analysis.

1

Birmingham: The City and its Churches

Religion and society in postwar Birmingham

On 7 May 1945 Birmingham citizens breathed a sigh of relief as the war in Europe ended. With the formal announcement expected for some days, the *Birmingham Post* reported that city-centre crowds received the news 'without excitement, almost, in fact, in a mood of complacency'. Soon however, flags appeared on civic buildings. Buses and tramcars were prepared for flood-lighting. By evening, the mood became more celebratory: in Victoria Square a group of 'mainly young people' sang hymns, whilst nearby in Stephenson Place, others sang 'the latest popular jazz tunes'.[1] Early on VE Day itself a 'quiet, Sundayish air' pervaded. Religious observance was mixed: 4,000 people attended a thanksgiving service in Birmingham's Anglican cathe-dral, whilst at Aston parish church extra services were hurriedly organised.[2] However, in the south Birmingham suburb of Cotteridge, 39-year-old house-wife Betty Foreman remembered only a small congregation for the short VE Day communion at St Agnes, while her husband and neighbour chose instead to celebrate at a local pub.[3] Later, a party atmosphere took hold in many residential districts, with bonfires and dancing to gramophone records in the streets, as if to chase away the shadows of the blackout.[4]

In Birmingham, as nationally, the immediate postwar mood blended cele-bration, war-weariness, foreboding at the scale of reconstruction ahead and determination to see this through. Whilst escaping the level of destruction suffered by its near-neighbour Coventry, Birmingham's industrial base was nevertheless heavily targeted by bombing – particularly in 1940–1 – resulting in high civilian casualties and extensive damage.[5] A serious housing crisis also loomed: the city's population was growing but a third of dwellings were unsuitable for habitation.[6] Economic prospects looked healthier: the small-scale, highly-skilled precision industries which had made nineteenth-century Birmingham famous as 'the workshop of the world' continued to thrive in

---

[1] *BP*, 8 May 1945, 1.
[2] *BP*, 9 May 1945, 3.
[3] IJ12CT.
[4] *BP*, 9 May 1945, 3.
[5] A. Sutcliffe and R. Smith, *History of Birmingham*, III: *Birmingham, 1939–1970*, London 1974, 26–36.
[6] This was despite some prolific inter-war house-building: ibid. ii. 222; G. E. Cherry, *Birmingham: a study in geography, history and planning*, Chichester 1994, 113.

the twentieth, often adapting successfully to growth in light and medium engineering. During the war, factories geared to the war economy had provided high wages, skilled work and full employment.[7] By 1941 Birmingham's municipal authorities were already looking ahead, drawing up ambitious plans for the clearance of 51,000 slum houses and a rejuvenated city centre[8] – a conscious and optimistic echo of Joseph Chamberlain's 'civic gospel' which had brought municipal gas, water and civic pride to the city in the 1870s.

Though the Chamberlains were gone and Labour was in the ascendant by 1946, the continued public and political influence of several leading Free Church dynasties – including the Kenrick and Martineau families (Unionist and Unitarian) and the Cadburys (Liberal and Quaker) – recalled Birmingham's late Victorian reputation as 'the nonconformist capital of England'. Then, celebrated nonconformist preachers such as R. W. Dale (of Carrs Lane Congregational Church) and George Dawson (of the Church of the Saviour) had gained the ear of both a large working-class audience and Birmingham's socially-reforming civic leaders.[9] In the 1940s Birmingham remained a centre of Free Church activity; notably through the adult education colleges of Westhill (Congregationalist) and Woodbrooke (Quaker). However, Birmingham's nonconformist reputation rested more upon influence than numbers: in 1851 nonconformist attendances in Birmingham were only 16.7 per-cent of the total (half that of the Black Country, if the unusually low Wesleyan returns for Birmingham were accurate[10]). In 1892 Free Church attendances accounted for 47.7 per cent of the Birmingham total, a greater proportion, but still lower than in many large English towns around that time.[11] In the 1940s attendances continued to decline though ministers regularly reported congregations in good heart.

Church attendance in Birmingham was nevertheless higher than in many English cities. The *Birmingham News* religious census of 1892 recorded that 32.4 per cent of the adult population attended church on census Sunday (compared with figures from 1881 showing 19.8 per cent in Liverpool, 23 per cent in Sheffield, 40 per cent in Bristol, 27 per cent in Bradford and 24.2 per cent in Nottingham).[12] However, local perceptions of institutional weakness

---

7 Cherry, *Birmingham*, 126.
8 C. Upton, *A history of Birmingham*, Chichester 1993, 195; Commission of the bishop's council for the diocese of Birmingham, *Faith in the city of Birmingham: an examination of problems and opportunities facing a city*, Exeter 1988, 16.
9 G. F. Nuttall, 'Dissent in Birmingham: the first two centuries', in G. F. Nuttall and J. H. Y. Briggs, *Dissent in Birmingham, 1689–1989*, Birmingham 1989, 5–6.
10 G. Robson, *Dark satanic mills? Religion and irreligion in Birmingham and the Black Country*, Carlisle 2002, 235, 277.
11 Gill, *Empty church*, 305, 321.
12 R. Peacock, 'The 1892 Birmingham religious census', in A. Bryman (ed.), *Religion in the Birmingham area: essays in the sociology of religion*, Birmingham 1975, 12–28 at p. 14. Because different measures were used, comparisons are only rough.

persisted. John Wesley had first preached in Birmingham in 1743 and found it 'a dry and uncomfortable place'.[13] Despite the city's exponential growth in the nineteenth century, a separate Anglican diocese for Birmingham had been established only in 1905, against some odds and thanks largely to the efforts of its first bishop, the leading Christian social thinker Charles Gore. For Anglican authorities in the immediate postwar years, the most pressing problem was an acute shortage of clergy, in 1954 prompting the newly-arrived Bishop Leonard Wilson to conclude that 'our situation … is, I think, more desperate than any other diocese in England'.[14] Even by 1965 the number of Anglican clergy per head of population was half the national average.[15] Birmingham's Catholic population had been small during most of the nine-teenth century and after the 'Murphy Riots' of 1867 had largely escaped anti-Catholic agitation.[16] From the late nineteenth century successive waves of Irish immigration contributed to significant growth in the Catholic popula-tion of the area covered by the archdiocese of Birmingham, which doubled in the twenty years after 1945.[17] The 1930s and 1940s saw a particular warming of local ecumenical relations and even some missionary collaboration.[18]

By 1945 Birmingham's Christian communities found themselves – like the city as a whole – faced with a major reconstruction task: catering for a shifting population, engaging in rebuilding programmes and re-establishing normal patterns of life and worship. Reconstruction – of both a social and a spiritual nature – became a prominent theme of the first postwar decades. In the city at large, rebuilding proceeded unevenly, with ambitious municipal housing plans initially constrained by land shortages and planning restric-tions. By 1949 only 270 'slum' houses had been demolished, with rebuilding lagging behind the national rate in the 1940s and 1950s.[19] Nevertheless, by the mid-1960s new council housing was being built at a faster rate than in any other city in Europe. By 1970 there were 81,000 new homes, many in new outer-ring estates such as Brandwood to the south, Bartley Green to the west and Castle Bromwich (a pioneering high-rise development) to the east. However, acute social deprivation persisted in both older inner and newer

---

13 As quoted in Upton, *History of Birmingham*, 50.

14 As quoted in Sutcliffe and Smith, *Birmingham, 1939–1970*, 262.

15 Church of England, *Facts and figures about the Church of England 3*, London 1965, section A table 1.

16 During these the anti-papalist campaigner William Murphy visited Birmingham. Even here, disturbances were largely contained: S. Reynolds, 'Roman Catholicism', in W. B. Stephens (ed.), *A history of the county of Warwick*, VIII: *The city of Birmingham*, London 1964, 397–410 at p. 402.

17 J.V. Healey (ed.), *The official Catholic directory of the archdiocese of Birmingham*, London 1945; E. Kirner (ed.), *The official Catholic directory of the archdiocese of Birmingham*, London 1965. Figures cover the whole archdiocese, which stretched across several surrounding counties.

18 E. Benson Perkins, *With Christ in the Bull-Ring*, London 1935, 89; J. Barnes, *Ahead of his age: Bishop Barnes of Birmingham*, London 1979, 303.

19 Sutcliffe and Smith, *Birmingham, 1939–1970*, 229–33.

outer areas, and by 1986 a quarter of the city's housing stock was once again deemed unsatisfactory.[20]

For the Churches, too, reconstruction was a long process. An existing shortage of church buildings was exacerbated by war damage to around a third of the city's churches. New church buildings thus became a key priority for Birmingham's Anglican and Free Church authorities in the immediate postwar years. By contrast, Roman Catholic archdiocesan authorities focused their initial missionary efforts on building schools in the expanding suburbs (fifty-three primary, fifteen secondary and four grammar schools by 1972), only constructing new churches in large numbers from the 1960s onwards as the Irish Catholic population began to disperse more widely from its inner city heartlands.[21] But if the mainstream Churches had kept pace with population movement up to the early 1970s, they were again lagging behind by the mid-1980s. *Faith in the city of Birmingham* (the local Anglican diocesan response to the Church of England's *Faith in the city* report of 1985) noted 'pressure for change and reappraisal of the role of the churches in the inner city areas, particularly in the context of large-scale immigration'.[22]

Migrant populations had lived in Birmingham since the nineteenth century.[23] However, from 1941, an acute labour shortage led the Ministry of Supply to invite workers from Ireland and the English regions to work in the city. Thousands responded. By 1961 the Irish-born population of the city numbered 58,000. Six years later John Rex and Robert Moore's famous study of life in working-class Sparkbrook found that, despite some prejudice, Birmingham's Irish community was integrating comparatively smoothly into the wider population, Catholic parishes frequently playing an important social role in the transition.[24] Small communities of Black and Asian migrants had also existed in Birmingham since the 1930s, with more (mainly from India and Pakistan) arriving in the late 1940s and 1950s, also often through government immigration schemes. The 1950s saw further new arrivals from the Caribbean, many regarding Great Britain as 'the mother land, sure to offer greater opportunities for employment, better conditions and self-improvement'.[25] In the early 1970s these were joined by ethnic South Asian refugees escaping persecution in Kenya and Uganda. By 2001, 29.6 per cent of the city's population was drawn from an ethnic group other

---

[20] *Faith in the city of Birmingham*, 69.
[21] P. Dennison, 'The Roman Catholic Church', in N. Tiptaft (ed.), *Religion in Birmingham*, Warley 1972, 136–51 at p. 150.
[22] *Faith in the city of Birmingham*, 24.
[23] C. Chinn, *Birmingham: the great working city*, Birmingham 1994, 81–5.
[24] Rex and Moore, *Race, community and conflict*, 84–99.
[25] S. Taylor, *A land of dreams: a study of Jewish and Caribbean migrant communities in England*, London 1993, 110.

than 'white European',[26] making Birmingham amongst the most cosmopolitan cities in the country.

For many first generation arrivals, early experience of life in Birmingham combined close-knit migrant community life, hard social and financial circumstances and a decidedly mixed reaction from the locals. Ethnic minority workers were often condemned to the lowest-paid unskilled jobs and faced prejudice from those amongst the white population who believed that immigration was straining an already overcrowded city (incorrectly, since the city's population had been declining from the 1960s).[27] Although the City Council operated no explicit 'colour bar', Rex and Moore believed that most ethnic minority applicants were disadvantaged when seeking municipal housing[28] and many new arrivals found themselves squeezed into poor-quality multi-occupancy tenancies in middle-ring neighbourhoods such as Aston and Handsworth. If racial tension never reached the same heights as in the overtly racist 1964 Smethwick by-election,[29] mistrust of immigrants nevertheless ran high, with a contemporaneous poll of Birmingham residents suggesting that 90 per cent of the population supported immigration controls.[30] Local church leaders were quick to urge welcome and assistance for immigrants, though congregational reactions to Black and Asian worshippers were more variable: sometimes friendly, elsewhere lukewarm or even hostile. Partly in response to the disappointing experiences of Britain's historic denominations and wider racial prejudice, but also as the continued expression of distinctive forms of Christian identity,[31] new Black-led churches sprang up, numbering around 100 congregations and more than 4,500 full members by the mid-1970s.[32] However, Black and Asian Christians also constituted an increasingly significant proportion of churchgoers in the city's historic 'mainstream' denominations.

If the problems facing Birmingham's ethnic minority communities were particularly acute, the mid-1960s were the start of two difficult decades for the city as a whole. A once-broad industrial base had become heavily reliant on manufacturing, which fared badly in the more depressed economic conditions of the late sixties and seventies. One of the first and biggest shocks came

---

26 HMSO, *2001 population census in Birmingham: ethnic and religious groups, country of birth*, London 2001, 13.

27 Sutcliffe and Smith, *Birmingham, 1939–1970*, 178.

28 Rex and Moore, *Race, community and conflict*, 21–7.

29 J. L. Wilkinson, *Church in black and white: the Black Christian tradition in 'mainstream' Churches in England: a white response and testimony*, Edinburgh 1993, 8.

30 Sutcliffe and Smith, *Birmingham, 1939–1970*, 397.

31 R. I. H. Gerloff, *A plea for British Black theologies: the Black Church movement in its transatlantic cultural and theological interaction*, i, Frankfurt-am-Main 1992, 23; Toulis, *Believing identity*, 270–4.

32 R. Gerloff, 'Black Christian communities in Birmingham; the problem of basic recognition', in Bryman, *Religion in the Birmingham area*, 61–84. Gerloff estimates that attendance is typically double the membership (p. 65).

in 1966, when 6,000 jobs were lost at the city's BMC (formerly Austin) car factory. By 1981 a total of 21 per cent of the city's workforce was unemployed (rising to 34 per cent amongst ethnic minority workers), with four-fifths of job losses in the manufacturing sector.[33] Four years later, investigators for the Anglican *Faith in the city of Birmingham* report placed 83 per cent of the city's inner neighbourhoods within the most deprived 10 per cent of census districts in England and Wales.[34] The Lozells disturbances of 1985 (though exaggerated by the media) did little to reverse the public perception of a city in decline.

Even so, the 1980s also marked new beginnings for Birmingham, as a measure of economic recovery set in, painful economic restructuring took place and national and European investment bore fruit. By the early 1990s Birmingham's service industries were the fastest-growing in the country, and flagship projects such as the National Exhibition Centre (opened in 1987) and International Convention Centre (1991) helped the city to become the UK's fourth most popular metropolitan destination for business and international tourism.[35] Indeed, Birmingham's renaissance was arguably as much cultural as economic, as a vibrant and more tolerant cosmopolitan culture began to emerge. In the arts, the City of Birmingham Symphony Orchestra enjoyed international repute under chief conductor Simon Rattle, whilst the city's shops, clubs and curry houses attracted visitors from well beyond the city. Recovery was precarious: flagship city-centre regeneration projects obscured continued social dislocation and deprivation in less prominent residential areas. In 2000 unemployment remained at twice the national average, with manufacturing particularly vulnerable. Nevertheless, by the end of the century Birmingham seemed at least to have recovered an element of civic confidence. As if to demonstrate this, May 1998 twice saw the city in the international spotlight (albeit for very different reasons), as host to both the Eurovision Song Contest and the G8 Summit of World Leaders. For many in the city's churches, the latter was particularly significant since it also brought to Birmingham the Jubilee 2000 campaign for the cancellation of Third World debt. When between 50,000 and 70,000 protestors formed a human chain around the city's inner ring road on 16 May, an estimated four-fifths of campaigners were members of Britain's Christian Churches.[36] The Jubilee 2000 protest sounded a common note of excitement through many conversations and activities.

---

[33] Chinn, *Birmingham*, 111; Taylor, *Land of dreams*, 200; Upton, *History of Birmingham*, 210. The latter figure refers up to 1984.

[34] Reported in *Faith in the city of Birmingham*, 4.

[35] Chinn, *Birmingham*, 116.

[36] A rough estimate as a participant, corroborated by a Christian Aid representative speaking at the 1999 Greenbelt Festival.

Mapping the Church at the end of the century

In 1989 the English Church Attendance Survey found roughly 12 per cent of the population of Birmingham in church on census Sunday.[37] In the century since the 1892 *Birmingham News* religious census, the proportion of the city's adults in church had more than halved – although in the later twentieth century the decline in churchgoing should be contextualised against a (smaller) decline in the population of the city as a whole and its relative strength compared to other major English cities (11 per cent in Leeds, 10 per cent in Greater London and Manchester, 7 per cent in Sheffield, though 15 per cent in Liverpool).[38] The Church of England remained relatively weak, consistently returning the lowest attendance figures per head of population of any Anglican diocese in the country between 1978 and 1997. Since the early twentieth century Roman Catholics had constituted the largest single churchgoing constituency in the city (largely through immigration but also some conversions) though attendances at mass also declined towards the end of the century. By contrast the larger Free Church denominations had experienced particular decline, although Birmingham's Baptist Churches were notable exceptions, their combined membership growing by 15 per cent between 1975 and 1992 (bucking a national denominational decline of 2.3 per cent over the same period).[39] New house churches, independent Charismatic and restorationist fellowships[40] constituted more than 4 per cent of attendances surveyed by 1989. This reflected the resurgence of evangelical Christianity nationally in the postwar period. Moreover, immigration from the Caribbean and Africa had led to the emergence of significant numbers of Black-led congregations.

Leaving aside denominational patterns, churchgoing also varied from locality to locality across the city, demonstrating the continued salience of social class to patterns of religiosity. A ward-by-ward profile of Anglican, Methodist, Baptist and URC attendance figures in 1991 (*see* table 2, column B) shows generally higher levels of churchgoing as a percentage of the local population in Birmingham's more affluent middle-class suburbs (such as

---

[37] P. Brierley and H. Wraight (eds), *CRA Factfile* 3 (Mar. 1997). The 1989 English church census is widely regarded as more comprehensive and so is preferred to the 1998 survey.

[38] Brierley and Wraight, *CRA Factfile* 3.

[39] Figures from West Midland Baptist Association *Yearbooks*, 1945–96/7, BMS International Mission Centre, Selly Oak, Birmingham, and P. Brierley and V. Hiscock (eds), *UK Christian Handbook 1994/5*, London 1993, 254.

[40] These labels describe a range of churches (often with Evangelical or Pentecostal roots) emerging outside the historic denominations from the 1960s onwards. Initially known as 'house churches' (because many first met in members' homes) these are now sometimes labelled 'new churches'. For 'Charismatic' see chapter 4 below. 'Restorationism' is a particular vein of charismatic Evangelicalism emphasising the 'restoration' of a New Testament pattern of Christianity.

Table 2
Combined Anglican electoral roll, Methodist, Baptist and URC membership in Birmingham churches as a percentage of total population and of 'external constituency', 1991

Ward	Column A Combined electoral roll and membership (n)	Column B n as a percentage of ward population, 1991	Column C n as percentage of 'external constituency' in ward population, 1991
Acock's Green	459	1.76	1.86
Aston	506	1.89	2.75
Bartley Green	420	1.9	1.92
Billesley	501	1.85	1.92
Bournville	733	3.02	3.08
Brandwood	147	0.56	0.57
Edgbaston	352	1.72	1.9
Erdington	869	3.58	3.67
Fox Hollies	186	0.8	0.88
Hall Green	1,051	4.23	4.74
Handsworth	528	2.13	3.8
Harborne	805	3.72	3.84
Hodge Hill		Data incomplete	
King's Norton	385	1.7	1.71
Kingsbury	218	1.12	1.13
Kingstanding	192	0.69	0.71
Ladywood	853	3.45	4.36
Longbridge	391	1.67	1.69
Moseley	980	4.44	5.4
Nechells	195	0.85	1.35
Northfield	825	3.41	3.43
Oscott	279	1.27	1.3
Perry Barr	263	1.2	1.26
Quinton	612	3.01	3.12
Sandwell	233	0.86	1.4
Selly Oak	860	4.03	4.31
Shard End	387	1.64	1.64
Sheldon	394	1.9	1.92
Small Heath	343	1.09	2.13
Soho	626	2.23	3.91
Sparkbrook	765	2.95	5.53
Sparkhill	797	3.03	6.29
Stockland Green	262	1.08	1.15
Sutton Four Oaks	1,431	4.74	4.81
Sutton New Hall	1,867	6.01	6.09
Sutton Vesey	1,443	4.96	5.06
Washwood Heath	489	1.73	2.49

Weoley	506	2.33	2.34
Yardley	602	2.6	2.7
Combined Figure	**34,661**	**3.61**	**4.17**

Note: Membership and electoral roll exclude most under-16s, many under 18s and all attenders not registered on electoral or membership rolls)

Sources: CERC Church of England CBF Stats: parish returns, 1991: Birmingham; Birmingham Methodist District returns 5: Birmingham (1992); *URC Handbook* (1992); *West Midland Baptist Association Yearbook* (1992)

Sutton Coldfield and Selly Oak) than in traditionally working-class wards such as such as Nechells and Kingstanding.[41] This partly mirrored historic patterns: in 1881 church attendance in Birmingham's upper-middle-class districts may have been around 40 per cent, compared to 33 per cent for other middle-class neighbourhoods and around 10 per cent in the poorest inner areas.[42] However, whilst social class was a significant index of religious practice, it was not the only one. In almost every case the lowest Anglican, Methodist, Baptist and URC attendances per head of population were found in Birmingham's 'outer-ring' wards with large, mainly white, housing estate neighbourhoods (for example, Brandwood and Fox Hollies).[43] By contrast, inner-city areas with large Afro-Caribbean populations such as Spark-brook and Sparkhill showed generally higher levels of attendance.[44] If the Asian population of each ward (mainly – though not exclusively – Muslim, Hindu and Sikh) is omitted from ward population totals, the percentage of churchgoers in multi-ethnic working-class or deprived communities within the churches' traditional 'external constituency' was comparable to that in the mainstream Churches' traditional white suburban strongholds (*see* table 2, column C). Certainly a significant number of Birmingham's inner-city churches – such as the Moseley Road Methodist and Grenfell Baptist churches featured in this study – owed their continuation to a more actively churchgoing African/Caribbean population. Congregations in Birmingham's mainly white, outer-ring estates (such as St Bede's, Brandwood) were more

[41] Figures are necessarily approximate since many attenders will cross ward boundaries to attend church. Nevertheless, within the seven case-study churches, about 70% of questionnaire respondents lived within two miles of the church building.

[42] H. McLeod, *Religion and society in England, 1850–1914*, Basingstoke 1996, 62.

[43] One analysis estimated Anglican attendance in 'upper-middle-class' Birmingham parishes at 32 per 1,000 of population, but only 4 per 1,000 in the city's outer-ring estates, some of whom commuted to church: W. Brown and M. Brown, 'The hidden poor: a report to consider the needs of peoples living in the large outer ring council estates of the Birmingham diocese', Birmingham [1995], 1, 16, 19.

[44] In 1998 'non-white' constituted 7.2% of the West Midlands population but 11.4% of churchgoers in the region: P. Brierley, *The tide is running out: what the 1998 English church attendance survey reveals*, London 2000, 138.

likely to struggle. Research on Birmingham Baptist congregations in 1988 further suggested that whilst white members of inner city congregations were disproportionately older, and commuted to church from the suburbs, newer attenders were disproportionately young, Black and living locally.[45]

Gender differences in religious practice also emerge from the available statistics. Detailed records for the Anglican diocese of Birmingham in 1960 (the only postwar year for which a full set of data exists) showed women to be numerically dominant in almost every area of church life, and increasingly so throughout the life course: female confirmation candidates constituted 59 per cent of the total amongst under-15s, 67 per cent amongst 15–20s, and 70 per cent of over-21s. Whilst girls only slightly outnumbered boys in church youth groups in 1960, three times as many adult women were involved in all-female church discussion groups as men involved in corresponding all-male groups.[46] Between 1955 and 1989 female confirmation candidates in Birmingham and Solihull parishes outnumbered male candidates by almost 2 to 1.[47] Such patterns reflect a wider trend for women's church participation to outstrip that of men by a similar proportion.[48] Callum Brown's assertion of the importance of working-class female religiosity before the 1960s is tentatively supported by what sketchy figures are available: a gender breakdown of Birmingham Anglican Sunday school participation in 1956 suggests that girls counted for around 59 per cent of attenders in broadly 'working-class' areas, but only 56 per cent in broadly 'middle-class' areas.[49]

However, other factors moderated women's numerical preponderance in Christian affiliation. The 1989 English Church Census found gender difference most pronounced amongst the historic 'mainstream' denominations and least amongst Evangelical and more theologically conservative denominations. Moreover, census data also suggests that gender disparity in religious practice was less pronounced amongst younger cohorts, even accounting for women's average greater longevity (see table 3). Andrew Perry's analysis of attendance patterns at St John's Sparkhill between 1945 and 1975 likewise indicates stronger church attendance by women than men before the early 1960s, but a narrowing of the gap thereafter.[50] National data from the 2006 English Church Census agrees that the proportion of men in church had

[45] The Birmingham Baptist Inner City Project, *Baptists in the inner city of Birmingham*, Birmingham 1988, 16–27.

[46] Church of England CBF Stats, Church of England Records Centre, Bermondsey, parish returns, 1960: Birmingham.

[47] Confirmation statistics, ibid. 1955–64, 1972–89.

[48] C. D. Field, 'Adam and Eve: gender in the English Free Church constituency', *JEH* xliv (1993), 63–79; T. Walter and G. Davie, 'The religiosity of women in the modern west', *BJS* xix (1998), 640–60 at p. 642.

[49] Church of England CBF Stats: parish returns, 1956, box 3: Birmingham.

[50] A. Perry, 'Anglican Christianity in Birmingham, 1945–1975', unpubl. MPhil diss. Birmingham 2010, 34.

Table 3
Female churchgoers by age and denomination (%), Birmingham, 1989

Denomination	1–14	15–9	20–9	30–44	45–64	65+
Orthodox	60.0	58.8	52.6	54.3	55.8	57.1
Anglican	54.8	57.0	60.6	60.3	68.6	68.0
Baptist	53.6	53.4	56.2	57.3	61.6	69.5
Roman Catholic	52.9	54.0	51.1	54.1	57.6	56.1
Brethren	57.5	53.5	56.2	54.5	60.3	66.3
Fellowship of Independent Evangelical Churches	61.6	42.9	53.1	64.2	63.7	66.5
House church	51.7	57.7	57.1	53.2	47.3	51.2
Independent (other)	38.5	50.0	45.8	51.5	56.1	74.4
Methodist	60.1	54.9	57.4	59.2	61.5	70.2
'Afro-Caribbean'	62.3	59.9	70.6	64.8	62.4	65.2
Lutheran	30.0	0	18.5	50.0	67.4	50.0
Quaker	50.0	50.0	60.0	70.6	57.7	68.7
Protestant (other)	46.3	37.5	56.5	57.9	57.7	61.1
Assemblies of God	61.5	59.6	56.4	60.4	61.1	70.1
Elim	44.5	33.3	44.2	51.8	60.8	67.3
Pentecostal (other)	26.6	100.0	45.5	42.1	78.8	57.9
United Reformed Church	61.1	61.4	50.0	64.1	64.1	67.9
Local Ecumenical Projects	52.1	54.8	60.7	64.5	60.9	73.5
Total	54.8	54.6	56.3	58.1	62.7	63.0

Note: Ordering of cases reflects ordering in original dataset

Source: P. Brierley, English church census, 1989 [Computer File], Colchester: The Data Archive [Distributor] (5 Nov. 1991), SN: 2842

increased slightly since 1998 (primarily because women over 30 were leaving in greater numbers), with boys now in a slight majority in the 14–19 age group.[51] Did practice simply reflect wider gender- and age-related patterns of religious belief?[52] Had younger cohorts more specifically abandoned an assumed connection between piety and femininity, as Callum Brown has argued?[53] Or were these patterns attributable to other factors? The oral evidence certainly suggests a trend for younger cohorts to seek a partner sharing their religious outlook,[54] leading to greater gender parity amongst the married adult churchgoing population – although single young adult

[51] Brierley, Nosedive, 131–5.
[52] Walter and Davie, 'Religiosity of women', 642–3.
[53] Brown, Death of Christian Britain, 181–92.
[54] This is also noted in P. Ward, Growing up Evangelical: youthwork and the making of a subculture, London 1996, 176–7.

Christians remain disproportionately female. Whichever is the case, it seems that age and gender were interrelated in patterns of church participation in the late twentieth century.

Further evidence for the significance of age is provided by the 1989 and 1998 English church censuses. Churchgoing in the 1990s was heavily – though not exclusively – an older adult activity, particularly when compared to the age structure of the population as a whole. Notably, whilst over-65s constituted only 16 per cent of the English population in 1998, the same age group accounted for 25 per cent of English churchgoers and 27 per cent of churchgoers in the West Midlands. If the elderly were disproportionately represented in church, the 20–44 age group was comparatively absent (35 per cent of the English population in 1998 but amongst churchgoers only 26 per cent across England and 25 per cent in the West Midlands). By contrast, the 45–64 age groups were in church in exact proportion to their strength within the wider population. (This cohort, born between 1927 and 1945, and supplying the greatest number of interviewees, has been more widely characterised as 'joiners' of organisations.) Under-19s were also present in church in proportion to their presence in the wider population, although this represented a marked contraction from earlier decades of large-scale Sunday school participation.[55] However, clear variations also existed between denominations (see table 4) In 1989 over 24 per cent of Methodist attenders in Birmingham were over 65, compared to only 3.7 per cent of attenders of 'New Churches' (although the survey may under-represent numbers attending Black-led churches). Most striking was the polarisation between churches with many children and young adults and those with few or none: roughly 70 per cent of under-19s attending churches in Birmingham and Solihull in 1989 were concentrated in only 25 per cent of congregations, whilst a third of congregations had fewer than ten under-19s. The figures for the 20–29 age group were even more stark: 27 per cent of congregations had no attenders in their twenties, whilst only thirty-six congregations across the city accounted for over half of all attendances by this age group. The highest attendances by children and young adults were frequently recorded by Catholic churches (partly due to the larger size of Catholic parishes), but Evangelical and Charismatic churches were also amongst the most successful at retaining twenty-somethings in the late 1980s. Such figures suggest a very strong polarisation of the age profile of local churches in the late twentieth century.

[55] Brierley, *Tide*, 124.

Table 4
Age cohorts as percentage of total Birmingham church attendances, by denomination, 1989

Denomination	<14	15–9	20–9	30–44	45–64	65+
Orthodox	21.7	7.4	8.3	20.0	33.5	9.1
Anglican	22.4	5.1	9.3	18.7	27.8	16.7
Baptist	22.4	6.2	11.3	18.4	25.8	15.8
Roman Catholic	17.5	11.7	12.3	18.5	23.5	16.5
Brethren	24.7	7.6	11.2	14.3	21.3	20.9
Fellowship of Independent Evangelical Churches	21.0	3.9	9.2	12.6	23.2	30.2
House church	22.7	11.9	27.1	23.4	11.2	3.7
Independent (other)	29.8	9.3	12.1	20.3	15.7	12.9
Methodist	24.3	5.0	8.1	14.0	24.4	24.4
'Afro-Caribbean'	26.9	11.3	17.5	18.1	20.8	5.3
Lutheran	8	0	21.6	9.6	36.8	24.0
Quaker	9.1	2.5	4.1	14.1	22.7	47.5
Protestant (other)	15.7	9.8	17.1	23.4	18.0	16.1
Assemblies of God	22.7	9.8	16.3	19.5	20.7	11.1
Elim	21.1	5.2	13.7	15.9	22.1	22.1
Pentecostal (other)	15.3	1.0	11.2	19.4	33.7	19.4
United Reformed Church	22.7	3.6	3.3	14.0	26.8	29.7
Local Ecumenical Projects	20.5	5.2	10.3	15.2	21.4	27.4
All churches	21.5	7.2	10.9	17.9	24.8	17.6
Population (1991 Census)	21.4	6.6	16.6	19.5	20.2	15.9
All churches as % of 1991 population	**4.8**	**5.2**	**3.1**	**4.3**	**5.8**	**5.3**

Note: Ordering of cases reflects ordering in original dataset

Source: Brierley, *English church census, 1989* [Computer File]

Seven Birmingham congregations

The complexity of the picture outlined here cautions against placing too much emphasis upon any single social variable, but also highlights the importance of age. However, the general patterns require earthing in the actual experience of congregational life. Seven local churches were selected as 'bore holes' into the life and concerns of Birmingham's postwar Churches. Research into these congregations blended oral history interviewing and traditional archival research with one month's participant observation of the contemporary congregation and a questionnaire survey of a sample of regular churchgoers. Here, a pen portrait of each congregation is offered, primarily focusing on the shape and character of the churches at the time of the original research in 1997–9 (accepting that much will have changed since). Particular attention is given to the place of age and generation in the 'ecology' of each congregation, as the book's central concern. Not every aspect of generational identity can be explored here, but some reflections on cohort, attitudinal, behavioural and affectual differences are offered. This creates the context for the oral evidence discussed in later chapters, but also illustrates the way in which age and generational questions had emerged as key concerns for local churches by the end of the century. (Quotation is attributed where derived from interview testimony but not where originating from participant observation.)

Moseley Road Methodist Church

Moseley Road Methodist was founded in 1872. The present building (erected in the late 1940s after bombing destroyed the original) stands on the main road through Balsall Heath, a deprived but regenerating district south of the city centre. A high proportion of local residents are Asian or Afro-Caribbean, and in the late 1990s the church's membership was around 90 per cent Black, mostly Caribbean, but with growing numbers from Africa. Without the relatively successful assimilation of new arrivals from the West Indies in the 1950s and 1960s, and the perseverance of Black attenders despite some racial prejudice, Moseley Road would almost certainly have succumbed to the white 'flight to the suburbs' which saw several other inner Birmingham churches close in the postwar decades. The church's motto in the late 1990s – 'commitment to community' – reflected the desire of both the (white, male) minister and an ethnically mixed core of active members to extend practical service to the locality (expressed, for example, through a long-running open youth project, family counselling centre, weekly Carib-bean lunch and several uniformed youth organisations). However, for most church members, personal spiritual growth and fellowship took precedence over systematic, collective social action.

Liturgically, a fairly traditional English Methodism had by the 1990s acquired a discernibly Caribbean flavour – most notably in the style of singing, and in a readiness to join in reciting familiar Bible verses quoted by preachers. Visual reminders of the Caribbean included a small whitewashed model church surrounded by palm trees, positioned on the communion table. To church members themselves, Moseley Road was a friendly and welcoming community. Newcomers to Sunday services were habitually invited to stand and introduce themselves, to applause from the congrega-tion. However, engaging church members in conversation after the service proved more difficult, partly due to my inexperience as a researcher in an unfamiliar cultural context; partly because Sunday services appeared to play an important role in bringing together families and friends, perhaps reducing the level of attention given to newcomers. Two ministers furthermore noted that Moseley Road had historically felt stigmatised as the 'poor relation' of the churches in the local Methodist circuit, leading to a low-level suspicion of outsiders (though the continued legacy of this was difficult to substantiate). Whatever the causes, interviews with church members were comparatively difficult to arrange, and the resulting congregational portrait was sketchier than for other churches.

Nevertheless, it was clear that age and generation (amongst many other factors) helped to shape congregational life and identity. By the late 1990s many local Methodist churches were struggling to attract a broad generational spectrum. In comparison, Moseley Road was regarded as a success story within the wider Birmingham Methodist District. 'It's very lively there', I was told by several local Methodists, 'lots of young people.' The young figured highly in the official vision of the church as well as its wider reputation: its minister had recently introduced an 'all-age' style service, whilst some younger church members had created a reggae-style processional using taped music. Young and old largely appeared to mix well, several commenting on the church's potential as a meeting place for all ages and ethnicities. However, concerns persisted over the lack of youth in the congregation (the minister estimated that 50 per cent of the congregation were of retirement age). Older Black and white members both expressed disappointment that the church's long-running youth project had not drawn new members into church (although project staff did not regard this as the primary purpose), leaving a sense of powerlessness to engage with the young. As one long-standing West Indian member commented 'it's no good me saying to them "come to church" 'cos they won't take any notice. But with a young person'. The conviction that a congregation needed young people to attract young people was widely-held across the case-study churches.

Major events in Moseley Road's history had also bequeathed distinctive perspectives to different strata of the congregation. The longest-standing church members (mainly elderly white upper-working/lower-middle class) in some respects constituted a distinct 'affectual' generation within the congregational eco-system, being the only ones able to recall the original church building, an older pattern of Methodist worship and Balsall Heath as a predominantly white working-class community. While not necessarily welcoming every new development (notably in worship and music), they were proud of Moseley Road's resilience and of their own loyalty when other white families had left for the suburbs – 'to improve themselves' (as one woman in her sixties added, with a note of sarcasm). Older, West-Indian-born church members constituted a second (and largest) 'affectual' generation, playing a major part in the changes occurring at Moseley Road between the 1950s and 1970s. Arguably their preferences shaped many aspects of congregational life by the late 1990s. Though part of the same birth cohort as the church's older white members, they were less self-conscious in their use of Christian language and imagery, more demonstrative in worship and often more conservative in theology. However, both groups shared a preference for hymns, older mission choruses and oratorical preaching which many younger members found more challenging.

Indeed, a different approach to worship helped to distinguish a third 'affectual' generation at Moseley Road – adults in their twenties and thirties. This third 'generation' within Moseley Road was generally more highly educated, mixed more effortlessly across cultures and appeared more liberal and politicised in theology and ethics. Several spoke of a 'double alienation' of young Black people from a church which was both historically white and subsequently shaped by the Caribbean church cultures imported by the older West Indian majority. The group nevertheless participated fully and enthusiastically in congregational life, seeking reform from within but sharing with older members a desire to create a more welcoming church. Whilst generational differences were therefore apparent, they could be modified by ethnicity, theology and congregational loyalty.

Cotteridge Church (Anglican/Methodist/URC local ecumenical project)

The Cotteridge Church was created in 1985, when three churches – St Agnes Cotteridge, Kings Norton Methodist and Kings Norton URC – came together as a Local Ecumenical Project after some years of careful discussion.[56] Housed in the extensive refurbished Methodist Church premises since 1989, the church stands centrally within the mainly white working-class/lower-middle-class south Birmingham suburb of Cotteridge. In 1998 the church had around 300 members, with about 200 attendances weekly. The many weekday activities hosted or run by the church included a daily coffee bar, two day centres for the elderly, the local MP's surgery, adult education classes, keep fit clubs, and Boys' and Girls' Brigades. For the church's two ministers (one Anglican, one Methodist) and many of the core congregation, such activities were as central as worship to congregational life and ministry, echoing the ethic of practical service central to the original ecumenical vision.[57] Likewise, as individuals, Cotteridge members were more likely to participate in wider social, political and charitable causes than respondents from the other six case-study congregations. When asked about these activities, church members saw them not as purely 'secular' pursuits, but as an integral part of being Christian and being Church.

A readiness to blur the boundaries between 'sacred' and 'secular', 'church' and 'community' was also integral to the united church's founding vision, which from the outset had conceived 'church' as both Sunday congregants and weekday users; the whole building and not just the main worship space. However, as at Moseley Road, some expressed disappointment that the Sunday congregation had not significantly grown as a result of the church's community service. Social differences also persisted between weekday users

---

[56] A local ecumenical project is a formal arrangement between churches of different denominations to merge as one congregation, sharing worship and structures.

[57] I. Bussell, 'Church placement: semester paper' [on Cotteridge Church], unpubl. paper, Queen's Foundation for Ecumenical Theological Education, Birmingham 1997, 6.

and regular churchgoers, with the latter more heavily drawn from middle-class backgrounds and travelling to church from greater distance, often in search of qualities unavailable in their previous congregation (for example, ecumenical cooperation, flourishing children's work or extensive community involvement). Mostly however, a positive outlook pervaded, and most Cotteridge members spoke enthusiastically about their church.

For many members, the broad age profile of the church was a key indicator of its health. In 1996 eighty-five under-18s regularly participated in Junior Church[58] (a larger figure than for most local churches). Cotteridge became a magnet for young families – particularly those disinclined to attend Evangelical churches (in which youth work was commonly strongest). One questionnaire respondent noted how she and her young family had 'shopped around' for a church when moving to the area, eventually settling upon Cotteridge. Choosing a church with children in mind was increasingly common in the period.[59] Young and old generally appeared to mix harmoniously, and were in certain respects accorded equal status (for example, some places on the Church Council were reserved for young people). Cross-generational harmony was also arguably reinforced by the presence of several committed church families where parents, grandparents and children were all involved.

Nevertheless, other areas of church life – such as worship – were more contentious. For many younger Cotteridge members, worship seemed primarily geared to the needs of older members. For Claire Lewry, in her late teens, even 'all-age' worship services seemed little different to standard Sunday fare, continuing to contain 'really horrible hymns – they've got no tune, and they're really long ... I know that old people like them, but you just get put off singing them'. [60] Nor was this feeling confined to teenagers: Paul Harris (b. 1963 and one of several younger members with an Evangelical background) recognised the need to balance the preferences of all sections of the congregation, but found worship 'unadventurous and risk-free', remaining stuck in the mid-1980s when the three churches had merged.[61] If divisions of opinion over music and worship commonly occurred along age cohort lines, 'epochal' generational differences could thus also cohere around key events in a congregation's history. At Cotteridge, the original members of the three churches, who had experienced the 'coming together' first-hand,

---

[58] 'The Cotteridge Church: a profile for prospective ministers' (1996), 5. 'Junior Church' was popularised as an alternative to 'Sunday school' from the 1960s onwards; the name change reflecting a shift in emphasis towards adults and children as part of the same Christian community rather than as populating separate institutions (the 'church' and the 'Sunday school').

[59] QC, 3.11; K. Stevenson, 'Gathering threads', in R. Cotton and K. Stevenson, *On the receiving end: how people experience what we do in church*, London 1996, 5.

[60] IJ9CT.

[61] IJ16CT.

were still by-and-large satisfied with the congregation's direction. However, those who had joined more recently brought a more detached perspective on the church's story, identifying shortcomings as well as attractions.

St Bede's, Brandwood (Church of England)

St Bede's is the Anglican parish church for the large mid-twentieth-century south Birmingham estate of Brandwood. The first church building – a pre-fabricated multi-purpose hall – was opened in 1960, part of Bishop Leonard Wilson's 'Circles without Centres' campaign to establish churches on new housing estates. The present building dates from 1994, replacing the original multi-purpose church destroyed by arson three years earlier. In 1998 St Bede's was amongst the smaller Anglican congregations in Birmingham, with an electoral roll of around seventy and forty to fifty weekly attenders (amongst whom women strongly predominated). Liturgically, St Bede's services in 1998 blended a sober but unstarchy middle Anglicanism with a more catholic emphasis on symbol and ceremony, and an openness to Charismatic renewal amongst some of the congregation. This was neatly symbolised by the sight of an elderly member of St Bede's small robed choir singing a well-known chorus with arms un-self-consciously raised in worship. This eclecticism of worship styles and traditions owed much to the influence of previous clergy (who had taken the church in often different directions), but also reflected the variety of wider circles in which St Bede's people moved.[62] Whilst differences of opinion could occasionally surface (not least over worship), most of the congregation felt that commitment to the fellowship and its mission overrode these differences.

Of all the case-study congregations, St Bede's was the most strongly *local* church. Two-thirds of the 1998 congregation lived within a mile of the church building, and mirrored the mainly white working-class/lower middle-class profile of the estate as a whole. Serving the local community (for example, through a weekly lunch club and pastoral visiting scheme) figured highly in church members' conceptions of St Bede's mission. However, unlike at Cotteridge, boundaries between 'sacred' and 'secular' were often sharply drawn, many church members understanding their task as one of personal and community transformation rather than merely service (perhaps echoing St Bede's origins as a mission church). However, to many church members this task appeared daunting, in part hampered by the comparative invisibility of the building itself (located on a residential street away from the estate's main roads). My own visit to St Bede's fell during a long inter-regnum, when the burden of leadership bore heavily upon a core group of committed regulars.

---

[62] 62% of church members surveyed regularly participated in church activities outside their own congregation, compared to an average of only 53% across the seven congregations.

Where at Moseley Road and Cotteridge young people were taken to signify a healthy congregation, their absence at St Bede's signified malaise. The 1998 congregation's only teenager had recently departed to university, leaving only a handful of younger children in Junior Church. The lack of young people inside the church was often contrasted with the groups of local young people regularly congregating outside the building in the evening, sometimes banging on the church windows to disrupt meetings (something further taken to epitomise the difficulty of community engagement). The apparent fragmentation of neighbourhood life and the difficulty of engaging with youth were clearest to the few members of the current congregation who remembered the church's origins as a Sunday school on a new estate with few other community activities. For this oldest cohort, involvement in St Bede's had been a natural extension of neighbourhood life, an assumption which continued to continue to inform their views. Although the original Brandwood neighbours and church members were an ageing and shrinking group by 1998, they could still function as a 'grapevine' through which the church learned of people in need.

By this date, however, *de facto* leadership of the congregation had passed to a younger cohort, then in middle age. Variously in early retirement, part-time employment or free from regular family commitments, this group devoted considerable time and energy to maintaining the life of the congregation. As a result, life at St Bede's clearly bore the mark of their preferences in worship and their assumptions about church and mission. Some had first come to active Christian faith through the efforts of a missionary-minded vicar, Bob Jenkins, in the 1970s (often at times of personal crisis). This had left many of them with a similarly strong concern for local outreach and pastoral care. Nevertheless, the pressure of being a church in apparently stony soil also led many (particularly the younger and middle-aged) to value alternative 'sites of energy' beyond the congregation (some individuals with Charismatic roots attended events at Christ Church Burney Lane, a focus for renewal in the city, whilst the more liturgically traditional could sometimes be found at evensong at nearby All Saints' Kings Heath). Even so, the challenges of maintaining church life in challenging circumstances made for a close-knit atmosphere amongst core members which transcended age and liturgical differences. Newcomers (myself included) received a warm welcome.

St George's, Edgbaston (Church of England)
St George's, Edgbaston, stands on an island ringed by the one-way system at the centre of one of Birmingham's most affluent suburbs. The parish had been largely non-residential since the 1960s, with businesses replacing families in many of the large Victorian townhouses dominating the locale. In 1998 the residential population of the parish stood at just 2,884, but St George's continued to flourish, with regular worshippers from a wide geographical area attracted by its strong choral and liturgical tradition. The regular congrega-

tion of 1998 was predominantly professional middle-class in character, but with a significant working-class minority, many older, some still living locally in the north of the parish beyond the Hagley Road. Most of the average 170 worshippers attended the 10.30 a.m. Sung Eucharist, although a quieter 8.00 a.m. Communion, and Sung Evensong at 6.30 p.m. (both Book of Common Prayer) also attracted smaller, regular congregations. In 1998 worship at St George's was best described as 'central' with some catholic elements. Worship was ordered but not stiffly formal: after one Choral Eucharist, the sight of two eager choirgirls racing each other to the altar to snuff out the candles prompted a ripple of laughter. United in their affection for 'traditional Anglicanism', many of St George's regulars expressed pride at the quality of their choir and organist at their Victorian gothic building (Grade II listed), and at the high intellectual standard of preaching. Long-standing members of the congregation also knew their parish history, speaking proudly of previous clergy who had departed St George's for higher office.[63]

Sunday services were focal to the spirituality of individual church members and the weekly life of the congregation: St George's questionnaire respondents were less likely to pray in private, read the Bible, or participate in Christian organisations outside the parish than respondents from other case-study churches. Informal conversations about God or Christian faith were almost entirely absent within earshot of this observer. Few congregational activities besides worship took place on a regular basis, the main gatherings being a monthly fellowship (largely social/educational rather than devotional) and a monthly lunch club. In part, this reflected the dominance of Sunday worship in congregational spirituality, but perhaps also (as the 1997 Parish Statement noted) that a middle-class congregation were 'accustomed to buying work from others ... not as willing to devote their time' but were 'consumers ... [who] look for high standards in their church experience'. This concentrated considerable responsibility on office-holders. Clergy were nevertheless treated reverentially and were expected to deliver high standards. Lay people participated in services, but only licensed individuals led worship. Mission was regarded less in terms of personal evangelism and social action and more in terms of chaplaincy to local institutions (including several schools and hospitals) and offering a cultural as well as spiritual focus to the neighbourhood ('where would Edgbaston be without St George's?' asked one long-standing member). Whatever the true answer to this statement, it nevertheless illustrated the extent to which many church members saw St George's as deeply embedded in the life of the area, as one of its few surviving civic institutions.

Bound by common attachments transcending other socio-economic divisions, age and generation seemed of little overt significance at St George's. On Sundays older adults predominated but a spread of ages attended. As at

---

[63] The most eminent was A.W.T. Perowne (vicar 1905–13), a future bishop of Worcester.

St Bede's, the day-to-day running of the church rested predominantly with a small core of middle-aged and recently-retired regulars. With no major disjunction in the life of the congregation (such as the 'wilderness years' at Cotteridge), it was difficult to discern any 'affectual' generational group within the church formed through common experience of a distinct phase of shared history. However, the age profile of St George's could worry church members when it affected the heart of congregational identity, for example, the difficulty of finding young people to sing in the church choir.

Grenfell Baptist Church, Alum Rock

Grenfell Baptist Church stands on a quiet residential street in the interwar housing estate of Alum Rock, a 'middle ring' suburb of east Birmingham. The church was formed in 1952, a union of the local Thornton Road Fellowship and a rump from the historic Heneage Street Chapel when the latter closed due to slum clearance in its original Bloomsbury district location. Then, Alum Rock had been a comfortable working-class/lower-middle-class neighbourhood. In 1998 it formed part of what the minister of the time described as a 'twilight zone' between the inner city and more affluent suburbs. On the positive side, socio-economic and demographic change had brought many Afro-Caribbean residents into church membership and had enriched Grenfell's worshipping culture (by 1998 around half of the congregation's sixty adult members were Black[64]). Negatively, a perceived decline in neighbourliness and rising social dislocation led many contemporary church members to feel that Alum Rock was now more difficult mission territory than before.

Evangelistic outreach amongst the local community had been a priority throughout the congregation's history. In 1998 the congregation organised regular neighbourhood visiting programmes and participated in evangelistic initiatives with other local churches (including a jointly-run Alpha Course[65]). Socially and spatially this was a solidly 'local' congregation: virtually all the congregation lived within two miles of church and many expressed strong attachment to the area. Several recalled feeling guided to the church on Sunday morning (either by a prompting voice or an otherwise improbable set of circumstances), subsequently rediscovering their faith.[66]

In 1998 Grenfell Baptist was predominantly Evangelical and Charismatic in ethos. In the 1970s several church members had experienced Charismatic renewal, and from the 1980s services became increasingly marked by the pop-influenced worship music and more informal styles by then associated with the movement. The increasingly Charismatic-Evangelical direction of the church was also in harmony with older Caribbean members' preference

---

[64] Minister's estimate, QC 2.8.
[65] This was, and is, a popular discussion-based course on Christian basics developed by the Holy Trinity (Anglican) Church, Brompton, London, widely used across the world by the late 1990s.
[66] For example, Merlene Watson, IJ46GB.

for lively, revivalist-style worship. Charismatic gifts (particularly tongues and prophecy) remained in evidence in 1998, though usually discreetly used. A strong emphasis on the power of God in individual lives reflected the debt of the two most recent ministers to the teaching of influential US pastor, evangelist and founder of the Vineyard network of churches John Wimber, in whose thought the unleashing of extraordinary manifestations of spiritual power was key to authentic Christian life and witness.[67] A worship band including keyboard and drums led the singing. A spirituality centred upon daily prayer and Bible reading was expressed through both sermons and congregational questionnaire responses (every single respondent reported praying every day – more than in any other case study[68]).

How far did age and generational issues shape the 1998 congregation? On one hand, a discourse of 'family' was central to the maintenance of unity, encompassing Black and white, long-standing working-class members and younger, often more educated or professional members. Minister and church members regularly referred to each other as 'brothers and sisters (in Christ)'. Though the largest single cohort in the congregation was aged mid-forties to early-sixties, young parents in their twenties and thirties and their children (initially mainly white, with more Black families in latter times) were also present in significant numbers. Some of these had grown up in the congregation and were influenced in their teenage years by the Charismatic renewal. The worshipping preferences of this cohort had become increasingly influential – initially since older members were prepared to accommodate new styles to encourage a younger generation in faith, subsequently due to the arrival of a younger minister who was himself Charismatic-Evangelical.[69] Services offered various opportunities for children to participate in worship (for example, in waving flags or rattling shakers during the singing). In one corner, chairs were arranged in a series of crescents for use by family groups. This contemporary variant on the 'family pew' was primarily a practical step to allow families to accommodate pushchairs and other equipment, but its existence illustrated the valued place of young families in the church. Despite concerns over the lack of teenagers in the congregation, significant numbers of young children and a flourishing mother and toddler group offered hope for the future. Indeed in 1998 some core members of the congregation even speculated that ministry to this age group might become Grenfell Baptist's distinctive calling. One active member, Jan Hughes, explained that

---

[67] See, for example, J. Wimber with K. Springer, *Power evangelism: signs and wonders today*, London 1985.

[68] This possibly reflected the centrality of the daily 'quiet time' in Evangelical spirituality, though interviews and observations suggested that the questionnaire results did not exaggerate the extent of private devotion.

[69] Some research suggests that a younger minister will attract a younger congregation: *Quadrant* (May 1997).

there's lots of churches in our area ... and each of them has a unique ministry; some with old people, some with the workshop for the blind ... Christ Church have got gifted youth leaders, and a big youth group up there, whereas we have got lots of babies and toddlers down with us ... now, it seems silly ... if we all duplicate.[70]

Such a local division of labour was increasingly common amongst English churches in the late 1990s.

Carrs Lane United Reformed Church

A dissenting chapel has stood on the site of the present Carrs Lane United Reformed Church since 1748. Throughout much of the nineteenth and twentieth centuries, Carrs Lane was an important stronghold of English Congregationalism and served by some of its most celebrated preachers – among them R. W. Dale, J. H. Jowett, Sidney Berry, Leyton Richards and Leslie Tizard. Carrs Lane's profile remained high within the United Reformed Church (created in 1972 following the union of the Congregationalist and Presbyterian denominations). However, the twentieth century had also witnessed a long, slow decline in church membership (to 160 in 1998, with weekly attendance around eighty-five). One significant local factor in this decline was the disappearance of any sizeable residential population in Birmingham city centre as a result of postwar planning initiatives. Carrs Lane's continued viability owed much to the commitment of its many long-standing members,[71] two-thirds of whom were over sixty in 1998 and 90 per cent of whom travelled at least two miles to church. This unusual stability of membership was a mixed blessing: church members spoke positively about the many strong friendships formed within the congregation, yet worried about the ageing profile of the congregation and the risk of becoming stuck in a rut. Whether or not such fears were justified, it was the attitudes and experiences of this cohort, born before the Second World War, which were most important in shaping congregational culture.

The dominant theological discourse within Carrs Lane was an inclusive liberal Protestantism which encouraged questioning and honest doubt. A few (mainly older) church members expressed affinities with Quakerism. In 1998 Sunday morning worship followed a common Free-Church pattern of hymns (many from the denominational hymnbook), sermon and prayers, with space for individual reflection and occasional material from other sources (notably from the Iona Community, partly reflecting a previous minister's close involvement). A minority of the congregation (mainly in their forties and fifties) acknowledged a personal debt to the Charismatic movement, although the renewal had made little impact on Sunday services.

---

[70] IJ50GB.

[71] Carrs Lane questionnaire respondents had on average been church members for thirty years (average across seven congregations: twenty-one years).

The congregation was predominantly white and professional middle class, although short-term worshippers from overseas regularly attended. By the late 1990s Carrs Lane also had a growing ministry amongst the homeless and those with addiction or mental health problems, some of whom regularly attended the small evening service.

The multi-purpose church and community centre which had replaced the old chapel in 1970 played host to a wide range of charitable and community initiatives, some run by church members themselves. By contrast, few regular week-night activities took place, mainly due to the age of members and the demands of travelling in. Nevertheless, Carrs Lane members were almost twice as likely to be regular supporters of charitable, voluntary or political organisations as members of other case-study congregations. The church's long pedigree of radical Christian social conscience also continued to evoke pride amongst the latter-day congregation. Nevertheless, several members contrasted their own, ageing congregation occupying the church's main worship space and the growing young African Independent congregation leasing a small downstairs room in the church complex. More than one 'Carrs Laner' quipped (only half-jokingly) that before long the two congregations would be swapping rooms. Some wondered if the church should adopt more contemporary popular styles of worship to attract the young, even whilst admitting that this was unlikely to appeal to existing church-goers. However, others felt that the church should concentrate on providing worship and activities more appealing to its current constituency.

St Mary's Roman Catholic Church, Pitt Heath[72]

St Mary's stands amidst a large mid twentieth-century housing estate in Birmingham's middle ring. Parish work began in the mid-1930s, with the present building dating from the 1950s (one of several erected in Birmingham during the expansion of that decade, and one of the last to reflect pre-Vatican II architectural assumptions). A Saturday/Sunday mass attendance of around 400 in 1998 (over three services) was slightly lower than in neighbouring parishes, but represented an increase on the equivalent figure a decade previously (a more difficult period in the church's history). Recent growth was a source of some pride amongst Sunday regulars, and was ascribed largely to the dedication of the current, much-loved parish priest

In liturgy and parish life, a contemporary Catholicism characteristic of the aspirations of the Second Vatican Council blended with older 'pre-Vatican' styles and assumptions.[73] Masses were mostly in English, and lay participation was evident in bible reading, leading intercessions and bringing the bread and wine forward to the altar for communion. Yet 'pre-Vatican' elements persisted, as in the partial use of Latin at the 11 a.m. mass, and

---

72 Both 'St Mary's' and 'Pitt Heath' are pseudonyms.
73 For the 'pre-Vatican'/'post-Vatican' terminology see M. Hornsby–Smith, *The changing parish: a study of parishes, priests and parishioners after Vatican II*, London 1989, 31ff.

also in the parish priest's preference to run the parish himself rather than collaboratively with a church council. An active core of lay parishioners undertook visiting, organised social events, raised funds and (in some cases) campaigned on social issues. For a (mainly middle-class) minority of the congregation, St Mary's was the focus for much spare-time activity. However, most regulars approached churchgoing with a 'pre-Vatican' mentality, mainly attending mass and occasional socials.[74] Sunday mornings seemed relaxed and friendly, yet comparatively few worshippers lingered after services to chat[75] or recognised me as a newcomer.

As with most Catholic parishes in Birmingham, St Mary's attracted a significant (though not unusually large) proportion of worshippers born in Ireland, a heritage which continued to inform shared identity, but also linked Sunday regulars with a wider penumbra of local working-class Catholic families (a dance and social which took place during my month at St Mary's attracted several hundred people – a level of local community support unimaginable to many non-Catholic congregations). However, St Mary's parishioners were also less likely than average to be 'joiners' of organisations (either inside or outside the church), although many were involved in charitable collecting.

The significance of age in the week-by-week life of St Mary's was more difficult to assess, since the idea of congregation-as-community was less strong than in the other six churches. There was age variation between St Mary's three main services: adults predominated at the Saturday-for-Sunday mass (the shortest, without music). The 11 a.m. Sunday mass attracted a similar congregation, albeit with a slightly higher proportion of older people, some of whom appeared to appreciate the 'pre-Vatican' elements in this service. The 9.30 a.m. Sunday mass attracted more young families (mainly due to the Children's Liturgy group running during the service, the success of which was clearly a source of encouragement to the adult congregation). Older parishioners sometimes hoped that such work might reignite the faith of parents as well as children, and cited examples where this had occurred.[76] However, many younger attenders felt that St Mary's remained insufficiently geared to their needs. As one active member of the congregation, Anna Carter (b. 1983) explained,

> I think that unless the church starts focusing on the youth more, it's just going to fade away ... you go into a church and you mostly see older people

---

[74] This often remained the pattern: D. Ryan, *The Catholic parish: institutional discipline, tribal identity and religious development in the English Church*, London 1996, 15.

[75] This was not unusual amongst Catholic parishes: M. D. Stringer, *On the perception of worship: the ethnography of worship in four Christian congregations in Manchester*, Birmingham 1999, 112.

[76] This may have been a general trend amongst late twentieth-century Catholic congregations (Ryan, *Catholic parish*, 32), although insufficient to reverse an overall decline in attendance.

... I think what Fr. Neill's got at the moment, having those two little sessions, in the middle of the Mass ... I think that's really important, to get them to understand when they're younger.[77]

Ms Carter and several others felt that the church had made real advances in catering for young people, but still had far to go. As in other congregations, two issues predominated. First, there was teaching of moral standards. Several expressed a preference for open discussion over a strictly didactic approach (particularly on questions of sex, marriage and divorce). A second matter of contention was music and worship. Just as some St Bede's members supplemented their own church's worship with occasional visits to a 'niche' church of their preference, younger Catholic attenders also regularly sought out dedicated extra-parochial youth ministries – for example, diocesan retreats, monthly youth masses at St Chad's Cathedral, and the annual 'Emmaus' youth day at Alton Towers. Nevertheless, whilst those with reservations about the church's approach to worship and moral teaching were disproportionately young, differences of opinion were not drawn solely along age cohort lines: for example, parishioners who had grown up before the reforms of Vatican II seemed fairly evenly divided over whether or not the full Latin mass was better than the present liturgy.

This chapter has highlighted the key social and cultural changes amidst which Birmingham's churches sought to pursue their common life and ministry: postwar reconstruction and population movement from the centre to the outskirts of the city; the decline of historic industries and the social problems arising in consequence; and the transformation of Birmingham into a multi-cultural city. Some key themes in postwar church life have also been identified: a general (though uneven) decline in formal affiliation; changing relationships with local neighbourhoods; the importance of congregational belonging to personal identity; significant differences on questions of worship and mission; and the challenge of pursuing a positive Christian distinctiveness in a post-Christendom society. These will be considered in more detail in the following chapters.

Throughout this chapter, questions of congregational history, current priorities for ministry and mission, or prognoses of the future frequently became focused around age-related issues. Consciousness of a long-term decline in attendance, particularly amongst the young, led to a strong intergenerational mix being seen as a key indicator of congregational health. This could influence decisions over worship style or even the primary pastoral or missionary direction of the congregation. The idea of generationally monocultural congregations was increasingly familiar – commonly as an accident of geography, membership or congregational style, but occasionally as a result of a more deliberate decision to focus ministry on one particular age group. Even

[77] IJ67SM.

where congregations were generationally diverse, the assumptions of certain cohort groups, or the memory of defining moments or phases of church and community life kept alive by those who experienced them, could exert a strong influence on the congregational ecology of local churches.

The generational stratification of the local church at the end of the twentieth century should not be over-exaggerated: age and generation were not always the most important variables in quantitative terms, and nor was generational change the only matter of concern to the congregations. Open inter-generational conflict was extremely rare and most churchgoers valued the church as a social space in which young and old could mix. However, the seven case studies suggest particular differences between an older group of church members, into adulthood by the outbreak of the Second World War and over 70 by the late 1990s; an intermediate group mainly born in the 1930s, '40s and '50s and then in middle age; and a younger cohort growing up during or after the 1960s then in late teenage and young adulthood. These divisions roughly correspond to the 'Builder', 'Baby-Boomer' and 'Generation X' scheme of social generations already familiar in existing literature on generations. Yet from the snapshot of late-1990s local congregational life presented in this chapter, it is already possible to note the plural and multi-layered character of generational identity, as it arose from a complex interaction of past experience, present context and future expectation. To understand the nature and development of these late twentieth-century patterns of generational identity further, and in particular to consider the extent to which contemporary age cohort patterns rested on more than life-course effects and attitudinal difference, it is necessary to move to a more historical exploration of four of the most important spheres of experience through which that identity was negotiated: family, congregation, community and wider society.

2

The Spectre of 'Decline'

One of the most significant recent developments in the historiography of Christianity in modern Britain has been the search for new narrative frameworks which broaden the scope of debate beyond questions of institutional decline.[1] As John Wolffe has argued, 'a rounded account of the history of religion in Britain ... needs to balance the language of decline and secularisation with an awareness of continuity, adaptation and new beginnings'.[2] Nevertheless, declining church attendance remains an inescapable feature of the history of postwar Christianity. From around 40 per cent of the population of England and Wales in church on Census Sunday 1851, this figure had dropped to 7.5 per cent by 1998 and 6.3 per cent by 2006.[3] In Birmingham, roughly 32 per cent of the population had attended church in 1892, but only 8.6 per cent by 1998 and 6.8 per cent by 2006.[4] Although the bald statistics are familiar, less is known about the impact and interpretation of decline amongst those who remained in church. If decline is a cultural as well as statistical phenomenon, then exploring experiences of living with decline should be important to our overall understanding. As a result, this chapter seeks to provide a more rounded account of the experience of growth and decline in church attendance at grass-roots level. In so doing, it brings Birmingham church attendance statistics into conversation with perceptions of congregational strength or weakness derived from parish magazines and oral testimony. Throughout the period clergy and congregations in Birmingham watched attendance figures closely, with gain or loss an important barometer of the Church's health. Significantly, from the 1950s, these explanations acquired an increasingly strong generational dimension and, by the end of the century, the generational profile of their congregation

---

[1] See particularly Cox, 'Master narratives', 201–17; Morris, 'Strange death of Christian Britain', 963–76; McLeod, 'Crisis of Christianity in the west', and 'Being a Christian at the end of the twentieth century', in McLeod, *Cambridge history of Christianity*, ix. 23–47, 636–47; and Garnett, Harris, Grimley, Whyte and Williams, *Redefining Christian Britain*.

[2] J. Wolffe, 'Religion and "secularisation"', in P. Johnson (ed.), *Twentieth century Britain: economic, social and cultural change*, London–New York 1994, 427–41 at p. 440.

[3] Rough 1851 estimate is from McLeod, *Religion and society in England*, 13. A precise figure remains elusive since the 1851 census counted attendances, not attenders: see K. D. M. Snell and P. S. Ell, *Rival Jerusalems: the geography of Victorian religion*, Cambridge 2000, 37, 432. Figures for 2006 are from Brierley, *Religious trends 6*, 12.2.

[4] Peacock, 'The 1892 Birmingham religious census', 15; Brierley, *Religious trends 6*, 12.105.

significantly influenced how positively individual Christians saw the past and future. Moreover, a strong relationship existed in the oral testimony between attitudes towards decline across different cohorts and interviewees' memories of the comparative health and/or malaise of the church in their formative years.

'Decline' in context

Declining church membership is such a familiar subject to early twenty-first century observers that it is important to note two particular reasons (beyond the bare facts) why decline became culturally as well as statistically significant. The first, inherited from the nineteenth-century heyday of denominational Christianity, was a preoccupation with quantification. In most periods of Christian history, measuring the Church was too difficult, too arcane, or insufficiently meaningful to be of widespread concern. From the eighteenth century, however, this began to change. As Callum Brown has demonstrated, the churches of the Evangelical revival kept careful records of membership and conversions, partly to demonstrate their success, but also to gauge the scale of the task remaining.[5] This absorption with religious statistics was further fuelled in the nineteenth century by the educated Victorian mind's fascination with measurement, classification and the prospect of a 'science of society'.[6] While membership grew, as it did for some denominations until the early twentieth century, numbers could be a source of encouragement (although even very high levels of churchgoing recorded in the 1851 religious census proved shocking and disappointing to many contemporary observers).[7] However, once numerical decline set in, the same statistical exercise provoked a more profound sense of crisis.[8] Both the quantification of observance, and growing concern over what the figures revealed, had thus become hardwired into many mainstream denominational cultures by the early twentieth century.

Arguably a second factor in the foregrounding of 'decline' in the churches was the onset of a much wider cultural pessimism in British society after 1945.[9] Prognoses of civilisational decline have been politically and culturally influential in every age,[10] but arguably assumed renewed prominence in

---

[5] Brown, *Death of Christian Britain*, 145–6.

[6] M. J. Cullen, *The statistical movement in 19th-century Britain: the functions of empirical social research*, Brighton 1975, 135–49. I am grateful to Arthur Burns for introducing me to this.

[7] McLeod, *Religion and society in England*, 55.

[8] This is perceptively charted in Cox, *English Churches*.

[9] The phrase is taken from O. Bennett, *Cultural pessimism: narratives of decline in the postmodern world*, Edinburgh 2001.

[10] For a brief survey see ibid. 1–20; H. White, *Metahistory: historical imagination in nineteenth century Europe*, Baltimore 1975, 108–31, 191–229; and White's inspiration

the later twentieth century. Confident predictions of steady human progress had become less sustainable in a century which had witnessed a catalogue of man-made horrors, including the Somme, the Great Depression, the Gulags, Hiroshima and Auschwitz. Domestically, too, thinkers of both Right and Left developed assessments of British economic and social life which Jim Tomlinson has subsequently christened 'declinism'.[11] Perceptions of decline may have been accentuated by the canonisation of other historical periods as the apogee of European civilisation or British greatness.[12] Explanations for decline varied with political allegiance, ranging from general economic stagnation to the loss of empire, the expansion of the welfare state and the culturally degrading effects of commercialisation and consumerism. In fact, Tomlinson suggests, 'over the last forty years of the century, almost every facet of life in Britain was alleged by someone to be the cause of decline'.[13] In quantifiable matters at least, the evidence is ambiguous, and depends on the indicators considered. However, regardless of reality, the idea of 'decline' remained culturally compelling.

Writing a cultural history of church decline is made more complex by the variety of interpretations found in the oral evidence. Understandings of growth and decline were partly shaped by perspective. As Robin Gill has noted, churchgoers have sometimes inferred a pattern of decline from the numbers of empty seats in their church building, whereas Victorian churches in particular were typically built to accommodate numbers well in excess of the regular congregation.[14] At Birmingham's Grenfell Baptist Church, where children's work was healthy, overseas missionary success was regularly reported and a providential theology predominated, prognoses were more optimistic than most. Juliette McLean (b. 1969) remarked that 'they say not many people do go to church … But maybe when you do go to church and [read Christian] literature and that, you see how many people have been converted, you don't have to hear about it on the news'.[15] In contrast, those who had seen dramatic decline in their own congregations and/or had fewer providentialist convictions were often more pessimistic. Joan Egan, of St George's, Edgbaston, in her sixties, felt that

> When you look at all the churches in that short distance, in twenty-five years' time, I can't see that they're going to be there. I think a church ought

for this, K. Mannheim, *Ideology and utopia: an introduction to the sociology of knowledge*, London 1952 edn.

[11] J. Tomlinson, *The politics of decline: understanding postwar Britain*, Harlow 2000.

[12] Mannheim, *Ideology and utopia*, 211–12.See also White, *Metahistory*, 22–6.

[13] J. Tomlinson, 'Economic growth, economic decline', in K. Burk (ed.), *The British Isles since 1945*, Oxford 2003, 63–89 at p. 83.

[14] Gill, *The empty church*, 10.

[15] IJ43GB.

to be there, but with young people saying 'I don't want to be bothered to go to church' I don't see how it's going to be viable.[16]

Decline could also become part of congregational folk memory even amongst those too young to have a long-term perspective. Interviewees under thirty-five found it particularly difficult to make assessments about the changing fortunes of the church from their own experience, offering what Schuman and Scott call 'flashbulb memories'.[17] Older interviewees appeared better-placed to consider the phenomenon of religious change, reflecting the greater facility of this age group in 'life review' modes of thinking.[18] The key here is not to expect oral history to provide what is better gleaned from other (that is, statistical) sources. However, perceptions of growth and decline were often as significant to congregational mood as actual numbers.

Before and after the war

As Callum Brown writes, 'during the late 1940s and first half of the 1950s, organised Christianity experienced the greatest per annum growth in church membership, Sunday school enrolment, Anglican confirmations and Presbyterian recruitment of its baptised constituency since the eighteenth century'.[19] In 1945, however, an imminent religious revival looked unlikely given the failure of the war to prompt a large-scale return to churchgoing. The Anglican report *Towards the conversion of England*, published that year, was (despite its optimistic title) fairly realistic about the scale of the evangelistic task.[20] Similar concerns were expressed by clergy at local level. In Cotteridge, in 1946, Thomas Tunstall, vicar of St Agnes, urged parish magazine readers to renew regular church attendance, warning that 'it is not merely a matter of filling the churches: still less is it a matter of coming for the sake of the Parson. The neglect of religion is having serious consequences on our national life'.[21] For some interviewees, the temptation to abandon regular churchgoing had clearly been strong in the immediate aftermath of the war. Joan Egan, of St George's, Edgbaston, recalled:

---

[16] IJ39SG.
[17] Schuman and Scott, 'Generations and collective memories', 351–81 at p. 375.
[18] Ibid.
[19] Brown, *Death of Christian Britain*, 172. For a more pessimistic interpretation of the statistics see Green, *Passing*, 242–72. See also chapter 5 below for discussion of the factors involved.
[20] Archbishops' Commission on Evangelism, *Towards the conversion of England: a plan dedicated to the memory of Archbishop William Temple*, London 1945, 37ff. For other, similarly cautious, assessments of the national religious temperature see Green, *Passing*, 242–72.
[21] SACPM xxxii/311 (Sept.–Oct. 1946).

Probably we became a little disenchanted with Establishment and church, and probably thought 'oh, we shan't go' for a bit, cos you were just trying to do something different; prove a point somehow.[22]

According to Andrew Perry, Anglican attendance in Birmingham certainly stagnated in the late 1940s,[23] with Roman Catholic mass attendance following suit until 1947–8. Baptist and Congregationalist membership fell in the same period (although a 'radical revision'[24] of membership rolls to remove the names of the lapsed or deceased probably made immediate postwar decline appear sharper than it really was).

Yet, if the first few years of peace saw local churches initially struggle to re-establish previous levels of attendance, there were some encouraging signs. Many congregations were boosted by the return of ex-servicemen from the war. Although some never returned to their prewar faith (Maureen Wall, b. 1944, remembered the war as crucial in her father's decision to cease church-going[25]), most research suggests that wartime experience only comparatively rarely prompted a crisis of faith (or conversely, conversion experience). More often, existing convictions, religious or otherwise, were deepened.[26] Devout young men returning from the forces could be a particular asset to their congregations, offering leadership skills and credibility amongst the young. Bill Hobbs, a lifelong worshipper at St George's, Edgbaston, returned from the army keen to recommence his involvement in the church, establishing a new parish youth club with a friend.[27] At Heneage Street Baptist, where forty-one men of the congregation had seen active service, a 'Comradeship Group' was established to welcome back returnees, though in April 1946 a letter in the church's magazine suggested that 'we would like to see more of them attending our services, and taking part in the work of the school or church. We need their help'.[28]

From the end of the 1940s several denominations began to record renewed growth in affiliation. For Roman Catholics, the expansion was dramatic: the Catholic population of the large swathe of the Midlands covered by the archdiocese of Birmingham grew by a third in just fifteen years, and Easter communions by nearly as much.[29] This followed large-scale postwar

[22] IJ39SG.
[23] Perry, 'Anglican Christianity', 26.
[24] WMBAY, 21.
[25] IJ29SB.
[26] B. Beit-Hallahmi and M. Argyle, *The psychology of religious behaviour, belief and experience*, London–New York 1997, 196; M. Snape and S. Parker, 'Keeping faith and coping: popular religiosity and the British people', in P. Liddle, J. Bourne and I. Whitehead (eds), *The Great World War, 1914–45*, II: *The people's experience*, London 2001, 397–42 at pp. 406–10; Parker, *Faith on the home front*, 73–9.
[27] IJ30SG.
[28] HSBCN, 183 (Apr. 1946).
[29] Figures from OCD, London 1945–59 edns.

immigration from Ireland which, in turn, may also have generated a small rise in conversions to Catholicism (as Catholic migrants increasingly often married non-Catholics[30]). Growth was also seen amongst the historic Free Churches: surviving figures for the Belmont Row Methodist Circuit (covering the central eastern quarter of Birmingham from the Coventry Road to the outer edges of Solihull) displayed substantial growth in the late 1940s and 1950s, from 1,634 members in 1946 to 2,347, a postwar peak, in 1965.[31] In this particular case, suburban drift helped to maintain numbers, but similar patterns were repeated in the Bristol Road and St Paul's Circuit, covering many well-established residential areas in south Birmingham. Nationally, Methodist membership also grew between 1949 and 1954, though it declined thereafter.[32] A full account of changing patterns of church affiliation in the Birmingham Anglican diocese has yet to be constructed, but Andrew Perry's analysis of eight contrasting congregations suggests an umambiguous rise in church attendance until at least 1958.[33] From the early '50s, clergy letters in church magazines became more optimistic in tone. In 1956 George Browning, newly-installed vicar of St George's, Edgbaston, wrote that

> Quite recently someone was speaking to me in a very gloomy way about the progress of the church in this country. But surely there was never a time when gloom and depression about the church were less justified ... There is discernible [sic] a gradual return to the church in many parishes ... careful observers are quite sure that they see a gradual but sure improvement. And what is only a small movement today may become quite a large increase tomorrow.[34]

Such cautious optimism was widely replicated across the mainstream denominations.[35]

The recovery of Sunday school attendance was particularly encouraging, even where adult membership stagnated. The most complete local figures available derive from local Baptist and Congregationalist records (*see* figures 1, 2). At their postwar peak around 1955, Sunday school membership in the Birmingham churches of the Warwickshire Congregational Union was 40 per cent higher than a decade earlier. Sunday schools in the city's Baptist churches grew by 26 per cent in the same period. (By contrast, adult Congregationalist and Baptist church membership had declined by 13 and 14 per cent respectively.) In part, growth in Sunday school attendance was attributable to an end to wartime disruption and to rising birth rates (though it

---

[30] The 'curve' in conversion numbers behaves in remarkably similar fashion to that of marriages solemnised in Catholic churches.
[31] Belmont Row Methodist Circuit, plans and directories, 1946–87, BCA, MB4/81–8.
[32] Currie, Gilbert and Horsley, *Churches and churchgoers*, 144.
[33] Perry, 'Anglican Christianity', 26–8.
[34] *SGEPM* (July 1956).
[35] Green, *Passing*, 252–6.

Figure 1
**Birmingham Baptist adult membership compared with
Sunday school and youth membership, 1945–93**

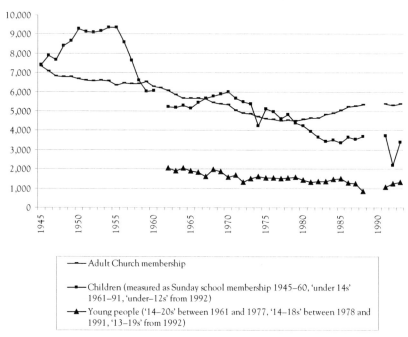

Source: West Midlands Baptist Association Yearbooks (1945–93)

never kept pace with wider population growth[36]). However, such considerations do not entirely explain why Sunday schools rallied more strongly than adult attendance.[37]

By the early 1950s growth in Sunday school membership was beginning to impact upon adult church membership, as the relevant cohort aged: figures 1 and 2 show a postwar bulge in local Sunday school attendance followed by a plateau in adult membership in the late 1950s.[38] More impressionistic evidence supports this picture. Church magazines of the 1950s (in contrast to those of the '40s and the '50s) often commented upon the healthy numbers of young people and younger adults involved in church. National and local

[36] This was noted in an internal National Methodist School Committee report of June 1951: Methodist Youth Department Sunday school committee, minutes, 6 June 1951, JRUL, Marc DDEY1/11. See also Green, Passing, 71, 260–1.

[37] For the factors involved see chapter 3 below.

[38] It is, however, impossible to confirm that the new adult members of the fifties were precisely those individuals who had attended Sunday school in greater numbers a decade earlier.

Figure 2
Birmingham Congregationalist and (after 1972) United Reformed Church and Sunday school membership, 1945–96

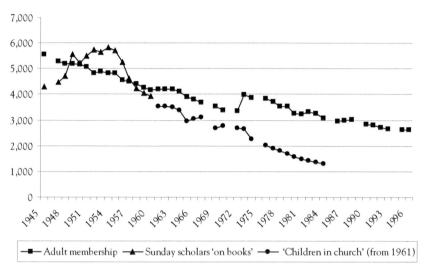

Note: Figures for church/Sunday school partipation by children are not given for years after 1984 since several changes in counting method renders it almost impossible to achieve a meaningful series of figures.

Source: Congregational/United Reformed Church Yearbooks, 1945–96

evangelistic initiatives certainly found their primary appeal amongst younger age groups: one study suggested that perhaps 60 per cent of those attending Billy Graham's Greater London campaign rallies of 1954 were aged under nineteen. Similarly, a 1957 report on the activities of Birmingham Youth for Christ (BYFC), the first UK branch of Youth for Christ, a US-based international organisation dedicated to spreading the Gospel amongst young people, calculated that 71 per cent of those making a commitment at recent meetings were teenagers.[39] Though many of these had some existing church contact, such events were often instrumental in activating or renewing a previously nominal faith. Several interviewees who had been in their teens during this period cited the importance of large evangelistic rallies in their own conversion stories. Doug and Margaret Hensman of Grenfell Baptist had originally met at a BYFC rally at which Doug had been a volunteer steward and Margaret had made her Christian commitment.[40] Local church leaders

---

[39] Youth for Christ worked with young adults as well as adolescents: BCL, Lp10.06, *Birmingham Youth for Christ: ten thrilling years, 1946–57: tenth anniversary brochure*, 19.
[40] IJ42GB.

also took encouragement from further afield: in 1956 George Browning informed his St George's parishioners that, according to a recent survey, church attendance at Oxbridge colleges stood at 51 per cent for men and 63 per cent for women, with dons noting a discernible increase in religiosity since the 1930s.[41]

High levels of youth participation in church were partly attributable to 'life course' effects, as well as wider generational trends. Since the spread of the Sunday school movement in the late eighteenth and early nineteenth centuries, regular attendance by young people had consistently outstripped adult participation.[42] Figures published by Geoffrey Gorer in 1955 likewise suggest that 29 per cent of under-18s in the West Midlands attended church at least weekly, compared to 18 per cent of 18–24s and (more vaguely) between 10 and 20 per cent of adults aged 25 or older.[43] Psychologists and sociologists suggest that adolescence (however else it has changed over time) has typically been a period of 'choosing faith', of testing opinions and aligning oneself to a respected 'other'.[44] Nevertheless, the evidence here strongly suggests a strongly observant inter-war birth cohort, present in large numbers in the late 1940s and 1950s (and still disproportionately numerous in the Church of the 1990s). One preacher visiting Carrs Lane in 1955 reckoned that 75 per cent of his audience was under thirty.[45] True or not, 'Carrs Laners' (both then and in retrospect) nevertheless believed themselves to have been particularly blessed with young adults during that decade. It was during the 1950s that membership of the church's dynamic '70 Club' (for the 18–30s) reached its peak. One member, Ken Poole, arriving in Birmingham as a postgraduate in the late 1950s, already knew of Carrs Lane by reputation, and soon found there a strong friendship group of his own age.[46] Jim West (b. 1924) had grown up in a non-churchgoing home and came to Carrs Lane through family friends after war service. He, too, joined the club:

> Being a member of the 70 Club, being one of the disciples, being one of the seventy that Jesus sent out, was an idea that very much appealed to me, because I couldn't cover the resurrection of the body, and the virgin birth, all this sort of stuff, but the idea of being one of the ones Christ sent out with a mission appealed to me.[47]

---

[41] SGEPM (July 1956). See also D. Bebbington, 'The secularisation of British universities since the mid-nineteenth century', in G. M. Marsden and B. J. Longfield (eds), *The secularisation of the Academy*, New York 1991, 259–77 at p. 269, and McLeod, *Religious crisis*, 199–201.

[42] Currie, Gilbert and Horsley, *Churches and churchgoers*, 90.

[43] G. Gorer, *Exploring English character*, London 1955, 451.

[44] The phrase 'choosing faith' derives from Fowler, *Stages of faith*, 151–73. See also Erikson, *Identity and the life cycle*, 87–98, and Beit-Hallahmi and Argyle, *Psychology of religious behaviour*, 58–65.

[45] CLJ liii/5 (May 1955).

[46] IJ57CL.

[47] IJ52CL.

Mr West's willingness to invest energy in his church despite his doubts perhaps illuminates a further aspect of this cohort's approach to organised religion. Despite the poet and critic John Wain's barbed observation that 'since 1946, nobody above the Jehovah's Witness level had believed in joining something in answer to the world's problems',[48] it is clear that the associational and institutional loyalty normally associated with the late Victorian and Edwardian periods remained a significant social force well into the twentieth century – long after religious and voluntary organisations had begun to experience difficulties.[49] The first postwar children and young adults were strongly encouraged to 'join', and evidently did so in large numbers. Moreover, those who joined a church often found a purposeful institution whose aims and methods appeared to be bearing fruit. Such experience appears to have left its mark on those who came of age during this period. Their formative Christian experience was frequently one of belonging to a growing, confident and purposeful institution, and their late twentieth-century interview testimony still contained an echo of this institutional confidence (despite having subsequently lived through the wintrier religious climate of the '60s and '70s). By 1998 many churchgoers of this cohort were in influential positions within the lives of their churches. Whilst on one hand this was due to the natural transfer of responsibility from one generation to the next, this cohort also displayed a strong tendency towards institutional loyalty carried forward from their formative years; loyalty, moreover, to an institution apparently resurgent at that time. Notably, national figures from successive English Church Censuses point to the smallest net decline in attendance amongst those born between 1936 and 1945 compared to any other birth cohort (5 per cent in 1985–95 and 2 per cent in 1995–2005, compared to overall declining attendance of 18 and 22 per cent respectively).[50] Not for nothing have contemporary generational typologies often labelled this mid-1920s to mid-1940s cohort as 'joiners' or 'builders'.[51]

Intriguingly, given that the postwar rise in church participation was strongly (if not exclusively) associated with children and young adults, the recovery of the 1950s was not at the time primarily understood in 'generational' terms. Exhortations to religious duty were aimed at the whole population; particularly adults. Religious commentators frequently noted declining church attendance in adolescence, but significantly, 'fifteen-year-itis' (as the Anglican vicar of Kings Norton labelled it in 1958[52]) was still largely understood as a normal life-course occurrence rather than indicative of more profound generational change. This was apparently with good reason. Where

---

[48] As quoted in R. Hewison, *In anger: culture in the Cold War, 1945–1960*, London 1981, 119.
[49] For this see Yeo, *Religious and voluntary organisations.*
[50] Brierley, *Nosedive*, 121.
[51] Hilborn and Bird, *God and the generations*, 112–21.
[52] *KNPM* (Mar. 1958).

comprehensive denominational data exists – such as for Methodism – the statistics suggest a persistent difficulty in replenishing adult membership from amongst the young.[53] Even during a time of comparative success, such as the early 1950s, fewer than two in seven children continued into adult membership.[54] However, for much of the 1950s many church leaders held parents and society as a whole responsible for weaknesses in youth church-going, rather than blaming the 'rising generation' itself.

'How long can the Church survive?': the crisis of church participation in the 1960s

If the early 1950s brought cautious optimism for many religious observers, the second half of the 1950s saw their mood darken. Formal indicators of church participation (such as Sunday school attendance, Anglican confirmations and Easter Sunday communicants) peaked around 1956–8 and thereafter began to stagnate, with decline accelerating sharply after 1963.[55] There is growing consensus that the early 1960s were critical years for the Churches.[56] Callum Brown's identification of decline with a 'long 1960s' from 1956 to 1973 (and a particularly acute fall during a 'short 1960s', 1963–70) also correlates remarkably closely with Arthur Marwick's suggestion that 1958 to 1974 (which he also calls the 'long 1960s') were the years of most significant cultural upheaval in society at large.[57]

Several sources on church participation in Birmingham suggest a similar trajectory. Whilst Roman Catholic mass attendance continued to rise across the archdiocese of Birmingham for most of the 1960s, conversions fell sharply after 1959, standing at only a quarter of late-1950s levels by 1970.[58] Local Baptist membership reached its postwar peak in 1959, thereafter registering a persistent decline not halted until the late 1970s. Methodist membership fared slightly better, growing until the mid-1960s, but also declining there-after. Statistics collected by Andrew Perry for selected Anglican churches similarly suggest a definite (though not dramatic) decline in the early 1960s, briefly stabilising in the late 1960s/early 1970s.[59] A sudden downturn in

---

[53] R. Currie, *Methodism divided: a study in the sociology of ecumenicalism*, London 1968, 101; *UKCH, 1994/5*, 262.

[54] Marc DDEY1/11, 4 June 1952.

[55] Currie, Gilbert and Horsley, *Churches and churchgoers*, 128–225; Brown, *Death of Christian Britain*, 161–92.

[56] A. Hastings, *A history of English Christianity, 1920–1990*, London 1991 edn, 580–6; G. Parsons, 'Contrasts and continuities: the traditional Christian Churches in Britain since 1945', in G. Parsons, *Growth of religious diversity*, I: *Traditions*, London 1993, 55–7; J. Munsey Turner, *Modern Methodism in England, 1932–1998*, Peterborough 1998, 21–4.

[57] A. Marwick, *The Sixties: cultural revolution in Britain, France, Italy and the United States, c. 1958–c. 1974*, Oxford 1998, 7.

[58] OCD (1945–98).

[59] Perry, 'Anglican Christianity', 26–8.

attendance after three years of growth at St Bede's, Brandwood, prompted the following exchange at the September 1963 Church Council meeting:

> *Church Attendance* – This was freely discussed, and various reasons for the decline in attendance were put forward. The church was not 'friendly', the complaint that [the curate] 'used people and dropped them'. But Mr Burns felt that unless people would come forward and give their personal reasons, it would be difficult to come to any conclusion. Mr Dutton felt that there should be more contacts and visiting, especially of the sick, and here it was pointed out that the clergy were not always made aware of sick people. Mr Sharp pointed out that the wardens' scheme should, however, help in this matter. Mr Dudley suggested that some people have problems about church and Christianity generally. Mrs Frost agreed and said there should be opportunities for discussion. Mr Simkiss suggested church activities should be increased, to bring people together. Mr Lovering felt that some fall off in attendance could be attributed to dissension among the immediate members of the church. Mr Simkiss thought apathy was a factor. Mr Ward pointed out that the fall in Evensong attendance was general throughout the country.

The discussion graphically illustrates the mounting sense of crisis in the local church, and bewilderment over the causes of decline. This hit hardest where one's own congregation was affected, just as rising attendances in the 1950s were frequently interpreted as a vindication of current approaches. Knowing that 'the fall ... in attendance was general throughout the country' could variously engender a feeling of powerlessness, of absolution from blame, or determination to respond.

The reaction of many clergy was to seek to maintain morale and convince doubters that some change was necessary. In 1961 Philip Lee-Woolf, minister at Carrs Lane Church, acknowledged that whilst

> A couple of generations ago, most churches were obviously more flourishing and socially influential than they are today ... I do not personally subscribe to the view that they were in fundamental ways stronger and healthier; obesity is after all a weakness, and the alienation of the majority of people in our country – 90% dissociated from church life – partly results from what the churches were like in those palmy days.[60]

Lee-Woolf's letter continued with a positive assessment of the contemporary ecumenical scene, and many other clergy letters of the time likewise exhorted church members to welcome other encouraging developments in the churches, nationally and worldwide. Nationally produced monthly church-magazine inserts bolstered this message. In the mid-1960s St George's, Edgbaston (by no means a hotbed of radicalism), subscribed to one of the more forward-looking publications, *Outlook*, dedicated to emphasising 'the

---

[60] *CLJ* lix/12 (Dec. 1961).

new movements stirring within the church today'.[61] Cultural ferment could be exciting: new theological ideas could engender enthralling debate, individual gifts were released in the service of the church, and new patterns of worship, ministry and mission emerged. Perceptions of change were not, therefore, entirely dominated by falling numbers.

Nevertheless, the early 1960s saw the loss of much of the confidence that the churches had regained in the 1950s. In many quarters, a mood of deep self-criticism set in. As one contributor to the *Birmingham Diocesan Leaflet* agonised in 1964:

> How long can the Church of England as we know it survive? ... Not long, we are told, unless we 'put our house in order': and then we shall probably be too late. The Church, it is said, has never won the town and has now lost the country. It is on its last legs, and has ceased to be relevant to life in modern England.[62]

Whilst emphasising that these were the views of the Church's critics, and noting that reform had already begun, the writer acknowledged that simply 'putting the house in order' might not be enough: 'the real trouble is that the church and the general public are on different wavelengths'.[63]

The rapid decline in church participation in the 1960s is easier to chart than to explain. However, two particular facets of change can be noted here. One was the widespread decline in evening church attendance (as noted at St Bede's). In small measure (but only in small measure) this related to a decline in 'twicing' – the practice of attending both morning and evening services, particularly in Free Church congregations. 'Twicing' had probably always been a minority activity, and was certainly declining amongst regular churchgoers by the late nineteenth century.[64] That it re-emerged in clerical commentary in the late 1940s probably suggests as much about local church leaders' efforts to maintain a spirit of unity and purpose in their congregations after the war as it does about new trends in religious practice. Nevertheless, by the 1960s 'twicing' appears to have been in decline even amongst highly-committed churchgoing families.[65] Free Churches (whose evening services were frequently the main act of worship) were particularly affected. In 1949 the *Heneage Street Baptist Church Newsletter* carried a communication from the area superintendent minister encouraging regular attendance, urging that if a 'one Sunday attendance only' pattern of churchgoing was becoming

---

[61] *Outlook* 1 (Jan. 1963).

[62] *BDL* (Oct. 1964).

[63] Ibid.

[64] The 1902–3 London *Daily News* census suggested 15.5% of attenders were 'twicers' – roughly 3% of the total population: H. McLeod, *Class and religion in the late Victorian city*, London 1974, 237.

[65] It experienced, however, a small resurgence between 1998 and 2005: Brierley, *Nosedive*, 145.

the norm, priority should be given to the evening service.[66] In fact, there appeared a general shift towards Sunday mornings – partly in response to experimentation with new kinds of Sunday morning service formats, but probably also because of the growing popularity of television.[67] Many interviewees born into devout churchgoing families in the 1930s still remembered (with June Knight of Cotteridge Church) 'church in the morning ... Sunday School in the afternoon and you went to church again in the evening'.[68] However, this pattern was much less common by the 1960s, as Edna Haybury of Carrs Lane (b. 1909) remembered:

> in the old church, I should say the evening service was well-attended – even later on, into the fifties, and even sixties, as well attended as the morning. My husband's mother, who was ... very strict ... and she used to stay with us ... and she used to go to church with us in the morning and with my husband in the evening ... I couldn't go because I'd got these two boys ... but when they came back, I can still hear my husband's mother saying 'isn't it funny how many people are oncers?' ... oncers meaning they don't go twice a day, which to her was the usual thing.[69]

As Mrs Haybury implied, the norm for committed churchgoers of her mother-in-law's generation seemed increasingly optional for her own. Keith and Joy Bradbury, originally Methodists and members of the Cotteridge Church (both b. 1942) were the youngest to remember 'twicing' as a rule during their own childhood. Although the practice was still evident at the end of the twentieth century, anecdotal impressions of the Birmingham evidence suggested it was now a matter of choice rather than convention, and largely confined either to those playing a specific role in one service and attending the other simply to 'receive', or to 'portfolio' churchgoers who might 'top up' their main church participation with a different style of service (often at a different church altogether) in the evening.

A second prominent feature of the collapse in church participation in the 1960s was the growing recognition of a 'generational' element to the trend. Whilst rates of childhood and adolescent church participation had outstripped that of adults for much of the previous century and a half, this had been reckoned normal; the key problem being to encourage more children to make the transition to adult membership. In the postwar period, this situation was dramatically reversed, with numbers of church-affiliated children dropping below that of adult numbers in most denominations. Moreover, statistics from Birmingham's Free Churches suggest that a decline in Sunday school membership after the 1950s preceded a drop in adult membership from the late 1950s and 1960s. Across the Birmingham Baptist District, for

[66] HSBCN, 224 (Sept. 1949).
[67] For the former see chapter 5 below, and for the latter chapter 7.
[68] IJ6CT.
[69] IJ53CL. Mrs. Haybury dated this conversation to the mid-1960s.

example, the number of Sunday scholars grew from 1945 to 1955, followed by sharp decline to the end of the century, only temporarily reversed in the mid-1960s and late 1980s. Adult membership, by contrast, held steady until 1959, thereafter declining until a short period of growth in the late 1980s. Amongst the city's Congregationalist churches, a rise in Sunday school membership after the war initially appeared to reap benefits in terms of adult membership, whose long-term decline in numbers was briefly halted in the early 1960s. At this point however, Sunday school membership began to fall dramatically, in 1961 standing at only 61 per cent of the total six years before. A similar pattern prevailed in the Methodist Church, for which the most comprehensive local and national statistics exist. Nationally, the postwar rise in Sunday school membership helped to halt a decline in adult membership, levelling out between 1945 and 1960 with around one in seven young people making the step into adult membership. National Methodist Sunday school membership reached its postwar peak around 1952, declining thereafter. In the early 1960s adult Methodist membership, too, began to fall. In each case falls in adult membership were preceded by declines in Sunday school membership.

Detailed figures from the Moseley Road and Sparkhill Methodist Circuit, south and east of Birmingham's city centre, offer a helpful illustration of these trends. In 1956 a report to the Circuit Meeting noted decreasing attendance amongst children and youth across the circuit; something partly attributed to removals to outer estates. However, the decline was uneven: whilst attendance amongst older teenagers remained firm, eleven- to fourteen-year-olds appeared to be deserting in unusually large numbers. Seven years later, in 1963, the most significant decline was again amongst the same cohort, now in late teenage. Adult membership, which had grown across the '50s, subsequently followed the downward trend earlier evident amongst the young, with minister Brian Duckworth reporting 'immense change' in patterns of membership by 1965.[70] As a member of the connexional Sunday School Committee, Duckworth was well-placed to recognise a wider trend at work. Figures presented to this national committee during the 1950s confirm a strong cohort effect: the 1940s population 'bulge' initially produced temporary gains amongst the 8 to 13 age group even as Methodist Sunday school membership began to decline overall.[71] Thereafter, declining membership in the youngest age groups was followed by fewer adolescent and adult members. Over the 1950s the Methodist Church saw a net loss of 1 per cent in adult membership, but 21 per cent of its Sunday scholars and 42 per cent of its Junior Members.[72]

---

[70] Moseley Road and Sparkhill Methodist Circuit quarterly meeting, minutes 1937–56, 1957–68, BCA, MC 9/3–4. Observations are derived from the minutes for the March 1956, March 1963 and June 1965 meetings.

[71] Marc DDEY1/11, 1 June 1955.

[72] This is based on figures in Currie, Gilbert and Horsley, *Churches and churchgoers*, 187.

Of course, membership trends were not entirely related to cohort behaviour – the 'curve' of adult membership does not precisely follow that of Sunday school membership a decade earlier (nor would one expect it to, given the range of factors involved in decline, and given that even a large influx of young adult members would only gradually alter the overall trajectory). Nevertheless, it remains reasonable to suggest that the growing pool of young church participants in the late 1940s and early 1950s contributed towards comparatively healthy adult participation in the late 1950s. Furthermore, sharp decline in Sunday school membership from the mid-'50s onwards shrank the key 'internal constituency' from which adult congregations recruited. As the 1960s progressed, the historic tendency for child participation to outstrip adult membership was reversed, with many adult congregations now larger than their Sunday schools. By the early 1970s a new kind of 'cohort chasm' which had not existed in the late 1950s/early 1960s had emerged – albeit with some variation – in most denominations in the UK and internationally. As early as 1976 Robert Wuthnow noted that in the USA 'the rate of secularisation since the 1950s has been more pronounced among younger than among older age strata ... both on religious practice and belief'.[73] A similar pattern in English religion was noted by Currie, Gilbert and Horsley in 1977.[74] In 1997 one multi-national study of the 'baby-boom' generation identified similar trends across the western world.[75] Most recently for the UK, Callum Brown has offered further evidence that a general decline in churchgoing was preceded by falling participation amongst the young.[76]

Though lacking the statistical information now available to historians and sociologists, many churchgoers who lived through the early 1960s also remembered the period as one of crucial change. For Keith Bradbury (b. 1942), a lifelong Methodist and member of Cotteridge Church, the most significant shifts came

> About 1963 – I say that cos I'd have been about twenty then ... the early sixties. I suppose, although I'm not old enough to pass judgement on the view, it was the tail end of the sort of collectiveness we had in the war, when they say there's nothing like a good disaster to fill the churches, cos people have been bordering or not on whether they should start going, this sort of thing was petering out at this point – youngsters were beginning to be more noticed, rather than just tolerated – they were individuals in their own right.[77]

---

73 Wuthnow, 'Recent pattern of secularisation', 861–2.
74 Currie, Gilbert and Horsley, *Churches and churchgoers*, 101.
75 Clark Roof, Carroll and Roozen, *The postwar generation*.
76 Brown, *Death of Christian Britain*, passim.
77 IJ14CT.

Interviewees frequently emphasised that even the normally ambiguous relationship between youth, Church and society had taken on an important new twist in the 1960s. Of course, one might expect the teenagers of the 'sixties to remember 'their' decade' as significant, since major contextual changes in adolescence and young adulthood frequently loom largest in recollections.[78] However, the significance of the 1960s in changing patterns of religious practice was also noted by interviewees of every cohort, albeit as a folk memory amongst the youngest.

One significant difference between the life stories of the oldest interviewees and those coming of age from the 1960s onwards was in the reasons given for leaving church. Ceasing regular church participation in teenage or young adulthood was a common historic pattern: in one study of church leaving and returning conducted in the early 1990s, 70 per cent of adult churchgoers who had also attended as children had spent time away from church, mostly leaving between eleven and fourteen.[79] Interviewees of various ages suggested that rebellion was part and parcel of adolescence, and where young people ceased churchgoing, this was regrettable but not unexpected. However, amongst the oldest interviewees, time away from church in late adolescence or young adulthood did not necessarily signify an abandonment of Christian faith and identity. Arguably this reflected contemporary assumptions that English society was itself basically Christian, in which view churchgoing was important, but only one possible expression of a wider cultural identity. As a result, the reasons cited for non-participation were mainly pragmatic – work, marriage or family responsibilities, study, or disagreements with clergy or fellow churchgoers. By contrast, an unusually large proportion of interviewees in middle age (born in the 1940s and 1950s) regarded their time away from church as a decisive break, many citing problems of belief, or the intellectual credibility of Christianity, as the most significant contributing factor. As Robert Grant, born in 1950 and in 1998 a member of Cotteridge Church, remembered,

> One morning we all poured into church – it was a Tuesday, the day of Aberfan – what responsibilities vicars have! – our school vicar … stood up in the pulpit and said this was all part of God's plan, so I took a conscious decision there and then to stuff God and didn't say the Lord's Prayer in church. Quite a radical decision … I might have gone through the motions for three or four years, but in reality I didn't believe – didn't want to know about it.[80]

In cases like this, non-participation could constitute a more deliberate break from Christianity itself. Whilst this reflected a wider cultural disenchantment with Christianity, it may particularly have been felt amongst the young.

[78] Schuman and Scott, *Generations and collective memories*, 361.
[79] J. Finney, *Finding faith today: how does it happen?*, Swindon 1992, 13
[80] IJ8CT.

First-hand experience of the 'haemorrhaging' of religious commitment in the 1960s and 1970s set apart those who had experienced it as a broad 'affectual generation' amongst the active church population. However, different age groups interpreted the decline in different ways. Some already into adulthood by the 1960s saw decline partly as a natural life-cycle process, often mirroring their own journeys into and out of churchgoing. Others, such as Philip Masterman (b. 1904) of St Mary's Pitt Heath, instead attributed decline to general religious apostasy:

> it doesn't seem to me that it's the failure of the Church so much; it's the failure of other people to listen – they're not interested, are they? ... People have lost a sense of religion altogether, haven't they? It's all materialism and the futile chase for what they think is happiness.[81]

By contrast, interviewees in their forties and fifties (teenagers during the 1960s) were much less likely to criticise non-churchgoers simply for not attending church. Whilst this group considered decline no less regrettable, they were more inclined to view it either as the fault of the church itself, or a fact of life to be worked with: as Jan Hughes, a committed member of Grenfell Baptist (b. 1949), reflected, 'maybe we're not going to see great growth, but maybe we're being obedient'.[82] Perceptions of crisis thus related not just to the degree of numerical loss, but also to interpretations of it. In some sense, the differences in attitude to the same events between pre- and postwar birth cohorts may by the end of the century have contributed to different 'attitudinal' generational identities.

Decline and renewal from the 1970s

Although for most denominations, church attendance continued to decline to the end of the century, the perception of crisis followed a slightly different trajectory. From the mid-1960s clergy letters in church magazines suggested some recovery of composure. This was most obvious at Carrs Lane, where ministers and members had felt the crisis of the early '60s more acutely than many other congregations (partly because many church members had taken the new intellectual challenges to Christianity of that decade particularly seriously). Introducing the national ecumenical initiative 'The People Next Door' in 1966, the *Carrs Lane Journal* suggested that the campaign offered 'a wonderful opportunity to find out what is wrong with our situation, and to put it right by acting on the results'.[83] In preaching his induction sermon

---

[81] IJ68SM.
[82] IJ50GB.
[83] *CLJ* lxix/11 (Nov. 1966). Planned by the British Council of Churches and the Council of Missionary Societies, 'PND' was a Lent study scheme encouraging churches

in 1970, the new minister Harold Tonks 'showed his awareness of the crisis of belief the church was facing, but he affirmed his belief in the Ministry and suggested it was wrong to be too pessimistic about the church's future'.[84] Meanwhile, by 1980, recently published Church of England statistics caused Donald Bradley of St George's, Edgbaston, to suggest that 'the church probably touched bottom, so far as religious observance was concerned, in the last decade, and a mild upturn now seems to have set in'.[85] Similar sentiments were expressed by leading clergy nationally.[86]

Certainly the actual rate of decline was slowing, with some patches of growth: from 1978, after a sixteen-year fall, Anglican confirmations in the diocese of Birmingham entered a ten-year plateau and though declining again thereafter, the drop remained less steep than in the early 1960s. Birmingham's Baptist Churches did even better, with membership growing by 17 per cent between 1980 and 1991, partly reflecting a rise in believers' baptisms to levels not seen since the 1950s. A peak of 371 baptisms in 1985 may partly be attributable to strong Baptist support for the 1984 'Mission England' campaign (in which Birmingham was a major centre of activity), since nationally Baptist membership declined slightly from the late '70s to the early '90s.[87] Generally however, the hope that decline had 'bottomed out' proved unfounded: in absolute numbers overall church attendance in Birmingham declined by 2 per cent between 1985 and 1989 (albeit against a general population decline of 3.54 per cent in the city between 1981 and 1991) and by 1 per cent nationally.[88] Mass attendance in the archdiocese of Birmingham, which had grown steadily until the early 1970s, declined dramatically and consistently across the period, with 47 per cent fewer mass attendances in 1998 than in 1971[89] (compared to a national decline of 38 per cent between 1979 and 1998). Despite a brief plateau in the early 1970s, Congregationalist/URC membership continued to decline steadily, confounding hopes of renewal generated by the 1972 union scheme. Local Methodist membership followed a similar trajectory. Child participation appears to have declined at a steeper rate than adult, contrary to the dominant trend of the 1940s and 1950s. Indeed, results from the English Church

---

to meet with each other and non-churchgoing neighbours to explore questions of mission (both at home and overseas), the secular society, ecumenism and 'the relevance of the worship and teaching of the Church': K. Sansbury, R. Latham and P. Webb, *Agenda for the Churches: report on the People Next Door programme*, London 1968, 15.

[84] *CLJ* lxxiii/9 (Sept. 1970).

[85] *SGEPM* (Mar. 1980).

[86] P. A. Welsby, *A history of the Church of England, 1945–1980*, Oxford 1984, 263.

[87] *UKCH 1994/5*, 254.

[88] Christian Research/Challenge 2000, *Churchgoers in England, district by district*, London [1991?], 14.

[89] *OCD*. Figures include the whole diocese, not just greater Birmingham. .

Censuses suggest that the loss of children from the Church in the 1990s was particularly severe.[90]

Despite numerical decline, however, a partial recovery of confidence was certainly experienced by many churches in the 1970s. One source of optimism was the growing influence of the Charismatic movement, which was widely regarded as a key source of hope for Christian renewal, particularly amongst the young. The fresh experience of God's presence and power brought by the Charismatic movement certainly appears to have inspired many lay Christians to renewed activity. Heather Francis (b. 1940) of St Bede's, Brandwood, remembered how in the 1970s and 1980s 'we used to have Bible studies and meetings and used to be going off in groups to different churches when they'd got things on … there seemed to be a lot happening'.[91] Statistically, renewed Evangelical churches were also amongst the most successful at fostering Christian commitment amongst teenagers. However, the renewal movement was also influential amongst those in early to mid-adulthood: of the eighteen interviewees touched by the renewal, twelve were in their twenties and thirties at the time and only two were older. This greater uptake of interest in the Charismatic renewal amongst those born in the immediate postwar years may partly be explained by the frequently observed phenomenon of re-commitment or 'second conversion' in early middle age.[92] A quarter of interviewees aged over forty had experienced some positive reappraisal of their faith at this stage of their life. For baby-boomers, early middle age coincided with the height of the Charismatic renewal's influence and energy in the late 1970s and 1980s. The Charismatic movement offered a clear alternative to those seeking a different direction at this stage in their lives. Interestingly, this cohort of interviewees was also the most sharply divided in their attitudes to the Charismatic movement, reflecting Mannheim's observation that sudden changes or unusual developments may result in the polarisation of any culturally-distinctive cohort into 'generation units'.[93] By contrast, most older interviewees said that Charismatic Christianity was simply not for them, whilst the youngest tended to accept it as part of the ecclesiastical landscape.

Even so, experiencing an active, Charismatic congregational life in one's formative years could still exert an important influence on church members and their interpretations of the health of the Church at large. For many interviewees in teenage and young adulthood in the 1970s and 1980s, renewal provided reassurance that even amidst numerical decline God was still present and active. Andy Sadler, part of a strong youth group at Grenfell Baptist during a time of Charismatic renewal in the 1980s, recalled that

---

[90] Decline amongst the under-15s, however, has slowed markedly since 1998: Brierley, *Nosedive*, 115.
[91] IJ25SB.
[92] Beit-Hallahmi and Argyle, *Psychology of religious behaviour*, 68.
[93] Mannheim, 'Problem of generations', 307.

'there really was a sense of a new wave sweeping across the land'.[94] Moreover, regardless of contact with the renewal, interviewees of this cohort frequently strongly argued for the continued relevance of Christianity within society (albeit now 'from the edges' rather than as socially or culturally dominant). Whilst many older churchgoers had also adjusted to the church's new position, an acceptance of having to live more counter-culturally was strongly embedded in the outlook of young Christian adults at the end of the twentieth century. Once again, an experience of change in the size and health of the local church appeared to have left its mark on the broad cohort that experienced it in their most formative years. At the time of writing, the public profile of religion is high and the rate of decline in church affiliation is slowing once again. But for churchgoers in Birmingham in 1998, a much hoped-for revival had failed to materialise, with the prospect of further decline on the agenda.

This chapter has traced some key postwar peaks and troughs in churchgoing and explored grassroots Christian responses to the facts of growth and decline, noting the increasing tendency to view fluctuations in generational terms (a tendency largely supported by the statistical evidence). This begs important questions of interpretation: why (even given the Churches' long-term difficulty in translating child participation into adult churchgoing) did the proportion of adults to young people in church shift so dramatically in the postwar period? Moreover, if, as this chapter has suggested, decline was linked to the experience of a particular social or cultural cohort, was it the result of large-scale teenage rebellion against religion, or of some other factor? To begin to answer these questions, the following chapter explores the changing relationship between Church, youth and family during the critical years from the 1940s to the 1960s.

---

[94] IJ61SB. The 'new wave' image was characteristic of much Charismatic and restorationist theology and song-writing of the period, for example in Dave Bilborough's popular song 'God of grace' (1985), which begins 'There's a new wave coming'. On this style see Ward, *Growing up Evangelical*, 133–40.

3

Church, Youth and Family from the 1940s to the 1960s

In 1965 Norman Power, vicar of the inner city parish of St John's, Lady-wood, published a hard-hitting reflection, *The forgotten people*, on a decade of sweeping change in his own local community (where slum clearances had radically altered neighbourhood life) and in the nation at large. Citing Professor G. M. Carstairs's description of the '"drab agony" left by the ebbing tide of Christianity in our land',[1] Power argued that whilst the disintegration of local community life was one salient factor, 'the main cause is the aggravation, by this disintegration, of the effect of the incredible indifference of many parents to the needs of their children'.[2] Power's Ladywood probably faced more daunting challenges than most, but his views reflected wider Christian concern that the health of Church, community and nation was fundamentally dependent on strong parental commitment to the rising generation.[3] Though hitherto receiving little attention from historians of postwar Christianity, youth and family were key issues of concern for local and national church leaders throughout the period. Where Christians' attitudes to the family have been considered, it has usually been to cast the Churches as bastions of 'traditional family values', without any real exploration of their motives or the nuances of their arguments.[4] True, most Christian commentators of the period assumed the importance of a particular conception of family life. However, for most, the strength of the family was not primarily an end in itself, but a buttress to social stability and a prerequisite to a form of generational continuity and cohesion apparently under threat in the postwar period, the disappearance of which was believed to threaten not only the Churches themselves, but also the very fabric of national life. This chapter explores how questions of youth and family life were of growing concern to many Churches in the postwar period, considers different inter-

---

[1]   Though I am unable to trace the source of the 'drab agony' remark, a similar point is made in G. M. Carstairs, *This island now: the BBC Reith Lectures 1962*, London 1963, 82–3.
[2]   N. S. Power, *The forgotten people: a challenge to a caring community*, Evesham 1965, 103.
[3]   I. Machin, 'British Churches and moral change in the 1960s', in W. M. Jacob and N. Yates (eds), *Crown and mitre: religion and society in northern Europe since the Reformation*, Woodbridge 1993, 223–41 at pp. 233–4.
[4]   For example D. Gittens, *The family in question: changing households and familiar ideologies*, Basingstoke–London 1985.

pretations of the increasing difficulty of engaging young people, and some important church responses to it.

The postwar visibility of youth and the focus on family religion

The 1940s to 1960s saw a marked rise in the social visibility of youth. This was neither sudden nor unprecedented. The 'problem of youth' has been discussed at length in almost every historical period, and even 'modern' conceptions of childhood and adolescence date from at least the nineteenth century.[5] Since the mid-1930s the young had become increasingly visible as consumers: higher wages, the extension of paid holidays and the return of fuller employment offering them (and particularly young women) increased financial independence from their parents and greater access to new consumer markets.[6] At the same time, a new 'youth consciousness' was stirring amongst middle-class youth and particularly student intellectuals.[7] Historians should thus treat claims about the novelty of postwar changes in youth and the family with extreme caution.[8] However, in the post-Second World War period there arguably remained an important sense in which, to quote Bill Osgerby, 'the "youth question" function[ed] as a medium through which fundamental shifts in social boundaries and cultural relationships were explored, made sense of, and interpreted'.[9] One immediate cause was growing wartime expectation about the postwar peace and a hope that the young would be both its chief beneficiaries and its guarantors.[10] As early as 1939, amidst concerns over a 'disruption in family life and loss of parental control',[11] the government had created a National Youth Committee to establish, for the first time outside the education system, a statutory basis for the formation of good character and citizenly values amongst the young. A second cause for optimism amongst many Christian commentators was the 1944 Education Act. This placed religion at the heart of postwar expectations for the rising generation, and reflected the 'general wish, not confined to representatives of the Churches, that religious education should be given a more defined place in the life and work of the schools, springing from the

---

[5] J. Walvin, A child's world: a social history of English childhood, 1800–1914, London 1982, 197–8.

[6] S. Todd, 'Young women, work and leisure in inter-war England', HJ xlviii (2005), 789–809,

[7] D. Fowler, Youth culture in modern Britain, c. 1920–c. 1970, Basingstoke 2008, 30–58,

[8] See M. Anderson, 'What's new about the modern family?', in M. Drake (ed.), Time, family and community: perspectives on family and community history, Oxford 1994, 67–87.

[9] Osgerby, Youth in Britain, 17–30.

[10] J. Davis, Youth and the condition of Britain: images of adolescent conflict, London 1990, 91–103.

[11] P. Addison, Now the war is over: a social history of Britain, 1945–51, London 1985, 197–8.

desire to revive the spiritual and personal values in our society and in our national tradition'.[12]

However, despite growing enthusiasm for state intervention, many postwar Britons continued to believe that the family remained the primary instrument of socialisation. Intellectually this view was expressed by the influential psychologist John Bowlby, whose *Childcare and the growth of love* (1953) emphasised the role of parental attachment in the creation of rounded individuals, and the corresponding dangers of neglect.[13] While such emphasis arguably re-enhanced the status of the family in the immediate postwar years, it also directed attention towards apparent shortcomings in family life. Official statistics added to such concerns: divorce rates exhibited a steep (albeit temporary) rise to 1947. Between 1938 and 1945, indictable offences rose by 223 per cent, with particularly sharp increases in juvenile crime.[14] If the perception of social breakdown (partly media-driven) was greater than the reality,[15] the impression of crisis none the less proved a sufficient spur to action. The threat from hostile totalitarian enemies abroad heightened concern that neglect of the rising generation was serious both for young people themselves and the nation at large.[16] Many, both within and outside the Churches, regarded the war as a struggle for 'western civilisation and Christianity' and saw the answer partly in terms of spiritual renewal. Even Winston Churchill (not usually known for his piety) remarked that 'all hopes will come to nought unless the structure of the New Europe is built firmly upon moral and spiritual foundations'.[17]

Youth was central to this vision. When the Roman Catholic archdiocese of Birmingham established a network of youth centres towards the end of the war, a working paper argued that Christian faith and good citizenship went hand in hand:

> For far too long clubs have been regarded as centres for amusement, with no other plan or purpose other than to provide a place for young people to escape from the streets. The newest conception of club life is that it should be a centre of every social, spiritual and cultural activity. The nation is determined that our youth shall not be allowed to drift aimlessly through the years

[12] This is quoted in G. Parsons, 'There and back again? Religion and the 1944 and 1988 education acts', in Parsons, *Growth of religious diversity*, ii. 161–98 at p. 167.
[13] J. Bowlby (ed. M. Fry), *Childcare and the growth of love*, London 1953 edn.
[14] B. Turner and T. Rennell, *When Daddy came home: how family life changed forever in 1945*, London 1995, 154; A. Marwick, *British society since 1945*, 3rd edn, London 1996, 60.
[15] P. Hennessy, *Never again: Britain, 1945–51* (1992), London 1993 edn, 445.
[16] A. Wills, 'Delinquency, masculinity and citizenship in England, 1950–1970', *P&P* clxxxvii (May 2005), 157–85.
[17] A message to a Christian Action rally chaired by Lord Halifax in Oxford in April 1948, quoted approvingly by Robert Aitken in *GBCN* (July 1952). For the rally see *The Times*, 26 Apr. 1948, 3.

between school and manhood, neglected and neglectful, playing no part in their own or their nation's welfare.[18]

Sometimes congregations (among them Heneage Street Baptist Church) registered their youth organisations with the city youth service, intent on developing 'the whole boy – mind, body and spirit'.[19] Elsewhere, personal conversion to Christianity was seen as the first step towards national spiritual renewal. Birmingham Youth for Christ, founded in 1946, worked amongst both adolescents and young adults, its monthly evangelistic rallies packing out the old town hall from 1948.[20] However, central to renewed postwar efforts to re-engage young people were attempts to foster family religious observance. In 1944 R. S. E. Knight, Anglican vicar of St Agnes, Cotteridge, urged his parishioners to support the incoming Education Act 'by shewing by our example that we ourselves value religion, not just in some vague and sentimental way, but by making it a definite part of our life. What we would specially like to see would be an increase in family worship – do not send your children to church, bring them'.[21]

Amidst the 'constant analysis'[22] of the young undertaken in the 1940s and 1950s, one notable example emerged from Birmingham's Westhill College, an important centre of training and expertise in church and school religious education. *80,000 adolescents*, written by prominent Methodist Bryan Reed, was a study of the attitudes and leisure habits of Birmingham youth aged 14–20.[23] Published in 1950, the report was reviewed in several church magazines and appears to have generated some discussion. Centrally, the report argued that whilst it was

> quite erroneous to suppose that there are large numbers of unattached adolescents roaming the streets or going to the cinema every evening or spending their leisure in vicious or anti-social ways ... what one does feel about the lives of many of these young people, ... is that they are very barren and restricted.[24]

Researchers discovered that a high percentage of those joining youth organisations had subsequently left, citing boredom or alienation. The much-vaunted city youth service drew particular criticism for its apparent lack of

[18] 'Objects of a Catholic youth centre' (n.d. probably early 1940s), BAA, AP, box 14, folder 13 (papers concerning youth organisations, 1942–60).
[19] *HSBCN* (Mar. 1942).
[20] D. J. Jeremy, 'Businessmen in inter-denominational activity: Birmingham youth for Christ in the 1940s–1950s', *Baptist Quarterly* xxxiii/7 (1990), 336–43 at pp. 336–7.
[21] *SACPM* xxx/297 (Jan.–Feb. 1944).
[22] J. Ryder and H. Silver, *Modern English society*, 2nd edn, London 1970, 208.
[23] B. Reed, *80,000 adolescents: a study of young people in the city of Birmingham, by staff and students of Westhill Training College, for the Edward Cadbury Charitable Trust*, London 1950. Reed was also a member of the National Methodist Sunday School Committee.
[24] Ibid. 131.

purpose.[25] Though in the early 1950s youth churchgoing was still buoyant (28.6 per cent of survey respondents reported attending regularly), the report's authors felt that young people's involvement in church frequently failed to translate into either purposive lives or into adult church participation. Churches and church youth organisations were castigated for their lethargy and introversion, and many young people were described as 'almost religiously illiterate'.[26]

How did local churches understand the causes of this situation, and what solutions were proposed? Many observers noted that the young had grown up in very different times from their parents. Wartime dislocation of family life was frequently blamed, as was rising prosperity: in 1958 a new vicar of St Agnes, Cotteridge, F. A. Carroll, ascribed falling church attendance in part to 'upset family life due to the war, Sunday working, greater opportunities for pleasure, care of a young family resulting in parents not being able to attend again'.[27] Although family breakdown was regarded as religiously disruptive, this did not always result in straightforward condemnation of parents who divorced. When in 1952 the Mothers' Union voted nationally to refuse fellowship at communion to divorced women, criticism came even from some theological conservatives. One such, Edward Ashford, vicar of Kings Norton, published an outspoken attack on the decision and (when the Mother's Union objected) closed down his parish's branch, likening the organisation's policies to those of Stalinist Russia and the medieval papacy.[28]

Indeed, the growth of state influence in private life was also regularly identified by clergy as a threat to the family (this was despite strong general welcome for the welfare state from many church leaders).[29] For Birmingham's Roman Catholic leadership, non-denominational state education was perceived as a particular threat to Catholic norms and values.[30] At the Birmingham Archdiocesan Reunion of 1949, Archbishop Joseph Masterson warned how 'the liberal secular state … claiming to be the embodiment of enlightenment and progress, not bound by the ordinary laws of morality, and recognising no authority higher than itself' had been making 'its assaults through the school and home; seeking to cast its citizens into a uniform mould and to eliminate sectarian differences it either banished God from the schools or admitted religion only in the form of an agreed syllabus'.[31]

Whilst state education itself was relatively uncontroversial in Anglican and Free Church circles, cross-denominational concern existed that

---

[25] Ibid. 27–30, 184–5.
[26] Ibid. 42, 187.
[27] SACPM xliii/382 (Apr. 1958).
[28] KNPM (June 1952).
[29] Welsby, *History of the Church of England*, 16–17.
[30] J. Keating, 'Faith and community threatened? Roman Catholic responses to the welfare state, materialism and social mobility, 1945–62', *TCBH* ix (1998), 86–108.
[31] *OCD 1950*, 151.

increased state intervention might erode a sense of personal responsibility amongst parents and children. The oft-heard accusation that 'the youth of today are spineless and spoon-fed' even became the subject of a debate at a Kings Norton Youth Fellowship meeting in 1953.[32] Whilst this was a harsh verdict, the label appears to have stuck: retrospectively, interviewees already into adulthood by the 1940s and 1950s often drew comparisons between themselves and the postwar cohort. May Gladding of Moseley Road Methodist (b. 1917) suggested that 'if you go through a war and come through it unscathed, it does something for you, in a way nothing else can ... I belong to a fighting generation ... the next generation were nursed'.[33] In her own way, Miss Gladding had made a similar generational characterisation as the historian David Thomson, who has described the mid-1930s to mid-1950s birth cohort as the first 'welfare generation'.[34] In contrast, the war remained a symbol of endurance and vindication against which subsequent generations would be judged.[35]

However, if the younger generation were sometimes perceived as lacking in character, many in the Churches believed that primary responsibility lay not with youth but with parents and elders. Commenting on recent riots by 'Teddy Boys' in Nottingham in 1956, Edward Ashford, vicar of Kings Norton, argued that 'although I am not excusing the Teddy Boy hooligans, I *am* going to say that the majority of them come from homes where parents are quite uninterested in their children's concerns'. Parents who left their children with child-minders in order to work or socialise were wrong, he believed, but 'equally dangerous as the parentless home is the God-less home, and that is a description which would apply to tens of thousands of homes in our country today ... I have hundreds of children here, whose parents have never darkened the doors of the church since I have been here'. Ashford's conviction of the importance of family religion to the rising generation (and the nation at large) was shared by clergy and active laity across the theological spectrum. This diagnosis was not entirely new: as Simon Green has shown, parental indifference to the religious socialisation of children had begun to be identified by some church leaders as a significant factor in declining Sunday school attendance in the 1920s and 1930s.[36] Nevertheless, throughout the 1950s, church elites became increasingly convinced that schools, youth services, and even church youth and children's organisations, were of limited use without strong Christian foundations at home. For Leslie Tizard, minister of Carrs Lane Church (and an altogether more liberal voice

[32] KNPM (June 1953). For similar fears nationally see Wills, 'Delinquency', 170.
[33] IJ2MR.
[34] Thomson, 'Lifetime of privilege?', 215–38 at p. 220.
[35] H. McLeod, 'Protestantism and British national identity, 1815–1945', in P. van der Veer and H. Lehmann (eds), *Nation and religion: perspectives on Europe and Asia*, Princeton, NJ 1999, 44–65 at p. 64.
[36] Green, *Passing*, 162.

than Ashford), 'the family – the *real* family – is the ideal of community'.[37] In one sense there was nothing new here: the 'godly home' had for centuries been considered a force for social good and a crucible of Christian nurture.[38] However, for many observers at the time, this required urgent reinforcement against new forces threatening family life.

This became an increasingly urgent theme of clerical comment in the 1950s. Clergy letters to parishioners frequently warned against parents adopting an over-indulgent or *laissez-faire* approach to their children's recreation and behaviour (though specific theories – such as those of John Bowlby or Benjamin Spock – were only rarely discussed). Sometimes clerical commentators explicitly identified a generational shifting in parenting – Ashford, for example, noted a tendency amongst his parishioners to say: 'I had a hard time, and I am going to give my children as easy a time as possible'.[39] However, material indulgence seemed less threatening than neglect of religious socialisation. For Birmingham's Catholic archdiocesan authorities, this was particularly exemplified in the increase in Catholic parents sending their children to non-Catholic schools and not providing Catholic teaching at home. Though choice of school was ultimately a matter of parental choice, permission from the archbishop was theoretically required. In practice these so-called 'permissions' were likely to be granted where there were both good educational grounds and parents who were committed to supplementing their child's (non-denominational) schooling with Catholic teaching at home. However, extant correspondence between parents, parish clergy and archdiocesan authorities suggests that many parents regarded religious instruction as the Church's responsibility. One parish priest from Tipton recorded that when he informed a certain mother that 'the religious education of the children was the duty of the parents and that Mrs. [X] was neglecting her duty, she suggested that even if she were, I still had my duty!'[40]

Across the denominations, clergy also cited a decline in family prayers as evidence of parental neglect. Family prayers were probably increasingly uncommon from the late nineteenth century. However, in the immediate postwar period attention refocused on the matter. In the 1940s Catholic clergy became particularly concerned over the decline of the family rosary, part of a wider apprehension that religion played only a superficial part in Catholic family life.[41] During Advent 1946 the Catholic archbishop of Birmingham, Thomas Williams, suggested in a pastoral letter to his arch-

---

[37] *CLJ* xli/6 (June 1944).

[38] L. Davidoff and C. Hall, *Family fortunes: men and women of the English middle class, 1780–1850*, London 1987; P. Crawford, *Women and religion in England, 1500–1720*, London 1993.

[39] *KNPM* (Jan. 1953).

[40] Revd George Gallagher to Fr. Kenny, 21 May 1958, BAA, DP, box 7, folder 2 (permissions to attend non-Catholic schools, 1944–5, 1957–61).

[41] A. Harris, 'Transformations in English Catholic spirituality and popular religion, 1945–1980', unpubl. DPhil. diss. Oxford 2008, 67–73.

diocese that a shortage of candidates for priesthood was hardly surprising if religion and vocation were never discussed at home.[42] Though Free Church ministers were generally more sensitive to the dangers of parents compelling children to say their prayers (thereby perhaps also alienating them from religion altogether), Carrs Lane Church's assistant minister Roy Clark nevertheless felt it 'a pity [that] the practice of family prayers seems to be a thing of the past' as it did 'establish the principle of family religion'.[43]

Most commonly, concern was expressed over apparent parental reluctance to send or bring children to church. For John Morris, curate at St John the Baptist, Longbridge, family church attendance was 'an idea we are in danger of losing almost completely in our modern age'.[44] In part, this highlighted issues over the division of religious labour between parents. For Callum Brown, the woman's role in creating a Christian home and family was crucial in maintaining Christianity's discursive dominance between the mid-eighteenth and the mid-twentieth centuries, whilst women's rejection of this role in the 'long 1960s' crucially impaired the transmission of Christian norms and values between generations.[45] In a climate still predominantly shaped by patriarchal norms, married women who worked could draw criticism from more conservative clergy who saw this as neglect of a woman's duty to remain at home and raise children. Even so, specific criticism of women remained sparse in clergy letters. In part this may simply bear out Elizabeth Wilson's observation that in the 1950s and 1960s 'theoreticians, popularising sociologists, doctors, vicars, schoolmasters and journalists engaged in prolonged and heated debate about the state of the family without ever seriously discussing the position of women at all'.[46] Nevertheless, it is worth noting that fathers, as well as mothers, could earn criticism. Frank Mort's contention that 'the bond between fathers and sons was not viewed as inconsequential by the agencies of culture and by individuals living in families'[47] certainly applies to church comment in this period (though more in the popular church press than in local clergy letters to parish or congregation). In 1958 the monthly church magazine insert *Church News* carried the cautionary tale of 'the Muddleheads', a family apparently uninterested in their children's upbringing. When a church youth group leader, 'Mrs Keen', enquires whether the Muddleheads could accompany their son to church on Sunday mornings, 'Mrs Muddlehead' replies 'Sunday morning's Mr Muddlehead's only chance to lie in … "I did my churchgoing when I was a nipper",

---

[42] 'Pastoral letter of Thomas, archbishop and metropolitan, Advent 1946', BAA, AC, 1946.
[43] *CLJ* lvii/3 (Mar. 1959).
[44] *KNPM* (Jan. 1956).
[45] Brown, *Death of Christian Britain*, ch. viii.
[46] E. Wilson, *Only halfway to paradise: women in post-war Britain, 1945–68*, London 1980, 61.
[47] F. Mort, 'Social and symbolic fathers and sons in post-war Britain', *JBS* xxxviii (1999), 353–84 at p. 355.

he says, "and now I'm entitled to please myself how I spend my day off".[48] The tenor of such cautionary tales was reflected in more scholarly writing: John G. Williams' influential book *Worship and the modern child* (1957), for example, suggested that boys were particularly influenced by the (non-) churchgoing habits of their fathers.[49]

Evaluating the importance of family context in religious change

Had the Churches identified a significant reason for declining youth partici-pation, or was parental neglect merely a scapegoat for a problem with manifold causes (including the Churches' own failures)? The answer lies somewhere between the two. On the one hand, family religion was an obvious target for local church leaders wishing to foster greater Christian commitment. Reported Sunday school membership was consistently higher than actual weekly attendance. Parents who remained at home or organ-ised family outings on Sunday mornings constituted an obvious explanation for declining participation. Whether or not patterns of family religion were changing, clerical expectations of nominally Christian adults certainly were: the late 1940s and 1950s saw renewed emphasis by clergy on the importance of personal fulfilment of religious duty. Conversely, there was increasing intolerance of the long-standing practice of 'religion by deputy' (whereby attendance by one family member – usually mother or child – was assumed to fulfil the religious obligations of the whole family).[50]

In fact parental support for children's religious participation remained relatively high into the 1950s (if nevertheless lower than earlier in the century). According to Geoffrey Gorer in 1955, just over half of parents reported sending their children to Sunday school, a third doing so regard-less of their child's wishes.[51] Several Birmingham interviewees born in the immediate postwar years remembered being sent to Sunday school by non-churchgoing parents, although Jan Hughes of Grenfell Baptist (b. 1949) was the youngest to feel that she 'seemed to represent the whole family – and they were most put out because I wasn't going to go'.[52] Though clerical refer-ences to working mothers, or fathers sleeping in on their day off, implies particular criticism of working-class parents, working-class children were if anything more likely to be sent to Sunday school than middle-class children, and only slightly less likely to be taught to pray at home.[53] Popular religious

---

48 *Church News* (Oct. 1958).
49 J. G. Williams, *Worship and the modern child: a handbook for parents, clergy and teachers*, London 1957, 58.
50 This phrase is derived from Williams, *Southwark*.
51 Gorer, *English character*, 454–5.
52 IJ49GB.
53 Gorer, *English character*, 454–5.

participation in family rituals remained evident in working-class neighbour-hoods into the 1960s and 1970s. Sharon Parker of St Bede's, Brandwood, whose children were born between the mid-1960s and late 1970s, remembered her mother insisting '"you've got to get [your daughter] baptised if she's gonna die tomorrow" … my mum was a stickler like that – she wouldn't let me into the house unless I'd been churched'.[54] Indeed, the widespread persistence of such assumptions eventually prompted St Bede's vicar, Stuart Matthews, to write to parishioners in 1967 correcting what he regarded as a serious misunderstanding of the rituals for the purification of women after childbirth described in Leviticus xii.[55]

However, the suspicion that family religious practice was in decline was not without foundation. This was a long-term trend: Jeffrey Cox, for example, has argued that the eclipse of late Victorian nonconformity was partly attrib-utable to the increased reluctance of churchgoing parents to impose their beliefs on their children.[56] Simon Green also tentatively suggests that across the middle third of the twentieth century, young, married, middle- and upper-working class women were amongst those most likely to cease regular church-going, with potentially significant implications for the religious upbringing of their own children.[57] The new parents of the '40s and '50s seem also to have been less directive of their children's religious practice than their parents had been with them. Whilst two churchgoing parents still invariably took their children to church or Sunday school, successive cohorts of non-churchgoing parents appeared increasingly unlikely to follow suit. One 1957 study of young mothers living on housing estates in Birmingham, Leeds and London by the Christian Economic and Social Research Foundation suggested that many interviewees found it difficult to make time to attend church for them-selves, given family illness, domestic pressures and the difficulty of arranging care for very young children on Sundays (reflecting the continued influence of domestic ideology, but also assumptions about the unsuitability of bringing young children to church – both of which the report's authors seemed to take as normal).[58] Sending children to Sunday school also appeared in decline: according to Gorer in 1955, around two-thirds of parents over thirty-five had done so, compared with just less than half of parents aged twenty-five to thirty-four.[59] Whilst teaching one's children to pray was still common among 1950s parents, the oral evidence suggests that this too was in decline: Martin Hargreaves (b. 1945) of St George's, Edgbaston, was the youngest to

---

[54] IJ22SB.
[55] SBBPM (Nov. 1967).
[56] Cox, English Churches, 223–52.
[57] Green, Passing, 80.
[58] Christian Economic and Social Research Foundation, Aspects of the problem facing the Churches: an analysis of certain findings of the survey of factors affecting setting up a home, made in Birmingham, Leeds and London in January, 1957, London 1960, 10–14.
[59] Gorer, English character, 454–5.

have been taught to pray by non-churchgoing parents.[60] Gorer concurs that certain types of prayer (notably saying grace before meals) were increasingly scarce amongst younger adults.[61] Even in families with two churchgoing parents, patterns of home religious observance may have been changing. Dennis Fricker of St George's (born in 1929 into a practising Methodist family) remembered how before the Second World War

> Sunday ... was a little bit boring – you couldn't do nothing. You got up in the morning, perhaps had your better clothes on – didn't go to eight o'clock service, and you didn't go to perhaps midday service – but then you went to Sunday school and perhaps evensong. There was not a lot you could do on a Sunday ... you couldn't even go to the park ... you could walk in the park but ... I don't know if people thought 'we're not going to stand for that going on'?[62]

Several of Dennis's age group also commented on the restrictive nature of Sundays during childhood, and remembered taking a different approach with their own children.[63] Kathleen Norton (b. 1921, with two sons born in the early 1950s) remembered how for her, 'Sunday was a quiet day – services, church' yet as a mother she had made Sundays

> more relaxed, you know – I mean certainly it would be morning worship ... back for the Sunday roast, and then in the afternoon, I think the boys would go off on their own, with their own friends, and I would do some darning. In the winter times maybe just reading.[64]

In her own oral history research, Elizabeth Roberts has noted a similar tendency for the parents of the postwar cohort not to 'reject or abandon the standards of behaviour under which they were brought up', but instead to be 'rather less strict in enforcing those standards and punishing breaches of them'.[65] Whilst Roberts acknowledges the possible influences of specific 'permissive' parenting techniques, she ultimately deems these of less significance than the emergence of a more general child-centred approach, emphasising emotional intimacy and greater freedom of choice.[66] Elsewhere it has been noted that working mothers of the period frequently deflected accusations of neglect by emphasising the value of children growing into independent individuals.[67] Regarding church youth work, the writers of *80,000*

---

[60] IJ36SG.
[61] Gorer, *English character*, 456.
[62] IJ30SG.
[63] See also Green, *Passing*, 143–61.
[64] IJ50CL. The tendency for postwar parents to seek a better life for their children is also noted in Sykes, 'Popular religion in decline', 287–307.
[65] E. Roberts, *Women and families: an oral history, 1940–1970*, Oxford 1995, 158.
[66] Ibid. ch. viii. See also Gorer, *English character*, 420, 427–33.
[67] D. Smith Wilson, 'A new look at the affluent worker: the good working mother in postwar Britain', *TCBH* xvii (2006), 206–29.

adolescents found that youth leaders frequently expressed a similar reluctance to offer moral guidance to young people (perhaps partly out of sensitivity to accusations of indoctrination – Goebbels, after all, was still a vivid
memory).[68] Simultaneously however, postwar parents appeared increasingly
to believe that the guidance of children was their sole prerogative.[69] This did
not always result in a rejection of religion, and amongst highly committed
Christian parents it was often quite the reverse. In Sutton Coldfield, the
Catholic archdiocese's decision not to increase further senior school provision led to a 'strong and virtually unanimous feeling in the district that
the Church is denying our children a Catholic Grammar School education', according to one frustrated parent in a letter of complaint to the
archbishop's secretary. However, the writer's observations also suggested
that parental choice could undermine as well as strengthen the Church's
influence: 'I do not think it is realised that a number of Catholic parents
whose boys are at non-Catholic schools in this district have never even
sought permission and that at least one had no idea that such permission
was necessary.'[70] If the cohort growing up in the immediate postwar decades
were less religiously assiduous than their predecessors, this may be as much
to do with the attitudes of their parents as with any large-scale revolt by the
younger generation. Callum Brown may thus be right to connect the sharp
postwar downturn in formal Christian affiliation with a break in the 'cycle
of inter-generational renewal'.[71] However, this process may well have begun
before the 'long 1960s' themselves, even whilst church and Sunday school
participation was experiencing short-term renaissance, and sometimes owed
as much to the choices of fathers as mothers.

Efforts to re-engage young people in the 1950s and 1960s

In the light of such changes, how did local churches seek to re-engage youth
and families? Initially, in the late 1940s and early 1950s, many churches
responded by re-emphasising traditional expectations of family religious
observance, assuming the root cause to be neglect of religious duty, rather
than any failure of the Churches. (This pattern of response was also characteristic of local church responses to many other pastoral challenges in the
1950s.) Within English Catholicism, one early strategy to address family
religion was a firm restatement of teaching on marriage – for example in
the English bishops' joint pastoral letter on marriage and divorce of 1952.
Clergy were also urged to exercise caution in applying for dispensations for
mixed marriages, to allow time to gauge the 'disposition' of the non-Catholic

---

68 Reed, *80,000 adolescents*, 185.
69 Roberts, *Women*, 160.
70 Norman Hardy to Fr. Kenny, 18 July 1958, BAA, DP 7, box 7, fo. 2.
71 Brown, *Death of Christian Brown*, 1.

partner. 'These will not be ordinarily granted', wrote Archbishop Thomas Williams in 1947, 'as there appears little chance in such cases of moral certainty regarding the keeping of these promises.'[72] Williams's assumption were partly correct: later research by Michael Hornsby-Smith suggests that whilst many committed Catholics marrying exogamously remained assiduous in their practice, 'mixed' marriage was also frequently indicative of an existing drift from the Church amongst those already practising only occasionally.[73] This was symptomatic of the wider erosion of the 'fortress' Catholicism of the late nineteenth and early twentieth centuries.

The prospects for reviving family prayer seemed more favourable. Late in 1947 the new archbishop, Joseph Masterson, made it the focus of his maiden tour of the archdiocese. The following Lent he asked 'all of our Catholic people, parents and children, to take up this work [of teaching children to pray] and in the name of God to try to spiritualise their homes: to make them truly little kingdoms of God upon earth'.[74] Within a year, the English hierarchy announced a teaching mission on family prayer. In 1952 this was followed by a Rosary Crusade, led by Fr Patrick Peyton, in which families were encouraged to spend at least ten minutes per day saying decades of the rosary.[75] Here again a connection was made between familial devotion and wider social well-being, Archbishop Masterson arguing that such prayer could 'bring to the earth the blessing of God, but in particular, three graces of which we stand badly in need; peace of heart, peace in the home, and peace among the nations of the world'.[76] The long-term effects of the crusade are difficult to gauge, but its regional climax – a rally at Villa Park football ground – was certainly well-attended.[77]

Anglican and Free Church priorities were somewhat different. With the home apparently an unreliable source of spiritual nourishment, the 1940s and 1950s saw many congregations turn their attention to Sunday services as a potential incubator of family religion. The spiritual benefits of parents and children worshipping together were widely restated. Advertising Heneage Street Baptist Church's morning service in 1948, its newsletter explained that

> we are naturally keen to inculcate a 'church consciousness' and churchgoing 'habits' in our young people, and so build a future. So please help us in every way you can, by encouraging your children to come, and by influencing any others with whom you have to do.

---

[72] *Ad clerum*, 11 Aug. 1947, BAA, AC 1947/8.

[73] M. Hornsby-Smith, *Roman Catholics in England: studies in social structure since the Second World War*, Cambridge 1987, 99–100.

[74] 'Pastoral letter of Joseph, archbishop and metropolitan, Lent 1948', BAA, AC 1947/8.

[75] 'Pastoral letter, May 1952, to announce the Family Rosary Crusade', ibid. 1952.

[76] 'Pastoral letter of Joseph, archbishop and metropolitan, June 1952', ibid.

[77] For a fuller assessment see Harris, 'Transformations in English Catholic spirituality', 167–73.

Quoting Mark x.13 ('they brought young children to Him that He should teach them'), the writer continued, 'that word "brought" should burn itself in our hearts, as a duty, and a discipline, and a delight'.[78] As attendance by children and young people declined in the later 1950s, this message was reasserted even more firmly. In 1956 the Church of England ran a national campaign, 'Operation Firm Faith', 'to bring before the country the grave dangers of the neglect of spiritual training of children'.[79] In a two-pronged strategy, dioceses and congregations conducted thorough reviews of youth and children's work, whilst sermons, pastoral visits and church magazines exhorted parents to foster a more Christian ethos at home.

One of the campaign's most enduring results was the popularisation of new styles of church service geared more explicitly to an 'all-age' congregation. In many churches for most of the preceding century, adults and children spent the greater part of their time in separate spheres, with services typically taking place morning and evening, and many Sunday schools in the afternoons (often in separate buildings). In the early twentieth century, this division if anything became sharper: P. B. Cliff suggests that around half of Birmingham's morning Sunday schools disappeared during the First World War.[80] Though the separation of church and Sunday school had been in many ways a successful arrangement, an enduring by-product was the failure of many children to translate juvenile participation into regular adult churchgoing. Conversely, children ended up 'out of sight, out of mind' of many adult worshippers.[81] A further factor militating against families attending church together was a widespread assumption that church was no place to bring very young children. Jim West (b. 1924) was one of several older interviewees to have stayed away from church for a period in order to stay at home with his young children, implying that this was a natural occurrence.[82] A similar pattern emerged from the 1957 Christian Economic and Social Research Foundation study of young mothers and churchgoing. Whether parents had decided for themselves that church was unsuitable for small children, were simply making excuses, or had been pressured to keep young children away was unclear – although the widespread expectation that worship required hushed concentration may have been a factor in deterring some new parents.

In order to integrate children more fully into the adult congregation, mid-century Christian educationalists experimented with several new Sunday service formats. Amongst the most influential was 'family church', devel-

---

78 HSBCN (Sept. 1948).

79 H. G. G. Herklots, *Operation Firm Faith for Christ and his Church: a practical handbook*, London 1957.

80 P. B. Cliff, *The rise and development of the Sunday school movement in England, 1780–1980*, Redhill 1986, 235.

81 Ibid.

82 IJ52CT.

oped by the Congregationalist minister H. A. Hamilton, lecturer at Westhill College, Birmingham.[83] Put simply, 'family church' emphasised the value of parents and children worshipping together through a service designed to cater for all ages. Besides benefiting children, it was also hoped to encourage greater involvement from parents.[84] Whilst the immediate demands of postwar reconstruction meant that these ideas mostly lay dormant during the 1940s, declining Sunday school attendances and growing concerns about the provision of religious instruction at home and school brought renewed emphasis on family churchgoing in the mid-1950s across the denominations. At St Nicholas's, Kings Norton, a new family service was introduced in 1957. Despite criticism from some regulars (particularly concerning the omission of sections of the Prayer Book), most Parochial Church Council members agreed that family worship was desirable in principle. One suggested that 'feeling against the innovations were expressed mostly by older people', and that experimentation should continue since there had been 'many new faces at the family services'. Another agreed that he 'did not understand the Service in the Prayer Book when he first went to Church, and would have welcomed the family service as such'.[85] Such experiences appear to have been common, and 'family services' became an increasingly prominent part of the liturgical landscape across the Anglican and Free Churches. Even where congregations did not adopt the full 'family service' model, it became more common for children to spend part of the service in church; typically a fifteen- to twenty-minute segment containing a favourite children's hymn or song, and a brief 'address'.

Concern to make Sunday church more child-centred also extended beyond the 'family service' itself. By the late 1950s church magazines suggested increased awareness (almost entirely absent in the 1940s and early 1950s) that church might appear stuffy, obscure or unfriendly to young people.[86] This was corroborated in a 1957 study of four Birmingham congregations by the New Zealand academic R. H. T. Thompson, who found many young churchgoers regarded themselves as a distinct group sharing little in common with their elders.[87] A more pronounced sense of adolescent alienation (this time apparent to churchgoing adults) was evident in a 1966 study of churches in 'Brookton', south Birmingham (probably Kings Norton), by another overseas visitor, the Ghanaian diplomat Kofi Busia.[88] In the time between the two studies, many churches had already begun to seek to accom-

83 H. A. Hamilton, *The family church in principle and practice*, London 1943.
84 See, for example, Archbishops' Commission, *Towards the conversion of England*, 89.
85 *KNPM* (Jan. 1958).
86 See also chapter 4 below.
87 R. H. T. Thompson, *The Church's understanding of itself: a study of four Birmingham parishes*, London 1957, 31.
88 K. A. Busia, *Urban churches in Britain: a question of relevance*, London 1966, 67, 116, 123.

modate youth and children more fully into church life and worship. In 1961 the church council at the newly-established St Bede's, Brandwood, agreed to print special orders of service to enable children to follow the liturgy more clearly.[89] At the quarterly meeting of the Moseley Road and Sparkhill Methodist Circuit the following year, congregations were urged to 'accommodate themselves to our younger people ... interest themselves in what our youth was interested in ... [and] work on the assumption that this may be the last opportunity'.[90] Even at the liturgically-traditional St George's, Edgbaston, George Browning asked parish magazine readers whether 'the services we know and love so well [are] the right ones for young people who are sincerely trying to grow in church life?'[91]

Nor were attempts to re-engage the young confined to services. Allowing space for young people to question and explore their faith was increasingly encouraged. For example, in February 1962 the St George's youth club 'the Dragons' discussed what might happen 'If the Dragons could revise the Prayer Book'.[92] The 'fun' element of church youth clubs – always present but usually officially secondary – was brought increasingly to the fore as youth leaders sought to combat accusations of stuffiness. Considerable (if sometimes awkward) use was made of the language and artefacts of contemporary youth culture. In February 1964 young readers of Kings Norton's parish magazine were encouraged to join the youth fellowship with the promise that 'whether you are a "Mod" or a "Rocker" I am sure we have something for you'.[93] An advertisement for the Grenfell Baptist Christian Endeavour group (established to nurture the next generation of church leaders) asked 'Are you a young person who is at a loose end on a Tuesday night; fed up with watching the telly; nothing new on the squawk box; no new records to listen to and don't feel like reading a book?' Instead, it promised 'something new, something different', including a 'big business meeting ... which you won't be interested in', a picnic, 'no one telling us to turn that -?! record player down!' and 'an informal chat from Mr Aitken [the minister]'.[94] The use of 'us' implies authorship by a youth group member, lending credibility to the sense of common cause against pop-music-hating parents.

Whilst such appeals could (as Callum Brown has noted[95]) simply turn into embarrassing attempts to appear trendy, some youth work could more authentically combine the styles and language of contemporary popular culture with more robust engagement with the challenges of young people's

---

[89] St Bede's, Brandwood, church council minute book, 9 Jan. 1961, BCA, EP110/5/4/1.
[90] Moseley Road and Sparkhill Methodist Circuit quarterly meeting, minutes, Dec. 1962, BCA, MC9/4.
[91] SGEPM (June 1962).
[92] SGEPM (Feb. 1962).
[93] KNPM (Feb. 1964).
[94] GBCN (Mar. 1963).
[95] Brown, Death of Christian Britain, 180.

lives. In 1965 the Anglican diocese of Birmingham appointed its first dedicated 'chaplain to the unattached', David Collyer, whose *Double Zero* club (for young bikers) was a pioneering example of engagement with the new youth cultures of the day: seriousness about the issues facing young adults combined with an acknowledgement that their spiritual development might necessitate new forms of Christian community – not just assimilation into traditional church.[96] Both this more indigenised approach to Christian youth work and the more superficial restyling of existing youth activities signalled a growing acceptance, from the 1960s onwards, that the 'generation gap' could not simply be ignored, condemned or treated with a strong course of family churchgoing. For Collyer, greater seriousness about young people's lives was crucial because 'today more than ever [they] are being forced by the community to develop a life of their own ... smaller family houses ... slight social meeting space ... adults wanting a social life of their own, mass media, combine together to make the young a separate group'.[97] Historians have subsequently questioned whether this 'generation gap' was as wide as some contemporaries believed it to be. However, Collyer was at least correct in identifying changes in family life as one important catalyst for youth's increasing cultural distinctiveness. Since the mid-1930s rising prosperity had brought the prospect of a comfortable, home-centred life within the means of many working-class families (nationally, owner-occupation rose from 26 to 47 per cent between 1945 and 1966[98]). Equally important was a shift in attitudes to family relations, with surveys reporting widespread aspiration towards companionate marriage and an increase in leisure time spent with the family.[99] In particular, several historians have identified a growing link between domesticity and respectability, many postwar mothers believing it a sign of good parenting to keep their child at home, away from the 'rougher' associations of the street.[100] At the same time, changes in family structure also contributed towards a partial polarisation of the family unit. Smaller family size, a shorter, more defined period of childbearing and fewer intermediate kin living in the same house produced sharper generational stratification in many 1950s and 1960s families.[101] Though in many respects parents were increasingly inclined to give greater latitude to their children, and few families resented the new possibilities for home-based leisure,[102] the increased

---

96 D. Collyer, *Double Zero: five years with Rockers and Hell's Angels in an English city*, Evesham 1983 edn.
97 *Church News* (July 1967).
98 Roberts, *Women*, 25.
99 G. H. Gallup (ed.), *Gallup international public opinion polls: Great Britain, 1937–75*, i, New York 1976, 415.
100 M. Tebbutt, *Women's talk? A social history of 'gossip' in working class neighbourhoods*, Aldershot 1995, 173; Roberts, *Women*, 41.
101 Benson, *Prime time*, 101–5. This polarisation was somewhat mitigated by a trend towards marrying younger.
102 Roberts, *Women*, 238.

proximity of two increasingly distinct familial generations spending more time at home together could combine to create new kinds of tension. The potential for inter-generational conflict was heightened by the appearance of new mass consumer markets with an explicit appeal to the young – particularly in music, fashion and broadcasting – rejecting the ideal of a common trans-generational culture sometimes implied in the mid twentieth-century cult of the home.

The adolescents of the late 1950s and 1960s – the first 'teenagers' – have frequently been portrayed as the shock troops of cultural revolution. Certainly this cohort of young people frequently differed from their elders in attitudes to worship, church, taste and behaviour. However, neither young people nor adults were completely homogenous social groupings: long-standing social class divisions and newer allegiances to emerging youth subcultures all combined to ensure that remained the case.[103] Although folk-lore gives a prominent place to mods, rockers, hippies and student protests, most young people in the 1960s were measured in their attitudes (when Rolling Stones Mick Jagger and Keith Richard were imprisoned on drugs charges in 1967, 85 per cent of teenagers questioned in a national opinion poll thought the sentence either appropriate or too lenient[104]). Sometimes local church leaders reminded adults that young people need not be regarded fearfully: the St Bede's Church magazine *Progress* emphasised that despite their love of rock'n'roll, the youth fellowship were nevertheless 'all worshipping members of the St Bede's congregation', most of whom 'play their part in the life of the church'.[105] However, if young people did not always differ from their elders, they were not culturally indistinct. Keith Bradbury (b. 1942), a lifelong churchgoer from Kings Norton, remembered how 'youngsters were beginning to be more noticed, rather than just tolerated – they were individuals in their own right'. He continued, 'everywhere you went and everything you did you were chaperoned at that time, and you'd seek the opportunity to get away from the crowd'.[106]

If the teenagers of the 1960s were distinctive partly because their adolescence seemed so different from that of their parents, they were also set apart because at this formative stage in their lives they absorbed more completely than their elders new ideas about tradition and change. For Arthur Marwick, the long 1960s witnessed an 'outburst of entrepreneurialism, individualism, doing your own thing', and were characterised by a corresponding suspi-

---

[103] Osgerby, *Youth in Britain since 1945*, 28; M. Brake, *Comparative youth culture: the sociology of youth culture and youth sub-cultures in America, Britain and Canada*, London 1985, 58–82.

[104] Benson, *Prime time*, 109.

[105] *Progress: the magazine of St. Bede's Church, Brandwood*, no. 1, Christmas 1962, BCA, EP110/7/1/2.

[106] IJ14CT.

cion of establishments and *a priori* authority.[107] Such attitudes arguably had enormous implications for the 'contract between generations'.[108] Rather than being an inherently valuable guide to present and future, the past became at best a cultural resource from which to pick and choose, but at worst an oppressive constraint on personal freedom. One key consequence was arguably to tip the balance of cultural power away from those with the greatest acquaintance with the past (the old) and towards those with the most potential to shape the future (the young, whose tastes and ideas could be propagated more extensively than ever in a climate of rising prosperity, changing social structure and increased specialisation of markets). In this sense, Marwick is right to see the 'unprecedented influence of young people ... the prestige of youth and the appeal of the youthful lifestyle' as equally central characteristics of 'the Sixties' experience.[109] For Martin Hargreaves of St George's (b. 1945), there were

> such changes in the mid-sixties ... the youth culture thing, which hadn't really existed – well, partly in the 1950s but really got its head in the sixties – of people thinking that youth had actually got all the answers in a way which I don't think was thought of in the forties and fifties at all.[110]

Here (in aspiration if not in practice) was historical change as revolution, not evolution; generational disjuncture rather than generational continuity.[111]

Whilst many local churches undoubtedly made strenuous efforts to adapt their worship and common life with youth in mind, there arguably remained a reluctance fully to embrace this 'changing contract between generations'. In this, great variation existed between congregations and also between denominations. Roman Catholic parishes arguably had least room to manoeuvre, given the extent of regulation governing the liturgy and historic inexperience in lay decision-making. Traditional Free Churches were, in theory, best prepared to give greater latitude to the young, given their historic attachment to individual freedom of conscience.[112] At one Carrs Lane Church conference in 1965, the Congregational Union's youth leadership training officer explained that for young people to develop in confidence and Christian fellowship, 'we must not force our convictions on them, but put our faith across by thinking and sharing together'.[113] That more cautious and open-ended approach to the transmission of faith seemed well in tune with

---

107 Marwick, *The Sixties*, 17.
108 The phrase derives from Bengston and Achenbaum, *Changing contract*, although my meaning is slightly different here.
109 Marwick, *The Sixties*, 17.
110 IJ36SG.
111 Garnett, Harris, Grimley, Whyte and Williams, *Redefining Christian Britain*, 119.
112 J. L. Altholz, 'The warfare of conscience with theology', in G. Parsons (ed.), *Religion in Victorian Britain*, IV: *Interpretations*, Manchester 1988, 150–69.
113 CLJ lxiii/9 (Sept. 1965).

the spirit of the age. Nevertheless, concern for the young generally remained subordinate to the trans-generational unity of family and congregation, an ideal graphically illustrated in a *Church News* photograph in January 1960, showing a mother, father and son, dressed in similar respectable fashion, walking up the church path together for Sunday worship.

Moreover, if the ideal of a 'common generational culture' held particular appeal for the Churches (for whom *traditio* – 'handing down' – was of the essence), it reflected a general aspiration in 1940s and 1950s Britain despite (or perhaps because of) significant divisions of class, taste and age.[114] Whilst in theory common generational culture could have centred around the preferences of young or old, the reality was that age took precedence. Mid twentieth-century Britain was a society founded upon the slow refinement of tradition rather than sudden, violent revolution. Concessions to youth were possible, but only if innovation was kept in careful balance with tradition. In ecclesiastical terms, such an assumption meant that if there were considerable willingness to permit new styles of youth service or extend young people's participation, the rising generation were nevertheless expected to wait its turn before effecting large-scale change. Thus in 1963 the Birmingham Diocesan Council for Family and Social Welfare ran what the Diocesan Leaflet described as '"preventative teaching" in schools, youth clubs and with adult groups' on subjects such as 'Why should I do what Dad says?' or 'Why should I not be a Beatnik?'[115] Other developments in church life could unwittingly reinforce the emphasis on common inter-generational culture. Besides the popularisation of the family service, the growing influence of the liturgical movement led to more churches (particularly within the Church of England) adopting the pattern of a single communion service for all worshippers on Sunday mornings, rather than allow for liturgical diversity. George Browning of St George's, Edgbaston, reflected the views of many fellow clergy in believing that the parish eucharist could be effective in retaining young churchgoers 'and I believe that we shall be doing a very good thing in training our children to understand and love this service'.[116] Though the idea of the young as 'adults in training' came under increased challenge in the postwar period, the assumption that children and young people were being prepared to carry forward not only theological truth, but also particular ecclesiastical styles, remained widespread.

In practice, this meant that the priorities and preferences of adults often remained paramount in church life. Experimentation was frequently dogged by concern that greater involvement of youth or consideration of their needs risked a decline in 'quality'. In 1962 Gordon Parkhouse, minister in the Moseley Road and Sparkhill Methodist Circuit, told the circuit meeting that

---

[114] Hewison, *In anger*, 181; P. Mandler, 'Two cultures – one – or many?', in Burk, *British Isles*, 127–55.
[115] BDL (July 1963).
[116] SGEPM (July 1962).

ministers and preachers should certainly become acquainted with the interests of youth 'but by doing so, not to lower the standards of work'.[117] Similarly, Robert Aitken of Grenfell Baptist Church noted that forms of worship targeted specifically at teenagers ('Christian skiffle groups and the adaptation of the Rock'n'Roll type of music') often generated accusations of 'gimmick religion'.[118] Such charges have often been levelled against innovation in times of rapid change. Nevertheless, they were expressed particularly often by prewar birth cohorts. This may partly reflect a tendency for spiritual needs and priorities to change across the life course. Older interviewees frequently emphasised the value of familiar liturgical patterns and a quiet atmosphere free from distractions. A 'period effect' was also apparent, in that concern over 'standards' drew directly upon contemporary assumptions about what constituted 'good' worship.[119] However, concern that concessions to youth might lead to declining standards perhaps also reflected wider assumptions about the proper relationship between youth and age. Whilst many adults were prepared to listen to youth, advocate change and discard cherished nostrums, a conviction nevertheless remained that tradition and innovation were a matter of equilibrium; that some generational continuity was important and that the priorities of the new generation should be accommodated through evolutionary, not revolutionary, change. Whilst this assumption seemed reasonable within an institution built upon timeless truth, it also placed the Churches on a direct collision course with the spirit of the age.

Rethinking youth ministry in the 1970s and 1980s

This basic dilemma continued to vex church efforts to reach young people, bridge the 'generation gap' and restore confidence amongst adult worshippers eager to accommodate young people but uncertain of the best approach. A 1980 report by the Children's Committee at St Bede's, Brandwood, noted 'the personal inadequacy and lack of training which many adults feel in dealing with young people whose lives and relationships are changing rapidly at puberty'.[120] Moreover, where once older teenagers would often have made a seamless transition from youth membership to youth leadership within the same church, declining numbers of twenty-somethings in church, increased geographical mobility and entry into higher education meant that fewer congregations had a ready supply of young adults to lead youth and children's work. As a result, increasing numbers of churches employed professional youth workers or gap-year volunteers. Carrs Lane and Grenfell Baptist churches both engaged outside help on this basis.

117 BCA, MC9/4, Dec. 1962.
118 GBCN (June 1963).
119 See chapter 4 below.
120 BCA, EP110/5/4/3, Jan. 1980.

Another strategy to increase youth participation from the 1970s onwards (though rarely discussed by interviewees) was the extension of full membership or communicant status to children and young people.[121] Though a logical extension of the family service concept, it also reflected the increased influence of child-centred approaches to education and ministry. As the influential Birmingham-based Christian educationalist John Hull wrote in 1984, 'those denominations which depend upon separate institutions ... for the Christian nurture of their children are tending to <u>lose</u> their children, whereas denominations in which children are being nurtured through a full and rich participation in the worshipping life of the denomination are tending to <u>hold</u> their children'.[122] In 1977 Kings Norton URC drew up new guidelines on children and communion, emphasising that even baptised infants should be seen as full church members, since 'heaven awaits us all'. In this view, communion was 'the sacrament of the start of adulthood', given to any child who had been properly instructed.[123] In 1991 St Mary's Pitt Heath trialled a 'faith friends' scheme, whereby first communion candidates were partnered with older churchgoing teenagers who would encourage them in their first attendance at mass.[124]

However, the most vexed question remained how to offer a clearly Christian yet non-pressurised home environment. A leading member of Carrs Lane Church preached on this theme in 1978, challenging church members that if they really believed that their values were pleasing to God, these should be passed on to their children.[125] By this time, the responsibilities of parenthood had passed to the postwar birth cohort, who seemed perhaps more eager than their elders to avoid the impression of indoctrinating their children. Some did so as a result of feeling that their child should be free to follow their own spiritual path. As Catherine Thorpe of St George's, Edgbaston, explained, 'I didn't christen my own children cos ... I wanted them to think about their baptism and do it for [their] own decisions, not mine'.[126] Sometimes parental hesitancy was more difficult to define: Martin Hargreaves, also of St George's, who had 'learnt to pray from my mother on her knee', nevertheless admitted that 'I don't think we've been as good at teaching [our children] to pray as my mother was with me, actually ... I don't think we've found that particularly easy to do'.[127] For those born in Ireland and raising children in Britain, a more secular cultural milieu could also

---

[121] In Roman Catholicism, first communion had traditionally occurred at an earlier age.
[122] This is quoted in *CLJ* lxxxvii/5 (May1964). Hull was, for a period, a member at Carrs Lane.
[123] *Kings Norton URC Monthly News* (Mar. 1977), BCA, CC20/2/1–8.
[124] Parish news sheet (14 May 1991) (in possession of parish priest).
[125] *CLJ* lxxxi/8 (Aug. 1978).
[126] IJ35SG.
[127] IJ36SG.

influence the degree to which children were taught to pray. Patrick Mannion (b. 1944) remembered how in Ireland:

> At night-time ... the father and mother went down on their knees, mother or dad would click on the rosary beads on the mantel-shelf. He'd start at the first dec, and you'd go on, down through the family ... it was more strict – very strict then – I don't know if the rosary's said now in Ireland or not.
>
> *[interviewer: what about here?]*
>
> I haven't come across it here, like. Like when my kids were young we used to say prayers, might say a decade of the rosary, something like that, but not as much as what we did in Ireland.[128]

For Catholics, two further factors may have exacerbated the decline in religious socialisation. As pupils at a Catholic school in the 1960s, Mary Mason and Theresa Wilby (sisters, b. 1951 and 1953 respectively) experienced sectarian bullying by pupils at a nearby school, and although 'away from church' whilst bringing up their own children in the 1970s, the Troubles partly influenced their decisions not to give their own children a Catholic education.[129] Of much wider significance was the Second Vatican Council. Whilst Catholic interviewees generally welcomed the resultant shift in emphasis in Catholic education 'from one based on fear to one based on love', it was also recognised that children growing up immediately after the Council may have been unsettled by the upheaval in Catholic life. Susan Williams, whose children attended primary school in the 1970s, believed that they had been 'very unlucky ... I think they used to get a lot of conflicting ideas from school ... it's hard to pass on something when it's changing, when you're completely unclear what the changes are yourself, or ... don't necessarily agree with them'.[130]

The challenge of passing on faith to the next generation persisted into the twenty-first century. Analysing British Household Panel and British Social Attitudes data, Alasdair Crockett and David Voas suggest that in the 1980s and 1990s the values of two religiously practising parents were transmitted to their children in only half of cases (and only 22 per cent of cases where there was only one religious parent), whilst absence of religious belief and practice was transmitted to children in almost every case.[131] This chapter has argued that in the postwar period, such patterns arose as much from the growing ambivalence of parents towards the religious socialisation of their children as to any revolt by the young *per se*. The 1990s saw further steep declines

---

[128] IJ70SM.
[129] IJ66SM.
[130] IJ65SM.
[131] D. Voas and A. Crockett, 'Religion in Britain: neither believing nor belonging', *Sociology* xxxix (2005), 11–28 at pp. 21–2.

in numbers of children and young people attending church. Although the rate of decline slowed markedly in the early years of the new millennium, the Churches' predicament was graphically illustrated in figures from the 2005 English Church Census, which found that 39 per cent of congregations had no attenders under the age of eleven, half had no eleven- to fourteen-year-olds and 59 per cent had no fifteen- to nineteen-year-olds.[132] Young people had disappeared from church on a scale scarcely imaginable in the 1940s. One significant feature of this situation was the increased determination of many Christian parents to find a church with a vibrant youth and children's programme for their children to join, and the resultant clustering of children and young people in a comparatively small number of congregations.[133] Amongst the churches attracting large numbers of young people, some had pioneered specialist youth congregations or ministries – a partial rejection of the 'all generations together' model dominant in the immediate postwar decades. Adult churchgoers could be ambivalent about such radical measures, regretting the separation of the young and old in worship and noting the difficulty of reintegrating youth congregations into the wider church. However, the growing popularity of generationally-specific solutions reflected the extent to which generational disjuncture had become an important, if not actually all-pervasive, expectation. Key to this were the religious and cultural shifts occurring over the 'long 1960s'. As the following chapters will suggest, contrasting notions of the relationship between youth and age, tradition and innovation, and continuity and discontinuity, continued to exert their influence on successive cohorts of the churchgoing population on a range of issues – from worship to congregational life, morals to mission.

---

[132] Brierley, *Nosedive*, 118.
[133] Idem, *Religious trends* 6, table 2.7.1

4

Life and Worship in the Local Congregation

Whilst Christian identity, belief and practice have always meant more than merely churchgoing, and many late twentieth-century Britons considered themselves Christian without regularly attending church, it remained widely accepted that Christianity (as officially practised) involved collective religious observance. Since this congregational dimension has frequently been omitted from discussions of English Christianity in this period, this chapter seeks to put worship and congregational life back on the map, acknowledging both the wider cultural, theological and ecclesiastical influences on local churches and the way in which the congregation functioned as an important prism through which wider social and religious change was experienced and interpreted. It is impossible here to survey every aspect of postwar congregational life. Instead, three key trends are considered, each discernible in oral and documentary sources: first, a growing expectation that lay Christians would be active participants in local congregational worship and leadership; second, a tendency for worship and church life to become less 'formal' in style; and third, increasing (sometimes controversial) experimentation with new forms of popular culture within worship. Running through each of these, but particularly the latter, was a tendency for change to generate heated debate, some of which reflected changing needs and dispositions across the life course, and some of which reflected wider social generational differences in taste, behavioural norms and church experience.

First however, some contextualisation may be useful.[1] The late twentieth century saw growing diversity within (and cross-fertilisation between) Christian denominations, contrasting with the more denominational direction of the late nineteenth and early twentieth centuries. Most historic denominations became more culturally and theologically pluralistic, with central authorities progressively less able (and sometimes less inclined) to enforce conformity. Cross-fertilisation related to ecumenical activity, particularly between the 1960s and 1980s, when hopes for full institutional union between denominations were highest. During this period members of different denominations began meeting together for worship and study, often for the first time. The national campaign 'The People Next Door' (1967) was

---

[1] See further I. Jones, 'Daily life and worship: introduction', in D. Dyas (ed.), *The English parish church through the centuries: daily life & spirituality, art & architecture, literature & music* (DVD-Rom), York 2010, section 6: Churches to the present day.

an early watershed, with 75,000 churchgoers across the country gathering ecumenically during Lent, including 150 such groups in Birmingham.[2]

As in many periods, renewal movements also transcended denominational boundaries, two of the most important in the late twentieth century being the liturgical movement and the Charismatic renewal. The former, originating in eighteenth-century Catholic France, sought a renewed understanding of worship as 'essentially corporate, the act of the parish community as a whole rather than an act of individual devotion'.[3] The practical legacy of the movement, which by the early twentieth century was influential within the Church of England and some mainstream Free Churches, included an emphasis on more frequent corporate observance of holy communion and the development of vernacular and participatory liturgies. Charismatic renewal, by comparison, was an outpouring of spiritual intensity proclaiming the possibility of direct and intimate experience of a loving God who intervened in the world and gave extraordinary gifts through the Holy Spirit for worship and service (for example, prophecy, healing and speaking in tongues).[4] Strongly indebted to earlier revivalist and Pentecostal outpourings, Charismatic renewal was also (as David Bebbington observes) a distinctively late twentieth-century phenomenon, proclaiming the continued activity of God amidst a disenchanted society whilst exhibiting a very contemporary counter-cultural emphasis on personal expressivity, ambivalence towards institutions and affinity with new folk and popular cultures. The movement's heyday was from the late 1960s to the late 1980s, inspiring new congregations (often labelled 'house churches' or latterly 'new churches') but also becoming influential within the historic denominations (notably the Anglican and Baptist Churches). In the 1970s around half of Anglican ordinands acknowledged some Charismatic inspiration.[5] Through songbooks, popular literature and a new generation of Christian festivals and conventions, Charismatic styles and culture became influential well beyond the renewal movement itself. Indeed, both within and beyond Evangelicalism, annual festivals, conferences and other extra-denominational places of pilgrimage became particularly important incubators of new Christian subcultures. Amongst the most influential, the Taizé Community in France (begun in the 1940s), Scotland's Iona Community (founded in 1938), the Greenbelt Festival (1974) and Spring Harvest (1978) were as stylistically recognisable to many churchgoers as the historic denominational allegiances which they transcended.[6]

---

[2] Sansbury, Latham and Webb, *People Next Door programme*, 12, 15, 68.
[3] M. D. Stringer, *A sociological history of Christian worship*, Cambridge 2005, 217.
[4] A good general survey is P. Hocken, *Streams of renewal: the origins and early development of the Charismatic Movement in Great Britain*, rev. edn, Carlisle 1997.
[5] Welsby, *History of the Church of England*, 243.
[6] See P. Ward, 'The tribes of Evangelicalism', in G. Cray and others, *The post-Evangelical debate*, Triangle 1997, 19–34..

Postwar congregational life and worship were also transformed as a result of the changing relationship between church, neighbourhood and wider society. Recruitment for choirs, committees and outreach activities became more difficult, partly due to declining Christian commitment and decreasing interest in voluntary and membership organisations in their own right. Changes in the life course were also significant: disproportionately elderly congregations could struggle to maintain historic levels of activity, whilst the growth of paid employment for women, and (towards the end of the century) greater numbers of the recently retired caring regularly for parents or grand-children, also reduced the pool of potential volunteers. The changing place of the church in neighbourhood and society also frequently prompted reassessments of priorities for congregational activity beyond Sunday worship. In the second half of the nineteenth century many churches had responded to competition from sporting, musical and other leisure activities by offering their own more 'rational' (or simply alternative) versions, establishing their own sports clubs, theatre groups or branches of uniformed young organisations.[7] At the beginning of the postwar period, many of these were still flourishing. St Nicholas's, Kings Norton, was a fairly typical active Anglican parish church of the early 1950s, having a Mothers' Union, Girls' Friendly Society, Boy Scouts, Youth Fellowship, Badminton Club, Men's Club and a Women's Working Party, alongside regular jumble sales, garden parties and summer fêtes.

Although many such activities continued into the twenty-first century, the postwar decades saw a decline in many church-based recreational opportunities, and a changed attitude to those which continued. Some disappeared through simple lack of support. Others, such as the jumble sale, were victims of fashion and a growing reluctance to rely on the goodwill of non-church-goers to support the congregation. Some, such as church amateur dramatic societies, shared in a wider decline in such groups in the face of competition from cinema and television. If church-based social activities were in decline, many local church leaders instead gave greater priority to building up the faith of the congregation. Week-night meetings for prayer and study in members' homes (often called house groups) became an established feature of the life of many churches in the period, partly because local church life was now focused more heavily on a committed core membership, and partly through a conviction that, if the Church was to be an effective presence in contemporary society, Christians needed to be better than ever informed, supported and confident in discipleship.

---

[7] P. Bailey, *Leisure and class in Victorian England: rational recreation and the contest for control, 1830–1885*, London 1987 edn, 102–11.

Becoming the whole people of God

Efforts to equip and educate congregations in Christian faith were just one aspect of a much wider emphasis on the laity across the mainstream Churches in the postwar period. Strong lay involvement in worship and congregational leadership was by no means new, having been foundational to Nonconformist polity and increasingly accepted in the Church of England since the late nineteenth century; for example in the re-establishment of reader ministry (1866) – a loose equivalent of the Methodist office of local preacher – and the creation of parochial church councils (1919). Even within the more clerical culture of the Roman Catholic Church, clergy had always in practice relied upon a measure of cooperation (or acquiescence) from the laity. Nevertheless, mainstream Christianity in mid twentieth-century England remained highly clericalised, making the flowering of lay participation in the postwar period remarkable. The immediate causes were a combination of pragmatic necessity, theological reassessment and wider cultural change. Ross McKibbin has argued that the 1940s and 1950s saw mass interest in transplanting the implications of democracy well beyond the purely political sphere.[8] Certainly greater lay participation reflected the less deferential, more egalitarian spirit of the times. The social status of the clergy had also been in long-term decline as clerical incomes declined and competition from other emerging professions and public authorities narrowed the Church's temporal influence.[9] An overall decline in vocations to ordained ministry also undoubtedly concentrated attention on the possibilities of lay ministry. However, predating pragmatic concerns (though slower to take root in congregational life) was a widespread theological reappraisal of the role of the laity. 'Everybody talks about us laity these days', commented a reviewer of the 1964 Carrs Lane Church conference. 'Cynics may say it's because of the shortage of parsons, but it goes much deeper than this. We know that *all* the people of God – clergy and laity alike – are called to an active life of God.'[10] The phrase 'the people of God' was significant, since it was also central to the theology of the Second Vatican Council, then taking place. Across mainstream western Christianity an understanding of the Church as a clerical institution was being challenged by a conception of the Church as 'the whole people of God'. Here, just two examples of the rising currency of the laity are considered: first, increased efforts by Churches in the 1950s to renew a sense of Christian duty amongst the populace and to encourage active lay participation in the life and mission of the Church; and second, a growing role for lay Christians in worship, not least (but not only) through

---

[8] R. McKibbin, *Classes and cultures: England, 1918–1951*, Oxford 1998, 533.
[9] R. Towler, 'The social status of the Anglican minister', in R. Robertson (ed.), *Sociology of religion*, London 1969, 443–50; A. Russell, *The clerical profession*, London 1984.
[10] *CLJ* lxii/9 (Sept. 1964).

the more participatory liturgies developed by several denominations between the 1960s and the 1980s.

In the 1940s and 1950s local church leaders most frequently conceived the role of the laity in terms of duty and regular observance. Thereafter, as 'duty' became an increasingly unfashionable concept in wider society, this was gradually succeeded by a focus on the individual gifts and callings of church members as part of the whole body of Christ. The partial discarding of 'duty' as a guiding principle raises an important question of what was intended by it and why it subsequently declined in currency. Exemplifying the immediate postwar focus on duty and observance was the 1955 *Short guide to the duties of church membership*, issued by the Anglican archbishops of Canterbury and York, the main tenets of which were widely published and discussed in church magazines.

> All baptised and confirmed members of the church must play their full part in its life and witness. That you may fulfil this duty, we call upon you:
> To follow the example of Christ in home and daily life, and to bear personal witness to him.
> To be regular in private prayer day by day.
> To read the Bible carefully.
> To come to church every Sunday.
> To receive the Holy Communion faithfully and regularly.
> To give personal service to Church, neighbours and community.
> To give money for the work of the Parish and diocese and for the work of the church at home and overseas.
> To uphold the standard of marriage entrusted by Christ to His Church.
> To care that children are brought up to love and serve the Lord.[11]

Though, theoretically, the *Short guide* emphasised a wide spectrum of duties, in practice some were emphasised more heavily than others; notably the religious upbringing of children and church attendance every Sunday. Such emphasis was mirrored in other denominations: Anthony Archer has written how in the decades before the Second Vatican Council 'to be a better Catholic was to go more often to church'.[12] This has bequeathed an image of the English Churches in the '40s and '50s as preoccupied with duty and convention. Near-contemporaries could also be critical: in 1963 the leading theologian Martin Thornton criticised the *Short guide* for being not 'a rule, an ascetical system' but merely 'a list of rules'.[13] If so, why did church leaders in the immediate postwar decades believe that the practice of regular churchgoing particularly mattered? For one thing, 'duty' continued to matter more widely in mid-century British society, even if Nazism and Communism

[11] Here quoted in *SGEPM* (Jan. 1955).
[12] A. Archer, *The two Catholic Churches: a study in oppression*, London 1986, 99.
[13] M. Thornton, *English spirituality: an outline of ascetical theology according to the English pastoral tradition*, London 1963, 264.

remained object lessons in the dangers of uncritical obedience. Second, most church leaders shared a belief that the social and spiritual task of postwar reconstruction relied upon the active support of all professed Christians. Thomas Tunstall, vicar of St Agnes, Cotteridge, reflected such views in a reminder to parishioners in 1952 that the Church was

> Not the building, neither is it a body composed entirely of bishops, clergy and officials. It is a body of people who feel that in Jesus Christ all the deepest needs of the human soul are met ... If the people do not take their part freely and willingly, the work of the church must remain undone.[14]

Challenging the baptised and confirmed to more regular attendance was thus partly about seeking to re-engage the 'occasionally and conditionally conforming' majority of the English population. Fulfilment of duty was also understood to unleash spiritual power. Introducing the bishop of Birmingham's 'Ten Year Forward Movement' campaign to St Agnes's in 1946, Tunstall challenged his readers to consider 'what a real spiritual force your parish church could be if it were filled Sunday by Sunday with people who were really worshipping God and seeking through prayer to know His Will'.[15] Likewise, a Moseley Road Methodist Church Christmas bulletin to Balsall Heath residents in 1953 urged readers 'always be in your place in the House of God, and if you cannot come let the House of God be in your thoughts and prayers. Remember that the wettest Sundays are the days your presence is most needed'.[16] Such assumptions, common across the Anglican and Free Church congregations studied here, recalled the ideals of the influential Parish Communion Movement, which placed considerable emphasis upon the local church, the 'House of God', as a beacon of light within a dark world. As A. G. Hebert, one of the movement's leading early thinkers, wrote in 1926, 'by the existence of a house called God's House, these other [houses] are all claimed for Him'.[17]

However, whilst clerical and lay elites may have been able to articulate a theological case for regular observance in these terms, regular church attendance was not universally understood in this way. For some churchgoers, attendance was either a primarily individual act of devotion, a weekly 'recharging of the batteries',[18] or 'support' for their church and clergy – a show of commitment to something valued. Moreover, to critics the emphasis on regular observance could instead appear mere thraldom to convention; the appearance of public piety at the expense of more worthwhile virtues. Simon

---

14 SACPM xxxix/348 (Nov.–Dec. 1952).

15 SACPM xxxii/311 (Sept.–Oct. 1946).

16 *Moseley Road Methodist Church Special Bulletin, Christmas 1953*.

17 A. G. Hebert, *Liturgy and society: the function of the Church in the modern world*, London 1935, 39, 191–2.

18 This was also noted in J. M. Hull, *What prevents Christian adults from learning?*, London 1985, 142–3.

Green has noted how such an understanding was already fairly widespread in both educated and popular opinion in the interwar period,[19] suggesting that a renewal of emphasis on duty in the postwar years was – if in some respects in keeping with the cultural spirit of the 1940s and 1950s – nevertheless a risky strategy. In 1950 Westhill College's *80,000 adolescents* study warned that the likeliest legacy of an over-emphasis on externals was the spiritual impoverishment of the young:

> some of the uniformed organisations are in grave danger of equating the observance of these virtues ['loyalty, obedience, punctuality and smartness'] with the discharge of religious obligations … A boy is not to be blamed if he comes to believe that such duty [to God] means not turning up late for parade, washing the back of his neck.[20]

It is easy to caricature. In many respects the 1950s were years of considerable activity and energy in the local church, with many examples of imaginative or costly discipleship. Indeed, from the late 1950s and early 1960s there was a growing sense amongst clergy and active laity that more was required from the 'average' churchgoer than mere observance or attendance. This was the tenor of a 1965 Kings Norton church discussion group meeting on the findings of a consultation on 'teenage religion' (possibly Harold Loukes's 1961 study of the same name[21]). Perceiving a general 'adolescent revolt' against organised religion, 'many also wondered whether the Church and professing Christians were to blame' by failing to 'make Christianity an exciting, attractive and infinitely worthwhile thing'. The Diocesan Youth Officer, leading the meeting, added that 'enthusiasm and joy were essential, but often lacking' in many churches, whereas 'young people should see members of the congregation carrying out their witness every day of the week'.[22] Such conclusions certainly reflected Loukes's own study (of secondary modern pupils): 'even those who profess themselves friendly to the church do not see that it is greater than their own feelings … as the community in which Meaning is to be found'.[23]

The Churches' credibility beyond their core membership was also a significant consideration (although neither the only nor the most important one) in the matter of liturgical change. Between the late 1950s and early 1980s, most major Christian denominations in England undertook large-scale revision of their formal liturgy. In Anglicanism and Catholicism this produced the most radical overhaul of the official rubric for worship in either denomination for over three centuries. Theologically, the inspirations were desire

---

[19] Green, *Passing*, 156.

[20] Reed, *80,000 adolescents*, 124.

[21] H. Loukes, *Teenage religion: an enquiry into the attitudes and possibilities among British boys and girls in secondary modern schools*, London 1961.

[22] KNPM (Dec. 1956).

[23] Loukes, *Teenage religion*, 77.

for spiritual renewal, greater consonance with early Christian forms, desire for ecumenical congruity and the rising currency of the laity in general. In practice, a more corporate vision of worship manifested itself in two particular concerns: first, for greater accessibility of the language in worship; and second, a fuller and more active part for the lay churchgoer in the formal liturgy.

For Roman Catholics, the biggest changes came in the aftermath of the Second Vatican Council (1962–5). Inspired by the council's charge to restore and promote 'full and active participation by all the people',[24] mass in the vernacular gradually replaced Latin, and communion in both kinds (bread and wine) became the norm for the laity as well as the clergy. Writing to his Birmingham archdiocese from the council in Rome during 1964, Archbishop Francis Grimshaw hoped that 'if all goes well as the Council has planned and decreed not only the Mass ... but all the services and ceremonies will become much more vividly than at present the means of instruction they were intended to be' and in particular, expressed in 'the language of the ordinary people'.[25] In practice, the ensuing period of reform was variously exciting, chaotic and disorientating for many churchgoers, as such a sudden rupture was almost bound to be. From the 1960s onwards one could find (at all levels in the Catholic Church) some who believed Vatican II had gone too far, and others who thought it had not gone far enough. Nevertheless, as Alana Harris has suggested, the overall weight of evidence points towards widespread acceptance of the reforms in most English parishes, and not the 'fresh stripping of the altars' that some of the council's critics have claimed.[26] Desmond Ryan's 1996 study of archdiocese of Birmingham paints a similar picture, finding a majority of clergy and lay interviewees in favour of post-Vatican II liturgy.[27] When the Tridentine Mass was quietly reintroduced on an occasional basis at St Mary's Pitt Heath in the 1990s, its appeal even amongst older members of the congregation was less than expected. Philip Masterman (b. 1904), a loyal traditionalist in most respects, nevertheless

> [thought I] should miss the Latin Mass, cos I was brought up to it and used to go almost daily, but I didn't, no. They had the Tridentine Mass at our church – used to have it on the Sunday. It wasn't published, but people came, and I went once, and I felt quite strange ...
>
> [interviewer raises eyebrows to express interest as to why]

---

[24] 'The sacred constitution on the liturgy (sacrosanctum concilium)', para. 14 in A. Flannery (ed.), *Vatican Council II: the conciliar and post-conciliar documents*, 7th edn, New York 1984, 8.

[25] 'Pastoral letter of Joseph, archbishop and metropolitan' (Lent 1964), BAA, AC. Shortly before his death in 1965 Grimshaw had become Chair of the Liturgical Commission for English-speaking Countries.

[26] Harris, 'Transformations in English Catholic spirituality', 34 and passim.

[27] Ryan, *The Catholic parish*, 40.

Yeah! Didn't appeal to me. I thought it would have done … but I think it's much better really that people know what's being said. Before, all they heard was the mutter of the priest – people got to like that, but I think it's much better now people hear every word and understand every word.[28]

Fellow parishioner Peter O'Rourke (b. 1960s) similarly recognised that whilst many older members of the congregation continued to express a preference for Latin, 'one of the priests … had a Mass and I think he said it in Latin – some of the old people were saying they turned up and they couldn't follow the Mass!'[29]

From the late 1950s greater lay participation and contemporary language liturgy also became increasingly widespread in Anglican and Free Church circles, albeit more gradually. In the 1940s, if the Birmingham sources are any guide, most Anglican parish clergy appear to have regarded the Prayer Book as basically fit for purpose, if periodically requiring cautious amendment. Consequently, calls for more radical revision could sometimes be interpreted as evidence of devotional laziness. This attitude was exemplified (albeit in unusually harsh terms) in a parish newsletter written by Thomas Tunstall of St Agnes's, Cotteridge, in 1954. Responding to those who complained 'why don't you bring religion up to date … speak in a language people understand … have services which people can follow easily and at times when they can come?', Tunstall suggested that such objections were really excuses, made by 'people [who] do not want a religion which will interfere with their recreation-pleasure or money-making'.[30] Within a matter of years, however, loss of worshippers and a growing climate of criticism had provoked a radical change in attitudes. Stuart Matthews, vicar of St Bede's, Brandwood, echoed the new mood when he wrote in 1967:

Is it any wonder that there has been a gradual decline in church membership when the vital message which the church is proclaiming is couched in language which people do not understand? St Paul and Thomas Cranmer were anxious that people should understand what faith in Christ is all about, so too, along with thousands, if not millions, of others, am I.[31]

Though the call for liturgical revision had by this time acquired an urgent tone, the theological momentum for change had been smouldering for some time. Anglican congregations had already begun to experiment with contemporary language liturgy in the late 1950s (a reminder that the decade had its own share of ecclesiastical revisionists). In 1957 St Nicholas's, Kings Norton, suspended use of the Prayer Book and Authorised Version of the Bible for family services, instead introducing a simpler liturgy and J. B. Phillips's

28 IJ68SM.
29 IJ71SM.
30 SACPM lxi/357 (May–June 1954).
31 SBBPM (Oct. 1967).

recent translation of the New Testament in plain English. Letters to the Kings Norton parish magazine suggest that opinion was initially divided: critics complained of 'sacrifices to the goddess brevity' and that 'at times the words are almost slang; to those who appreciate literature to listen is sheer agony'.[32] However, one advocate responded that s/he 'did not mind the form of the service being changed in such a good cause and only hope that it will succeed in bringing the family to church'. Another contributor thought modification essential since 'the regular church-goer could tend to become, as it were, a member of a closed shop, and it was difficult for the outsider to break in'.[33] Eleven years later the congregation experimented again, this time with the Church of England's new 'Series II' communion service (an experimental liturgy following the pattern of the Prayer Book, but in a more contemporary idiom). A follow-up questionnaire on preferences in worship gives some insight into congregational opinion. Significantly, the breakdown of responses was given according to age. An overall majority welcomed increased lay participation in reading intercessions (with particular support amongst those aged between twenty-one and fifty, i.e. born 1918–47). However, certain innovations clearly divided the congregation: whilst over 80 per cent of under-fifties preferred the new Series II services, only 51 per cent of the over- fifties agreed. Support for contemporary bible translations also decreased with each successive age group, being supported by 75 per cent of under-twenties, 57 per cent of those aged twenty-one to thirty-five, 52 per cent of those thirty-five to fifty, and only 46 per cent of the over-fifties.[34]

How far such patterns reflect wider Anglican opinion requires further research. However, evidence from the other case-study congregations supports a picture of generational polarisation over certain aspects of worship, within a more general welcome for increased lay participation *per se*. Indeed, the lessening of liturgical controversy over time was partly due to increased familiarity with particular forms, the passing of an older cohort used only to the Prayer Book and Authorised Version, and the coming to adulthood of younger cohorts for whom liturgical variety was simply part of the ecclesiastical landscape.

From 'reverent dignity' to expressive informality?

For many interviewees, one of the most noticeable changes in congregational life since the Second World War was in dominant norms of behaviour within the worship space. Church became, for many, less 'stuffy' and more 'informal'. This was a long, gradually evolving trend, albeit one which

---

[32] *KNPM* (Jan. 1958).
[33] *KNPM* (Feb. 1958).
[34] *KNPM* (Dec. 1968).

gathered momentum after the 1950s. Even the oldest interviewees, growing up in the 1930s or before, felt that they had taken a more relaxed attitude towards behaviour in church than their parents' generation had done. Though in retrospect interviewees almost universally welcomed the trend, it had at times been controversial and arguably more complex than references to formality/informality might imply. Three aspects demand particular attention: first, the gradual abandonment of distinctively late-nineteenth/ early twentieth-century norms of 'reverence' in worship; second, the growing influence of a more expressive and spontaneous approach to worship, particularly (though not exclusively) associated with Charismatic renewal; and third, a concerted attempt from the mid-1950s to instil a friendlier and more welcoming ethos into Sunday mornings. Underlying these trends (though not wholly explained by them) was a desire to engage more effectively with the rising generation, in the light of perceptions that children and young people had been marginalised within congregational life and increasingly alienated by an atmosphere of stiff formality.

A degree of formality is intrinsic to any organised act of worship, but (as Simon Green has argued) personal conduct in church had become unusually highly regulated in the late nineteenth and early twentieth centuries. Reflecting a wider intensification of the policing of public space, late nineteenth-century concerns for respectful behaviour in church developed into an increasingly sophisticated discourse of 'reverence' in worship. Just as civility in the concert hall was increasingly felt to demand silence during a performance and restrained applause after it, so due reverence in church presupposed sobriety of behaviour and hushed concentration before, during and after the service. Excessive noise, emotional ecstasy and obvious reminders of 'the world' were considered distractions.[35] Despite an undoubted relaxation of behavioural norms over the first part of the twentieth century, 'reverence' remained a highly influential concept in mainstream church culture in the 1940s and 1950s. A report of Grenfell Baptist Church's inaugural service in January 1952 recorded the satisfaction of guest minister Superintendent Klaiber with 'a dedication act exactly what such a service should be in reverent dignity'.[36] Doug and Margaret Hensman of Grenfell Baptist remembered how, in the 1950s, they had habitually removed their children's shoes at the church door to prevent their footsteps disturbing the hushed atmosphere within.[37] At Carrs Lane, the Revd Leslie Tizard expected the same kind of quiet, sober restraint, asking church members to prepare quietly for worship, to avoid conversation which might distract one's neighbour, and to refrain from a 'grabbing of hats' before the closing organ voluntary.[38]

---

[35] S. J. D., Green, *Religion in the age of decline: organisation and experience in industrial Yorkshire, 1870–1920*, Oxford 1996, 293–324.
[36] GBCN (Jan. 1952).
[37] IJ41GB.
[38] CLJ xlvii/1 (Jan. 1950).

Indeed, the regularity of appeals for hushed concentration suggests that it was difficult to enforce. Moreover, for some, 'reverent dignity' was far from an accurate description of the prevailing atmosphere in church. In 1954 a series of Lenten house meetings hosted by the Church of the Epiphany (later St John the Baptist), Longbridge, found that amongst non-churchgoers 'it was more than once complained that [services] are archaic and meaningless to the ordinary sort of chap, and, worst of all, that they are often so deadly dull, mournful and miserable'.[39] Retrospectively, many regular churchgoers concurred: Betty Foreman (b. 1906) of Cotteridge Church contrasted the atmosphere of the present-day congregation with the 'po-faces' at church in her youth, when 'that was the done thing, you see, they were brought up like that – and you'd got to be quiet and didn't talk in church, and your children didn't talk in church, and all that's altered now'.[40]

This transition did not always occur smoothly, and sometimes provoked considerable debate. The adoption of Charismatic worship styles in a growing number of churches in the 1970s and 1980s proved a case in point, partly because of the more openly expressive approach often taken by Charismatics, partly because of the newer styles of music which sometimes accompanied it. Grenfell Baptist Church first began to experiment with new forms of worship in the 1970s. By the early 1980s, several church members had been touched by Charismatic renewal. The nationwide 'Mission England' campaign of 1984, partly focused on Birmingham, also functioned as a catalyst for change. Around that time, some Grenfell teenagers formed a worship band, playing songs from the campaign songbook.[41] Before long, pop-influenced worship songs, clapping and raising hands had begun to filter into Sunday worship.[42] Many current church members in young or mid-adulthood in 1998 dated the renewal of their faith to this period – sometimes in contrast to their earlier, more negative, attitudes to emotive worship. However, at the time, not all church members were so content: one participant in a passionate church meeting debate in 1984 complained that people 'came to church for peace and uplift' but that 'at present many over-40 find themselves irritated at church too: reverence lacking, hippodrome mentality, too much moving about prior to service, music rehearsals – not a lot of peace'.[43]

Even so, a majority of the 1984 meeting conceded that change was necessary for the congregation's survival. One member noted that 'we have a large group of young born-again Christians who deserve our support'. Another

---

[39] *KNPM* (May 1954). For the growth of such criticisms in mid-century England more generally see Green, *Passing*, 136–51, 270.

[40] IJ12CT.

[41] The songbook, combined with two supplementary volumes as *Mission praise* (London 1990), constituted one of the most widely-used church music resources in England in the late 1990s.

[42] GBC, church meeting minutes, 16 Oct. 1984.

[43] Ibid. 17 Apr. 1984.

expressed herself 'delighted to see the young people. We are a large family and should consider all members of the family'. Whilst many older Grenfell members saw the question primarily in terms of the best way to cater for the young, younger members themselves were reluctant to play the 'youth' card: 'we should be one generation united, but the church needs to be alive', pleaded one teenager.[44] As in other churches, differences of opinion along age-cohort lines could be mitigated by a wider sense of congregational vision. At Grenfell, church members were united in attaching primary importance to mission in the local community,[45] and differences over worship could ultimately be subordinated to this end. The church's older West Indian members may have aided the transition, having originally joined the church because its worship style appeared more 'lively' than in some other local Free Churches.[46] However, where no such mitigating factors existed, and congregational identity was primarily bound to existing patterns of worship, church members could find changes in service style an unacceptable price to pay for the prospect of attracting new members.

Besides growing expressivity in worship, greater informality was also partly associated with perceptions of increased friendliness amongst congregations and concerted efforts to improve the welcome given to newcomers. Churches in every age have been sites of friendship and hospitality, quarrelling and cliquishness. Nevertheless, the Birmingham evidence suggests a growing conviction in the 1950s that bad experiences of church were driving away both newcomers and existing congregants (concerns largely absent in the same church magazines a decade earlier). In 1957 the youth club leader of St George's, Edgbaston, informed parishioners how, on one recent Sunday, 'a young lady came with a friend of hers to our evening service ... No one welcomed them, and nobody spoke to them, and as they were leaving the church the friend said, "well, if this is Christianity we do not want it"'. The youth leader continued: 'Is it true that we are unfriendly and unwelcoming? It must certainly not be true.'[47] R. H. T. Thompson's study of four Birmingham parishes that same year suggested the problem was not merely confined to newcomers: 'a large number of people felt unwanted and out of place even though ... regular churchgoers'. Young people expressed particular isolation, although older worshippers sometimes shared similar experiences (one woman remarked: 'Of course I don't know many of the people – you see I'm new to this parish, I've only been here seven years'[48]). When Hilda Robbins (b. 1923) first attended Carrs Lane Church in the early 1970s,

---

[44] Ibid.
[45] D. Grace, R. Hey and others, 'Grenfell Baptist Church: the history of Grenfell Baptist Church and people's attitudes on the role of the church in society', typescript, photocopy, 1990, Grenfell Baptist Church.
[46] IJ39GB; IJ45GB.
[47] SGEPM (Dec. 1957).
[48] Thompson, *The Church's understanding of itself*, 82–3, 31–2.

no one spoke to her for a fortnight. On the third week, determined to make new acquaintances, she resolved to remain behind in the foyer to be greeted even if this meant being the last to leave.[49] Not all were so persistent.

However, by the 1990s, most interviewees felt that a gradual yet discernible warming of local church life had taken place. Intriguingly, successive age groups remembered the church of their youth as less friendly than that of their adult life. If this partly reflected the tendency for congregational culture to be shaped by long-standing members, there are nevertheless good historical grounds for identifying a general increase in warmth of fellowship in many local churches in the postwar period. One factor was the progressive softening of class distinctions. Although rarely explicit in church magazines of the time, mid twentieth-century England remained a profoundly (if inconsistently) class-conscious nation.[50] For R. H. T. Thompson, 'congregations reflected rather than reconciled social divisions', with the Church's appeal resting on 'social compatibility rather than doctrinal conviction'.[51] In many neighbourhoods, congregational life could still reflect social distinctions. Joan Egan remembered how at Edgbaston Old Church in her childhood,

> every pew was labelled – and if you sat in the wrong one you were hauled out, make no bones about it!
>
> *Interviewer: 'By churchwardens, or...?'*
>
> Oh no – by Sidney W. Freemantle, the Beadle [laughs] who wore a livery and things, and if you went and sat in Mrs Bloggs' pew by mistake, you were told summarily, move! Well, I mean after the war, that went, you see.[52]

Located in wealthy Edgbaston, the Old Church was unusual, but more subtle class distinctions were evident in more modest residential districts into the 1960s. Janet Nicholson remembered how at Kings Norton Methodist Church in the '60s and '70s, it had been 'very difficult to do certain jobs ... you had to be quite well-to-do to get one, you know. To be a steward – very upper middle class! Not quite as bad as in some churches, but there was snobbishness'.[53] By the 1990s, however, most churchgoers felt class distinctions of this kind were almost entirely absent. Socio-economic variation still patently occurred (such as in the stark differences in churchgoing by ward). However, the virtual absence of comment on class and social status in the oral testimony remains none the less remarkable.

One preliminary and partial explanation (it is a subject which deserves

---

49 IJ59CL.
50 Bourke, *Working class cultures in Britain*, introduction; McKibbin, *Classes and cultures*, chs i–v; K. O. Morgan, *The people's peace: British history since 1945*, 2nd edn, Oxford 1999, ch i.
51 Thompson, *The Church's understanding of itself*, 82–3, 85.
52 IJ38SG.
53 IJ10CT.

fuller investigation elsewhere) suggested by the Birmingham evidence was a growing sense of the actively Christian population as a distinct constituency within wider society, sharing some basic affinities which transcended other divisions. Whilst sectarian or world-denying religious groups had always regarded themselves as socially marginal and consequently cultivated a close-knit community life, this mindset was still arguably quite alien to Anglican and Free Church congregations in the 1940s and 1950s. Whilst every congregation had its committed core whose lives and friendships revolved around church, a larger penumbra of regular churchgoers appears to have assumed that general social expectations of neighbourly civility also sufficed in church. As Lilian Rayner, a long-standing member of Moseley Road Methodist, recalled, 'it was assumed you just got on in church' – no special effort was needed.[54] Interviewing Birmingham churchgoers in the mid-1950s, Thompson likewise found 'little apparent difference between the values and behaviour of those outside the church and those inside'.[55] Whilst from one perspective this was scarcely surprising in a society which generally regarded itself as Christian, the lack of obvious Christian distinctiveness also made the Churches vulnerable to the popular expectation that true Christians should model a more exemplary lifestyle than others. As Lilian Rayner remembered, this attitude of detached civility caused particular dismay to those newly-arrived from the Caribbean in the 1950s and 1960s. Visiting an English church for the first time, many of her West Indian friends had been shocked that no one had welcomed them, invited them to dinner or sought to make friends.[56] Whilst racial prejudice was undoubtedly a factor in many negative experiences, differing expectations of congregational culture may also have played their part: what passed for normal neighbourhood relations amongst many white mainstream church attenders was experienced as coldness and rejection by many Black churchgoers. Significantly, racial and cultural assumptions appeared less significant in Birmingham's free Evangelical and Pentecostal congregations where cultural conventions were more likely to be overridden by a shared identity as true believers set apart from 'the world' and its values.[57] In this sense it might tentatively be suggested that the cultural marginalisation of Christianity as a whole within late twentieth-century society may have hastened the erosion of racial and cultural distinctions within the historic mainstream Churches.

---

54 IJ1MR.
55 Thompson, *The Church's understanding of itself*, 36, 177.
56 IJ1MR.
57 P. Jarvis and A. G. Fielding, 'The Church, clergy and community relations', in Bryman, *Religion in the Birmingham area*, 85–98 at p. 97.

Church music and popular culture

Amongst the many areas of debate over worship and congregational life in the postwar period, music was one of the most controversial. This should not be a surprise: meaning is often most profoundly located in the realm of the 'unsayable', and, as Susan Tamke has written, 'familiar hymns make a special appeal to the memory'.[58] Whilst controversy has beset church music in many periods, this has particularly been so at times when fundamental conceptions of 'beauty and truth' were themselves changing significantly. Between the mid-1950s and early 1990s, controversy centred overwhelmingly upon the Churches' encounters with new forms of popular and folk music. Again debates over popular music in worship were not unprecedented: from Palestrina in the sixteenth century to Charles Wesley in the eighteenth century and Ira Sankey in the late nineteenth, composers incorporating popular or folk idioms into church music were regularly accused of vulgarity or worse. Similar accusations were heard in the second half of the twentieth century.

Notable early experiments, including Geoffrey Beaumont's 1956 *Folk mass* and hymns by Patrick Appleford, employed swing and light music styles. In the late 1950s and early 1960s some congregations hosted experimental 'skiffle' or 'beat' services, mirroring the new chart music of the day. Through the 1960s and early 1970s, the folk revival proved a rich seam of inspiration to church musicians including Charismatic chorus-writers, Catholic liturgists and Liberal Protestant hymn-writers such as Sydney Carter, famous for *The Lord of the dance*. In the 1970s and 1980s Evangelical song-writers such as Graham Kendrick wrote extensively in pop and soft rock styles, creating soundscapes and performances reminiscent of the stadium rock of the day. In the early 1990s 'alternative worship'[59] groups were beginning to experiment with electronic dance, rave and ambient music reflecting the buoyant clubbing scene. Though the most radical experimentation typically occurred on the margins (for example, Christian festivals, youth events and special services), pop- and folk-influenced worship music was adopted extensively, even within the mainstream Churches, within a matter of decades. Background research for the Archbishop's Commission on Church Music in 1988 found that over 50 per cent of Anglican churches nationally used choruses or worship songs alongside or instead of hymns and choral music. A fifth of Anglican congregations (and a higher proportion in urban areas) had an instrumental music group in addition to organ or keyboard.[60] Likewise a 1976

---

[58] S. S. Tamke, *Make a joyful noise unto the Lord: hymns as a reflection of Victorian social attitudes*, Athens, OH 1978, 158.

[59] See n. 76 below.

[60] Church of England, *In tune with heaven: the report of the Archbishops' Commission on Church Music*, London 1992, 274–5.

survey of the Roman Catholic diocese of Portsmouth found that a third of parishes were using a folk mass setting.[61]

Yet these new forms could also provoke strong reactions amongst guardians of the western classical tradition of church music. A first peak of controversy came in the mid- to late-1950s, prompted by experimentation with swing and light music for worship. Though such experiments were mostly cautious in nature, critics feared that they represented the top of a slippery slope of capitulation to vulgarity, risking a century and a half's progressive refinement of the English church music tradition. A second peak of controversy came between the 1970s and early 1990s, during which time the adoption of contemporary music in churches was more widespread and frequently part of a wholesale reorganisation of Sunday worship, sometimes undertaken to accommodate new orders of service, sometimes in response to the growing influence of the Charismatic movement. At a loss to explain the movement's ascendancy, Lionel Dakers (former head of the Royal School of Church Music), suggested:

> maybe the associated music is a factor, much of it reflecting that of the secular world. If this is so perhaps it points to the need for those more traditionally orientated to guide the young towards the more lasting benefits that quality music can bring for the betterment of worship.[62]

Dakers's comments are illustrative of the many commentators on postwar Christianity who regarded popular music and Christian worship as unnatural bedfellows. Historians, too, have sometimes concurred: Callum Brown, for example, has described the Churches' adoption of pop and folk styles in the 1960s as a desperate 'compromise' measure designed to appeal to the young.[63] Both views contain a grain of truth: pop's appeal to teenagers was certainly a factor for many local church leaders. Moreover, pop and folk certainly constituted quite different musical languages to the vast majority of the music used in mid twentieth-century churches. Yet both these views appear to assume that popular music for worship was somehow inherently 'unnatural'; an alien incursion by the 'secular' into a watertight 'religious' cultural form. This also fails to acknowledge the possibility of an alternative theological aesthetic (in which the popular and the holy could be partners) or the possibility that Christians wrote, played or sang the new styles primarily because they wished to worship in their own musical *lingua franca* (in fact there were many who did so). With that in mind, it is as important to explain the degree of resistance to popular music for worship as to account for its increased popularity.[64] The challenging nature of folk and pop styles

[61] J. Ainslie, 'English liturgical music since the Council', in J. D. Crichton (ed.), *English Catholic worship: liturgical renewal in England since 1900*, London 1979, 93–109 at p. 103.
[62] L. Dakers, *Beauty beyond words: enriching worship through music*, Norwich 2000, 142.
[63] Brown, *Death of Christian Britain*, 180.
[64] I. Jones with P. Webster, 'The theological problem of popular music for worship in

to many (particularly older) churchgoers therefore remains a key part of the story of church music in the postwar period, but here is explored as a set of historically and culturally contingent responses rather than being assumed to be a 'natural' reaction.

Throughout the period, debates over popular music for worship acquired a strong generational dimension. Whilst age and birth cohort were not a fault-less guide to musical preference, interviewees growing up before the early 1950s were more likely to dislike pop music in church, whilst those growing up since the 1970s tended to be the most accommodating. This partly related to familiarity: the worshipping culture in which pre-war birth cohorts were formed was one of organs, choirs and hymns. Whilst some older churchgoers embraced the new styles many did not. For post-1960s birth cohorts, guitar-led worship songs were part of the ecclesiastical landscape, even where absent from their own regular churchgoing experience. However, mere 'familiarity' with traditional church music is insufficient to explain the controversy that popular music for worship could generate amongst some older churchgoers. Four assumptions common amongst prewar birth cohorts require particular exploration. First, that popular music might be morally corrupting or at least carry unhelpful associations with 'the world'; second that it carried strong (and for certain Christians, unpalatable) associations with revivalist Evangelicalism; third, that it challenged the high-art aesthetics that had dominated English church music over the previous century; and fourth that it was 'young people's' music and therefore unsuitable for adult congregations.[65]

The first contention (that popular music was too closely associated with the 'worldly' and even the satanic) appears to have been the least important, despite the claims of some music historians that clergy were unreservedly critical of rock and pop.[66] That thesis tends to rest upon highly selective quotation from newspaper accounts, for example the case of one vicar in the late 1960s who threatened to excommunicate his parishioners if they attended a rock concert in the local town hall.[67] In contrast, documentary evidence from the case-study congregations reveals almost no clerical criticism of rock'n'roll. At the very least, clergy perhaps felt that there were more pressing issues to discuss, and that gratuitous criticism could be pastorally counter-productive. Even the usually combative Ashford of Kings Norton (who had initially expressed suspicion of rock'n'roll's 'degrading rhythms')

---

contemporary Christianity', *Crucible* (July–Sept. 2006), 9–16.

[65] Whilst each of these themes emerged in my own early research, the development of my understanding of them owes a considerable debt to my more recent research collaboration on church music with Peter Webster, which I am delighted to acknowledge here: see nn. 72, 81 below and bibliography.

[66] J. Street, 'Shock waves: the authoritative response to popular music', in D. Strinati and S. Wagg (eds), *Come on down? Popular media culture in postwar Britain*, London–New York 1992, 302–24; M. Cloonan, *Banned! Censorship of popular music in Britain, 1967–92*, Aldershot 1996, 235–57.

[67] Cloonan, *Banned!*, 237.

wrote not disapprovingly in 1959 of the latest Teddy Boy fashions, suggesting that

> It is the duty of Christians to seize upon the best of the lovely things God gives to each generation ... The time has gone when Christians should be frumps ... God needs cheerful and gay Christians, abreast of their times in thought and fashion, and the more of such Christians we have in our parish the better it will be for the cause of Christ.[68]

Rock and pop certainly had its religious critics: the late 1950s witnessed a flurry of discussion amongst leading church musicians about the 'primal' (and thus apparently corrupting) rhythms of the new rock-based genres. One cartoon in the July 1960 edition of *Church News* compared the young people of the 'rock age' (a leather-jacketed boy swinging his dancing partner over his shoulder) to those of the 'stone age' (a leopard-skin clad hunter dragging his club with a women slung over his shoulder). Evangelicals of a more traditional disposition were sometimes wary of the Charismatic adoption of contemporary music for worship, and the birth of heavy metal in the 1970s excited some concern over possible demonic references in the lyrics. However, such views, if they were held amongst the congregations studied here, featured little in the oral and written records. Indeed, as rock and pop became part of mainstream culture for successive cohorts of churchgoers, it became easier to make critical distinctions between individual songs rather than generalise about each genre. In fact, for some mid-century church musicians, and for some older interviewees into the 1990s, popular music's more general associations with 'the world' appeared more problematic than any more specific hint of spiritual or moral depravity. Thus in December 1945 Carrs Lane church's organist explained that certain types of music were undesirable in church due to their 'associations with situations foreign to, and likely to prove disturbing in, the atmosphere of worship'. As a result, he continued, 'is it not even more essential that the songs of the church should rise above, and be kept above, the environment of life's entertainments, whether they be light opera, cinema or wireless?'[69] Such views appeared to reflect not only the common assumption that church was a distinct space requiring special behaviour, but also a widely-held conviction that 'Church Music' (sometimes capitalised) was a distinct subgenre within western classical music, distinguishable from the secular even whilst sharing certain characteristics. In practice, this seems to have engendered a marked reluctance amongst many clergy and organists to experiment with styles falling outside a recognisable genre of 'sacred music', and a feeling that to do so was to succumb to gimmickry. In October 1944 a lay member of Grenfell Baptist Church thus wrote that whilst the congregation must 'reveal more

---

[68] *KNPM* (Aug. 1959).
[69] *CLJ* xlii/12 (Dec. 1945).

vitality and depth in their services' rather than allowing 'public worship to remain unbearably dull and uninspiring', this did not mean acceding to 'a temptation to remedy this by "stunts"'.[70] However, if a strong demarcation between 'sacred' and 'secular' music enhanced the distinctiveness of the worship space, it also distanced Christian worship from a popular culture increasingly influenced by radio and the commercial music industry, and particularly targeted at the preferences of the young.[71]

If its associations with 'worldly values' caused some older adults to struggle with new popular music in worship, its associations with Evangelical Christianity could prove equally challenging. Whilst in reality Evangelicals were not alone in experimenting with popular music in the postwar period, the imaginative link between the two was nevertheless firmly established amongst many English churchgoers by the early 1970s, largely due to the Charismatic movement.[72] John Chandler (b. 1929), a theologically Liberal member of Carrs Lane church, remembered one occasion during the 1980s when

> the singing group took the service, rather than having an organist – it was a time people were encouraged to come ten minutes earlier to practise some of the kind of songs one associates with the Billy Graham meetings ... And very like a number of other people, I tended to steer clear of that time.[73]

In fact, associations with revivalism probably drew upon memories long predating rock 'n' roll. For much of the late nineteenth and early twentieth centuries the primary use of the short gospel song (or 'chorus') was evangelistic; for rallies and revival meetings where a simple message and popular style could help engage non-churchgoers. Choruses might feature occasionally in Sunday worship, particularly after an evangelistic campaign, as a familiar landmark for newcomers and to evoke memories of revival amongst existing worshippers. However, before the 1960s, choruses were mainly occasional music, even in Evangelical congregations. As Doug Hensman (b. 1920s) of Grenfell Baptist Church remembered, 'there used to be a CSSM chorus book ... in those days if you had a chorus [in a service] it was strange. Now, if you have a hymn it's strange!'[74] By contrast, interviewees growing up from the 1970s onwards expressed no sense that 'choruses' were for evangelistic meetings only. Whilst sometimes recognising the genre's recent associations with Evangelicalism, younger interviewees seemed less bothered by traditional party lines in choosing music. Katie Ellis, of Cotteridge Church (b. 1980),

---

[70] HSBCN, 165 (Oct. 1944).
[71] Marwick, The Sixties, 73–4.
[72] P. Webster and I. Jones, 'New music and the "evangelical style" in the Church of England, c. 1956–1991', in M. Smith (ed.), British Evangelical identities, i, Milton Keynes 2008, 167–79.
[73] IJ53CL.
[74] IJ41GB.

in many ways suspicious of Evangelicalism, nevertheless remembered how a few years previously their youth group

> wanted to get something like *Mission Praise* or *Junior Praise*, cos everybody knows all the ones in there, and they're more kind of happy clappy … if you talk to some people they just so much *do* want ['lively hymns'], but I think there's quite a lot of resistance.[75]

As for Katie, teenage and young adult churchgoers of the 1990s frequently expressed exasperation at having to choose between theological liberalism and liturgical traditionalism on one hand, and theological conservatism and contemporary popular music on the other. Indeed, such eclecticism of theology and worship was particularly characteristic of new kinds of renewal movements, variously styled 'alternative worship' and 'emerging church', which became significant during the 1990s, particularly amongst young adults.[76]

A third common strand to older interviewees' criticisms of the new music was that it lacked depth or musical quality, and thus represented a decline in standards. As Bill Hobbs (b. 1920s), a keen church musician from St George's, Edgbaston, commented: 'Think of the beautiful old hymns, and then think of "Give me Oil in my Lamp" – it doesn't go! Not with me, but I'm old-fashioned.'[77] (That Mr Hobbs took an old gospel song as his example of modern music for worship illustrates the degree to which 'traditional' and 'modern' were often used as ciphers rather than precise categories of analysis). Likewise for Bernard Scutt (b. 1917) of the Cotteridge Church, 'these choruses – they're a bit shallow I feel … they repeat the words over and over again. I don't feel they've got the depth that some of the hymns have – but that's personal taste … some people enjoy some of the choruses don't they?'[78] Personal taste invariably played a significant part in responses to the new styles. However, even 'personal taste' is always to some degree culturally constructed, and it is therefore important to explore the wider cultural assumptions according to which popular music proved aesthetically challenging to significant numbers in the postwar churches.

In the late nineteenth and early twentieth centuries, the writing and performance of church music within the main Christian denominations was dominated by high art aesthetics (albeit sometimes modulated by the

---

[75] IJ5CT.
[76] Theologically and liturgically eclectic, these diverse movements were also characterised by strong emphasis on personal authenticity in worship, ambivalence to institutionalism and a conviction that a thorough-going engagement with contemporary culture was essential for faithful Christian life and witness in a post-Christendom society. See P. Roberts, *Alternative worship in the Church of England*, Cambridge 1999, and Guest, *Evangelical identity and contemporary culture*, 134–67.
[77] IJ29SG.
[78] IJ13CT.

117

growing use of folk and popular forms). Considerable effort had been invested in raising the standards of church music across parishes and congregations; for example, in the foundation of the Royal School of Church Music in 1927. By the early 1950s most observers felt that this had resulted in an increasingly impressive and refined musical tradition. A particularly significant fusion had occurred between church music and an evolving, distinctively English, tradition of classical composition. It is significant how many leading composers of the early to mid-twentieth century – including Ralph Vaughan-Williams, Benjamin Britten, Herbert Howells and Gerald Finzi – were committed to writing sacred music despite their personal agnosticism. In part, this rested upon a belief in common culture as a shared basis for national life.

'Common culture' is a slippery phrase: in reality England was divided (as it always had been) by distinctions of class, taste, education and influence.[79] How 'common culture' should be produced and by whom were likewise matters for debate. However, most mid-century thinkers (religious and otherwise) assumed that common culture would reflect (or at least be mediated by) the standards and preferences of elites, even where it owed a conscious debt to folk idioms, as was commonly the case in the early twentieth century. Echoing Matthew Arnold, 'high' culture was widely understood not only as a yardstick of quality and taste but also as an important source of education and civility – one which might even form the cultural foundation for a shared national life in an era marked by international strife and domestic disharmony.[80] Christian, especially Anglican, worship (as enshrined in the Prayer Book, the Anglican choral tradition and a large body of well-known hymns and carols) was regarded as integral to this cultural foundation by many commentators beyond as well as within the Churches. Conversely, for many mid twentieth-century liturgists and church musicians, the 'best' in high art, literature and music also seemed the most appropriate for worship, not merely for the 'learned' but for all classes and generations. And although from the 1920s composers and liturgists had increasingly turned to vernacular song and speech for inspiration, western European high culture remained the touchstone of quality well into the 1950s.

At that very point, however, the hegemony of the western classical tradition was coming under renewed challenge on two fronts: on one hand from an intellectual *avant-garde* scornful of deference, convention and romantic ideas of beauty; and on the other from new, confident forms of popular culture, inspired by the conviction that individuality of expression was a

[79] Hewison, In anger, 181; Mandler, 'Two cultures', 127–55.

[80] See, for example, H. Wiebe, 'Benjamin Britten, the "national faith" and the animation of history in 1950s England', Representations xciii (Winter 2006), 76–105. My thanks to Frank Mort for introducing me to this article.

surer guide to human aspiration than inherited notions of quality. [81] Both in different ways challenged the idea that truth could best (or only) be expressed through the western high-art tradition. This wider musical contest was also played out within the Churches. Whilst the *avant-garde* made occasional, sometimes controversial, incursions into church life, a far bigger impact was made by increased experimentation with popular and/or vernacular forms. For many church musicians schooled in the classical vein, the stakes were high, and departure from classical norms was widely interpreted as a decline in standards. Admittedly the quality of popular music for worship was initially variable (in the mid-'50s rock and pop in particular were then exotic languages spoken haltingly by many but fluently by relatively few). Nevertheless, the tendency for the English church music 'establishment' to treat popular music as monolithic rather than discriminate between 'good' and 'bad' examples suggests a more wholesale aesthetic predisposition against it. Even the normally temperate Erik Routley, probably his generation's most influential commentator on church music, wrote in 1959 that guitar music was a 'lamentable substitute' for the choral and organ tradition, and risked introducing into church an 'atmosphere of callous slovenliness and emotional brainwashing'.[82]

Besides questions of faithfulness to the western classical tradition, a fourth key factor in reluctance to adopt popular music for worship was the strong associations of 'choruses' and popular styles with Sunday school and youth-club religion.[83] For some older churchgoers, simple popular songs performed a useful function in teaching children Christian faith and worship, but were consequently unsatisfactory as adult fare. Thus at Carrs Lane Church in 1949 Leslie Tizard rejected suggestions that the second hymn of the service be a 'children's hymn' since he believed that there were insufficient good children's hymns to avoid leaving adult worshippers feeling short-changed.[84] This reflected the wider assumption that a viable common worshipping culture should primarily reflect the needs and preferences of adults. As Tizard also acknowledged the following year, children were 'probably ... sometimes a little mystified by the hymns and prayers and lesson', but 'they are with their parents and in the family of the church, and they are becoming accustomed to the place where they will one day worship as grown-up men and women'.[85] Though on one level all forms of socialisation involve some element of behaviour modelling by elders, Tizard's words also

---

[81] I. Jones and P. Webster, 'Anglican "establishment" attitudes to "pop" church music in England, c. 1956–1990', in K. Cooper and J. Gregory (eds), *Elite and popular religion* (SCH xxxxii, 2006), 429–41.

[82] E. Routley, *Church music and the Christian faith*, London 1978 edn (first published in 1959 as *Church music and theology*), 107

[83] Ward, *Growing up Evangelical*, 107.

[84] *CLJ* xlvii/10 (Oct. 1949).

[85] *CLJ* xlviii/2 (Feb. 1950).

arguably reflected a more specific assumption of the day that change in the Church (as in culture more generally) was best achieved through slow evolution, starting with induction into existing norms and traditions. Yet with growing radio and television ownership and cheap recorded music, it arguably became increasingly possible (as well as socially acceptable) to by-pass that initial induction process and exercise greater individual autonomy in choice of music (at least within the limits set by broadcasters and record producers). Different styles of music were also now increasingly marketed at the young. As Martin Hargreaves (b. 1945) of St George's remembered, pop music was often quite deliberately 'something which [teenagers] like and their parents probably don't'.[86] In this light, popular music could appear a noisy eruption into a slowly-evolving common generational culture based on the needs and preferences of adults.

Some contemporary historians and liturgical traditionalists have claimed that contemporary music was foisted on an unwilling Church by clergy desperate to appeal to non-churchgoing youth. However, the evidence suggests that growing numbers of young churchgoers themselves began to express a preference for worship in contemporary cultural styles. In 1964 George Browning, vicar of St George's, Edgbaston, referred parishioners to the findings of a Bournemouth clergyman's survey of one hundred 11–15-year-old boys and their criticisms of church. These centred upon the need to align worship more closely with contemporary culture: organ music should be abolished and replaced with 'swing hymns', the Prayer Book revised (particularly the Psalms!), clergy taught to preach more briefly and more clearly, and church buildings equipped more like cinemas, with comfortable furnishings and sloping floors.[87] Browning was unlikely to have been in wholesale agreement with such views, but may have quoted them partly to admonish parishioners for opposing his recent proposal of a new songbook with younger churchgoers in mind. Recognising that 'we are very slow to change' and 'uneasy about anything new', he continued:

> If there were just ourselves ... to be considered, we could have everything in all our services that practically everybody knew and liked. But that would be a dying church ... we have to think of bringing into church life and active churchgoing the young people who have come up out of Children's Church and also people who for the first time in their lives are starting to come to church. Most of the schools from which our young people have come use *Songs of Praise* as their hymnbook and this means that most of our young people know far more of the hymns from that book than their mothers and fathers know.[88]

86 IJ36SG.
87 SGEPM (Sept. 1964).
88 SGEPM (Apr. 1964).

Browning's words highlight not only the increased difficulty of pleasing all generations in a single service, but also the need for experimentation to be cautious lest existing members be alienated (by 1964 *Songs of Praise* was already almost forty years old and hardly revolutionary[89]). His comments also reflected a growing conviction amongst many of his clerical contemporaries that not changing risked alienating some regulars as well as non-churchgoers – and especially the young. One 1972 survey of St George's own worshippers found that whilst 66 per cent of under-eighteens wanted to see more pop music in church, this dropped to 40 per cent of eighteen to forty-year-olds and only 8 per cent of over-forties.[90]

It is easy to overstate the case. For many teenage churchgoers, music was only one amongst many stumbling blocks to feeling at home in church. By no means all young people wished to abandon an older musical heritage: when the youth group of St Anne's, West Heath, featured an evening of 'rock'n'roll hymns' in 1964, members 'descended on [the performers] like an avalanche when they saw their guitars' but in the end apparently 'turned out to be the most conservative of all in their attitude towards hymn tunes'.[91] Adults were by no means universally opposed to the new music either: most parents to the teenagers of the 'long 1960s' did not prevent their children from listening to rock'n'roll and occasionally shared their interest.[92] 'Beat' and 'skiffle' services were also to some extent reliant upon adult (and clergy) support.

Nor did the question of music for worship later remain as generationally polarising as it was between the late 1950s and early 1990s. By the end of the twentieth century congregational conflict over church music lessened, partly because most congregations had now faced the issue of music style at least once in their recent history and had opted for either a 'traditional' or 'contemporary' style or a blend of both, often attracting new worshippers on that basis. As the sheer variety of musical options grew, and 'pop' itself fragmented as a genre, even applying 'traditional' and 'modern' labels to songs and hymns became inadequate to express the infinite gradations of musical style to be found from church to church (even if the labels frequently stuck). Moreover, by the 1990s, a greater proportion of church members had grown up with popular music (even if it was not to their taste): contemporary worship music thus became one of a range of possible musical choices rather than a threat to 'church music' *per se*. This more relaxed attitude was epito-

---

[89] Its compiler, Percy Dearmer, intended the book to be 'a national collection of hymns for use in public worship': J. R. Watson, *The English hymn: a critical and historical study*, Oxford 1999, 523.
[90] *SGEPM* (Apr. 1972).
[91] *KNPM* (Jan. 1964). St Anne's, like St Bede's, originated as a daughter church of St Nicholas, Kings Norton.
[92] For example IJ22SB.

mised by Catherine Thorpe (b. 1944) of St George's, Edgbaston, a lover of traditional church music who nevertheless found value in a more contemporary service that she had attended. At the church in question, worship had included 'tambourines and hymns – not even hymns, songs rolling up on a screen'. This was 'a very viable service – lots of family and lots of children, but it wouldn't do for me'.[93]

This more *laissez-faire* attitude contrasted markedly with the polarised atmosphere of the 1960s and 1970s, when rock and pop had been new and strikingly different. The fact at this stage that it was also obviously associated with young people left many older churchgoers torn between wishing to encourage young people in church attendance and concern lest a highly developed body of music tradition be set aside in the process. It is this particular connection between rock and pop and the first 'teenagers' that has led Lawrence Grossberg to describe rock as 'not merely the music of the generation gap. It draws a line through that context by marking one particular historical appearance of the generation gap as a permanent one'.[94]

This chapter has brought to the fore some key areas of debate and experimentation within postwar congregational life. The degree of greater lay participation, the correct balance between 'formality' and 'informality', and the relative merits of high art and popular culture were questions which marked out different expressions of organised Christianity as surely as denominational allegiance or theological standpoint. What a local congregational perspective brings to these familiar topics is a sense of how and why the balance of tradition and innovation generated such debate at grassroots level at this particular juncture. For example, if the question of what made the best music for worship rested in part on competing cultural and theological aesthetics, it also rested upon a much wider cluster of assumptions about music in relation to place and context, ecclesial style and age and generational difference (although throughout it has been noted that such differences did not necessarily occur neatly along age cohort lines). The chapter has sought to show how changes in congregational life and worship were not merely knee-jerk reactions to secularisation, yet also how local church life was profoundly shaped by wider cultural change. For example, changing attitudes to personal deportment in church were influenced by a wider softening of class distinctions and changing assumptions about public behaviour as much as by new thinking on the nature of the local church as a community. Even so, aware of the fragility of Christianity's appeal within the wider population, experimentation in worship and congregational life was often undertaken with at least one eye on its likely reception amongst

---

[93] IJ35SG.
[94] L. Grossberg, 'Another boring day in paradise: rock and roll and the empowerment of everyday life', *Popular Music* iv (1984), 225–56 at p. 230.

non-churchgoers, and particularly amongst the young. With that in mind, this book now moves the circle wider to consider the interactions of local churches with that wider context – first of all within their own neighbourhoods and then with wider social and cultural trends.

5

Church and Neighbourhood:
Four Congregational Stories

The duality of 'Church' and 'World' is an inherent source of tension within Christianity, and was no less so in the late twentieth century as Christianity became a more distinct cultural constituency within English society. One particular aspect of this which has too often been overlooked in general histories of the period is the changing relationship between congregation and neighbourhood, a sphere of life through which wider trends were often most immediately experienced. Individual congregational stories are brought to the fore as lenses through which to explore the impact of three major changes in the life of postwar Birmingham which affected the city's religious life: the depopulation and redevelopment of the city's central area, the creation of new outer-ring suburbs and the ethnic diversification of many middle-ring neighbourhoods following the large-scale population migrations of the 1950s and 1960s. Yet these particular local issues also enable us to explore wider postwar developments in local church engagement with neighbourhoods through evangelistic mission, social action and the use of church buildings. Throughout, as a result of both wider community change and the ongoing rethinking of the mission of the local congregation, church-goers of different ages brought with them, and sometimes acquired, different perspectives on how the Church should relate to its locality.

Urban areas had long been considered stony ground for the Churches. Against the traditional view that the Churches were slow to respond to urbanisation, many historians now make a more positive assessment of the concerted efforts made in the early nineteenth century to remedy the lack of religious provision in growing cities.[1] At the time, however, the perception of failure was deep-rooted and its causes simple: away from tightly-knit rural societies where Church and community were inextricably linked, religious commitment was bound to decline amidst the impersonal rootlessness of urban life. Whether this assumption is correct has been the subject of long-running debate. A. D. Gilbert, Steve Bruce and Alasdair Crockett have been amongst the strongest recent proponents of the view that modern

---

[1] C. G. Brown, 'Did urbanisation secularise Britain?', *Urban History Yearbook* (1988), 1–15; Robson, *Dark satanic mills?*.

urban society has been inherently bad for religion.[2] Jeffrey Cox has instead emphasised the agency of the Churches in their success or failure,[3] whilst K. S. Inglis and others have questioned whether it was only lack of church provision which lost the Churches the working classes.[4] More recently, Sarah Williams and others have emphasised the persistence of Christian-based popular religion in urban communities (both inside and outside the Churches) well into the twentieth century.[5]

In 1945 most church leaders shared with their Victorian forebears a conviction that urbanisation and population movement posed serious pastoral challenges. For Birmingham in the 1940s and 1950s the most immediate causes of population movement were slum clearance, large-scale inward migration fuelled by the city's booming industries and massive suburban expansion: by the late 1960s Birmingham had more council housing than any other local authority in the country.[6] For Edward Ashford, whose south Birmingham parish of Kings Norton encompassed several large new estates, the transformation was 'nothing short of breathtaking ... one must rejoice to see children playing in the wider streets and fresh, almost country air, when one has seen them sitting in the gutters by their often squalid homes in the heart of the city and industrialism'.[7] However, whilst overwhelmingly positive about progress in housing,[8] clergy also recognised the medium-term challenges of providing places of worship for the new populations of outer-ring estates. St Mary's Pitt Heath, Grenfell Baptist and St Bede's, Brand-wood, were amongst the dozens of new churches built as a direct result of church campaigns to establish a formal Christian presence in Birmingham's new suburbs. However, clergy were also alive to the fate of those people who remained in the cleared, depopulated or redesigned inner areas. For Canon Norman Power, whose Ladywood parish was stripped of slum terraces and rebuilt in high- and low-rise concrete in the 1960s, these were part of a global population of 'forgotten people' in large cities who 'have neighbours but ... no neighbourhood, no local pride, and ... no roots'.[9] This chapter thus turns first to the stories of those churches which continued to serve the city's inner areas.

---

[2] A. D. Gilbert, *Religion and society in industrial England, 1740–1914*, London 1976; S. Bruce, *Religion in the modern world: from cathedrals to cults*, Oxford 1996; A. Crockett, 'Rural-urban churchgoing in Victorian England', *Rural History* xvi (2005), 53–82.

[3] Cox, *English Churches*.

[4] K. S. Inglis, *Churches and the working classes in Victorian England*, London 1963, passim.

[5] Williams, *Southwark*.

[6] Sutcliffe and Smith, *History of Birmingham, 1939–1970*, iii. 222; Upton, *History of Birmingham*, 204.

[7] KNPM (Oct 1956).

[8] For the interwar background see R. Lloyd, *The Church of England in the twentieth century*, II: *1919–1939*, London 1950, 126–8.

[9] Power, *The forgotten people*, 16.

The social gospel for the city centre: Carrs Lane's story

In an influential study of US congregations' experiences of change, Nancy Ammerman notes that rapid shifts in neighbourhood social ecology typically present congregations with a choice either to stay put and seek to develop a distinctive ministry appropriate to the new context, or to relocate to new areas along with their members.[10] Whilst Heneage Street Baptist Church took the second course, Carrs Lane, Moseley Road and St George's, Edgbaston, pursued the first. Carrs Lane was first to face important decisions. Birmingham's city centre had been slowly depopulating since the late nineteenth century, and by the 1940s most regular worshippers in city-centre churches travelled in from the suburbs.[11] In 1944 its minister, Leslie Tizard, offered his congregation a choice: to close the building and disperse to other churches, or to continue a city centre ministry.[12] The congregation chose the latter course, partly for the symbolic value of a continued Congregationalist presence at the heart of Birmingham; partly to continue the work started by Dale, Jowett and others; doubtless partly through nostalgia; and partly because the immediate future seemed assured. Well into the 1950s Carrs Lane's nationwide reputation as a centre of good Congregationalist preaching continued to ensure healthy congregations. Julia Poole, who came to Birmingham in 1962, remembered the church as a magnet for young Free Church Christians seeking a theologically open, socially committed faith.[13] Nevertheless, even in 1948 the church's bicentenary history prophesied that 'the progressive centrifugal movement towards distant residential suburbs' and an 'uncertain future for preaching' meant that important choices lay ahead.[14] So it proved. One blow came in 1958 with the early death of Leslie Tizard – Carr's Lane's last oratorical preacher of great repute – an event which Richard Collins (b. 1948) felt had badly shaken the congregation.[15] By the late 1960s the church's future was once again under debate, most immediately because the planned new Birmingham central ring road was to pass the chapel's front door, and more generally because Carr's Lane members appear to have been particularly affected by the wider crisis of confidence in that decade over the Church's relevance to modern life. The dilemma was summed up in a Congregational Union pamphlet *The next ten years*, discussed by Carrs Lane's 'Fireside Groups' in 1960:

[10] Ammerman and others, *Congregation and community*, 107.
[11] Peacock, 'The 1892 Birmingham religious census', and G. K. Nelson, 'Religious groups in a changing social environment', in Bryman, *Religion in the Birmingham area*, 12–25, 45–59; *CLJ* lvii/8 (Aug. 1959). Similarly in 1998, two-thirds of respondents lived between two and five miles from the church; a quarter over five miles.
[12] *CLJ* xli/5 (May 1944).
[13] IJ56CL.
[14] A. H. Driver (with a contribution by H.W. Gosling), *Carrs Lane, 1748–1948*, Northampton 1948, 102, 107.
[15] IJ46CL.

What exactly is our church in High Street or Park Road aiming to be and to do today? This minority group within a mainly secular agnostic community, what is its main purpose, and how is that main purpose being served by what it does on Sunday and on weekdays?[16]

For many Carrs Lane members, a partial answer was offered by the clarion call to be 'the church for others' – a common motif in Liberal Christian thought in the 1960s. This was reflected in comments made at a 1965 church conference on Carrs Lane's future:

> There are many needs in central Birmingham – for a working man's club, for somewhere for married couples to go. These people may never join our worship, but the Church would be of service to the people we thus contact. A need for spiritual fellowship stems from service, so the outgoing activity is brought back in worship to the Church.[17]

Although no working men's club nor married couples' facilities ever materialised, the following year saw the church establish a counselling service, and when a new church building was opened in 1970 it contained purpose-built accommodation for overseas students and community organisations – a bold attempt to forge a distinctive new city-centre ministry. If social action was the priority, 'evangelism and "hot gospelling"' were 'out of fashion and unacceptable to the present generation', according to one contributor to the *Carrs Lane Journal*. While 'action without words is not a full expression of our mission', service was key: 'an opportunity will be found ... only after one has entered into a genuine relationship with one's neighbour'.[18]

The patterns established during this period remained influential for the congregation's subsequent direction, with 'obedience ... in terms of social concerns and social responsibility' regarded as one of the most vital signs of God in the world.[19] These assumptions also remained critical for the young visionaries of the 1960s who became the dominant cohort in the church of the late 1990s, many of whom remained suspicious of evangelism, despite several ministers' attempts to restore it to the agenda in the light of declining attendance. In 1998 older interviewees regularly attributed the church's lack of growth to the continued depopulation of the city centre or competition from Evangelical churches.[20] In comparison, younger Carrs Lane members were also enthusiastic for a radical, city-centre social action agenda, but nevertheless regretted its pursuance at the expense of seeking to nurture new Christians. A high proportion of under-sixties also advocated greater crea-

---

16 Quoted in *CLJ* lxix/4 (Apr. 1960).
17 *CLJ* lxxiv/9 (Sept. 1965).
18 This is quoted from the report of the Swanwick Congregational Forum Conference on 'The People Next Door', *CLJ* lxxv/10 (Oct. 1966).
19 *CLJ* lxxiv/12 (Dec. 1965).
20 IJ51CL; IJ52CL; IJ55CL; IJ57CL.

tivity in worship (which they believed was too conventional to be widely appealing) and more active outreach amongst city centre workers and shoppers. All remained committed to the church and convinced that Carrs Lane had been right to remain in the city centre. During the late 1980s and 1990s visiting schemes to local shops and flats were piloted, but no new members resulted. The exasperation felt by one long-standing Carrs Lane member, Jim West (b. 1924), reflected a common frustration amongst many congregations of the period:

> when you get to our age, you're going round these problems for about the third time. We had [a visiting preacher] ... I remember him giving a report to the Church Meeting as a result of a commission he had given to him, to go around the shops and offices and to go M&S and try to get them interested in the church. Now, we did that twenty-five years ago, and we have been doing it ever since.[21]

Though as a city-centre church Carrs Lane's story differed in many respects from the experience of suburban churches, it nevertheless illustrates several important aspects of local community engagement by congregations in various contexts. First, there was a gradual realisation from the 1950s that the church could not assume a ready audience simply by its presence. Second, in the 1960s and 1970s the recognition of this marginal position was the catalyst for much creative (but at times agonised) discussion about the 'relevance' of the church to its neighbourhood, often resulting in new initiatives. These were frequently pioneered by a cohort already into adulthood in the immediate postwar decades, but often in response to the perceived needs of 'the rising generation'. Third, the 1970s and 1980s marked a further period of reappraisal, with the following (postwar) cohort of churchgoers reaffirming the value of such outward-looking work, but questioning their elders' reticence in seeking new church members or speaking publicly of their Christian faith. Despite the reforms of the 1960s and 1970s, the hoped-for revival of churchgoing had not occurred. This, too, left its mark on attitudes to local mission in the 1990s.

Evangelism in a transplanted church: Grenfell Baptist's story

Whilst Carrs Lane Church continued a distinctive city-centre ministry, Heneage Street Baptist Church, in the nearby slum district of Bloomsbury, chose a different path. In 1952 a city council decision to clear the area's dilapidated housing stock forced the closure of the historic chapel and prompted a decision to relocate in the suburb of Alum Rock, recently built towards the eastern side of the city. Here a rump of the Heneage Street congrega-

---

[21] IJ51CL.

tion merged with the local Thornton Road Fellowship to become Grenfell Baptist Church, opening a new building that same year. Evangelistic mission was accorded high priority from the outset and through the experience of this church several important themes can be explored in both changing attitudes to evangelism and the experience of transplanting congregations.

For most English churches through the 1950s and 1960s 'mission' primarily meant three things. First, it meant support for 'overseas mission'. At Grenfell, this was taken particularly seriously – the chosen name for the new church was homage to George Grenfell, the nineteenth-century Baptist missionary to the Congo, born in Birmingham and converted at Heneage Street. However, overseas work also dominated conceptions of mission in the Churches at large – so much so that Busia's 1966 'Brookton' survey found churchgoers scarcely able to conceive of 'mission' in any other way.[22] Moreover, whilst a congregation might occasionally produce an overseas missionary from within its own ranks, most churchgoers supported mission through prayer and donations to missionary societies. A report on the Grenfell Missionary Circle compiled in 1954 described a typical meeting (although possibly with the social dimension exaggerated to encourage new joiners): '[we] have a very happy time and enjoy the social intercourse. We talk about our daily worries and sympathise with those of our number who have heavy trials and burdens. We have letters read from missionaries and discuss problems and conditions on the BMS stations'.[23]

A second strand to Grenfell's missionary effort was youth and children's work. This too was typical of the period. As Currie, Gilbert and Horsley have argued, a shrinkage in the 'external constituency' of potential church members tends to place greater importance on recruitment from amongst the church's 'internal constituency', the children of existing members.[24] At Grenfell, 'the need for all young people to decide for Christ while young' was underpinned by regular 'children's rallies', a 'decision day' and the annual 'young people's day'.[25] However, Sunday schools and youth organisations were also regarded as an important bridge into the community. Doug Hensman, a former Sunday school teacher over many years, remembered how each Sunday teachers would drive around the neighbourhood to advertise the day's activities, collecting any child wishing to participate.[26] The third conception of mission articulated at Grenfell in the 1940s to 1960s was that of support for large-scale evangelistic campaigns. Several church members supported the monthly 'Youth for Christ' rallies held at Birmingham Town Hall, a number making faith commitments as a result.[27]

---

22 Busia, *Urban churches*, 132.
23 GBCN (Oct. 1954).
24 Currie, Gilbert and Horsley, *Churches and churchgoers*, 51.
25 GBCN (Nov. 1954).
26 IJ41GB.
27 IJ41GB; IJ44GB.

Whilst all these facets of mission remained important to the end of the century, there were also signs by the early 1960s that assumptions were changing. In 1954 the announcement of Billy Graham's Haringey Crusade received a very straightforward call for support from Grenfell Church's leadership. However, during the Great Midlands Crusade at Villa Park in 1960, minister Robert Aitken felt obliged to suffix his challenge to win converts with a justification for such large rallies: 'such a crusade is bound to have its critics', he wrote, 'some of them sincere and others simply acting from hostility to the Gospel. But there can be no doubt in my mind that evangelistic methods on this scale, using the best modern methods of publicity, can be greatly used of God to the true conversion of many'.[28] Within eight years, however, limited success and declining church attendance led Aitken to rather different views. Evangelism, he wrote to his congregation, should be not be regarded as the church's 'summer sale' but as its 'daily business': '"special efforts" often have clouded this in the minds of many. The great crusades of well-known evangelists have perhaps been made a substitute for day-to-day evangelism which is the responsibility of us all'.[29]

The evolution of Aitken's thinking symbolised a wider shift in evangelistic methods in the late 1960s and 1970s away from large-scale campaigns (though these continued) and towards personal contact and invitation. Mainstream Evangelical Churches such as Grenfell also shared in a wider broadening of thought on the nature of mission, coming to regard both preaching and practical action as essential.[30] 'If you are not a better person for being a Christian ... then you can have nothing effective to say', wrote Aitken during a series of 'minister's letters' on mission in 1966. Along with prayer and study, an exemplary lifestyle was the bedrock of witness. Speech was to be 'quiet, wise, opportune, friendly, no sense of superiority. No heated argument. Yours is to <u>win</u> the man, <u>not</u> the argument'.[31] The hard-sell approach became widely regarded as more alienating than attractive. A key strategy at Grenfell from the late 1960s to late 1990s was that of regular neighbourhood visiting, initially to invite residents to services, but increasingly also to offer practical service. In 1990 the church's gap-year placement team conducted a survey of local residents and found widespread concern about lack of local amenities and neighbourhood decline,[32] something the church subsequently sought to address, for example, in the provision of a mother and toddler group.

---

[28] GBCN (May 1960).
[29] GBCN (Nov. 1968).
[30] Supremely in the Lausanne Covenant of 1974: D. Bebbington, 'The decline and resurgence of Evangelical social concern, 1918–1980', in J. Wolffe (ed.), *Evangelical faith and public zeal: Evangelicals and society in Britain, 1780–1980*, London 1995, 175–97 at p. 188.
[31] GBCN (Feb. 1966).
[32] Grace, Hey and others, 'Grenfell Baptist Church'.

The new approach was particularly (though by no means exclusively) associated with a large, active group of teenagers and young adults who came to the fore in the late 1960s and early 1970s, many of whom remained members into the 1990s and beyond. In 1966 some of them had started a gospel singing group,[33] touring local churches and schools. A house-to-house visiting campaign was instigated around the same time. In many respects, the priorities of this group came to dominate the church's approach to mission over subsequent decades. As Jan Hughes (b. 1949) explained, the intention was to

> go out with a servant attitude really ... and we get chatting to people – 'is there anything you'd like us to pray for?' and people are absolutely amazed and people say 'oh could you pray for me nan, cos she's not very well'... because those people are totally disarmed, because you're not asking them for anything, you're not threatening them ... to show that we're not stuck-up supercilious people who are just looking at them, and ... we care about the area, we want to show ... God to that area.[34]

Some older church members were less certain. Whilst on one level embracing the more relational approach to evangelism, some expressed disappointment that it was not producing new converts. Others retained a fondness for old-style evangelistic rallies. There was particular concern, notably amongst older West Indian members, that some ministers avoided preaching uncomfortable sermons. As Violet Best explained,

> to go back to West Indies, evangelists from especially America used to really preach the Gospel, you know – what you'd call, um, fiery preaching – down to earth, fiery preaching, and you used to shake! – give you food for thought. But I find a lot of the ministers nowadays want to water down the Scripture. The good thing about [our current minister]; he speaks the truth about the Bible – really gives it to you.[35]

However, by the 1990s the dominant orthodoxy at Grenfell was that whilst fiery preaching was acceptable for sermons, the business of making converts required a gentler approach, without hint of manipulation. Evangelistic services with an altar call were replaced by newer initiatives such as the Alpha Course (10,500 of such courses had taken place nationally by 1998[36]), in which enquirers were invited to discuss Christianity in the more relaxed surroundings of a meal. Such initiatives contrasted sharply with the approach of Grenfell's founding generation. Jan Hughes, who remembered that generation from her teens, recalled

---

[33] Among them was Roger Jones, prolific composer of biblical musicals and at that time member of Grenfell Baptist.

[34] IJ49GB.

[35] IJ39GB.

[36] S. Hunt, *The Alpha enterprise: evangelism in a post-Christian era*, Aldershot 2004, 11.

a 'we've got something and you ought to have it, ram it down your throat' kind of attitude ... I'm sure it put me back a long time in my Christian walk – I had people, very lovely Christian people, who knew and loved the Lord, who'd back me up a corner and say 'are you saved sister?'... I'd never approach anyone in that way, you know, you've got to earn the right to be heard[37]

'Earning the right to be heard' became a key concern within all the case-study congregations, but particularly for those churchgoers growing up in (or particularly influenced by) the intellectual and cultural climate of the post-1960s period. Breaking down those barriers demanded a listening ear, practical responses to individual and community concerns, and an acceptance that (unlike in traditional Evangelical discourse) 'belonging' might precede 'believing'.

New arrivals from overseas: stories from Grenfell Baptist and Moseley Road

Since the mid-1950s changing local demographics presented a series of pastoral challenges for Grenfell Baptist Church. Whilst the original Bank-dale Road population had been largely stable, younger white married couples increasingly relocated to the outer suburbs whilst more young churchgoers began moving away to university, cutting short their commitment to the congregation.[38] At Moseley Road a similar movement towards the suburbs took place. In their place, many neighbourhoods (Balsall Heath and Alum Rock among them) became home to substantial West Indian and Asian populations, some of the former wishing to join a local church. Temporarily leaving aside the specific experiences of Grenfell Baptist and Moseley Road, the welcome that Black Christians received when they appeared at English churches was often cool and sometimes hostile, as several studies (including several on Birmingham[39]) have shown. Many started their own churches instead, sometimes affiliating to denominations originating in the Caribbean and USA. By 1975 Birmingham's Black-led churches attracted around 4,500 full members and considerably more attenders.[40] Though the development of a separate Black church 'movement' is not solely attributable to rejection by white churchgoers, it was a significant factor. However, as Claire Taylor has written, whilst 'it is undoubted that many migrants did experience painful rejection from churches' the response of numerous congregations was 'far

---

[37] IJ49GB.
[38] GBCN (May 1967); (June 1968).
[39] Wilkinson, Church in black and white.
[40] Gerloff, 'Black Christian communities', 61–84 at p. 65.

more positive and happened far earlier than that of society in general'.[41] The experiences of Grenfell Baptist Church and Moseley Road Methodist – though by no means universally replicated – add weight to Taylor's contention.

In the 1940s and 1950s denominational hierarchies were often comparatively quick to respond to the influx of new arrivals from the Caribbean. Already by 1950 Birmingham's church leaders had jointly established an 'Organising Committee for Overseas Nationals'.[42] In the following years a 'hostel and social amenities for coloured people' were established, and by 1959 the Anglican diocese of Birmingham had also appointed a 'Chaplain to Overseas Peoples', Paul Burrough, whose eight-year ministry was still fondly remembered by Black Anglicans decades later.[43] However, such denominational responses frequently owed their origins to the experiences of clergy ministering in areas where substantial migrant populations had begun to settle. In December 1954 the Moseley Road and Sparkhill Methodist Circuit considered a report from the Revd J. J. Whitfield, who had been engaged in 'work on behalf of the coloured people of Birmingham' and who requested that congregations donate to the hostel appeal.[44] During my visit to Moseley Road Methodist in 1998, many older Caribbean members appeared reluctant to address experiences of discrimination in detail, but one white member of the congregation recounted episodes of harassment that her Black friends had experienced from neighbours; one family had faeces pushed through their letterbox. At the church itself, the welcome was warmer. Violet Best, now at Grenfell Baptist, remembered Moseley Road – her first church on arrival in England in 1955 – as 'lovely up there when we went up there first, and a lot of West Indians used to go there as well'.[45] Five years later a report on recent neighbourhood visiting campaigns similarly 'rejoice[d] that the patient ministry to coloured people from Moseley Road is winning a confidence evidenced by increasing numbers of West Indians at worship – over sixty were present on Easter Day'.[46]

Integration was a slow, experimental and sometimes tense business. In 1962 Moseley Road tried informal class meetings hosted by West Indian church members at nine o'clock in the evening, with the hope of reaching out to the local Caribbean population. At Sparkhill Methodist Church a special Morning Prayer was arranged once a month, which became popular with West Indians 'who delight in a service to which they are so well accustomed'. In both cases, ministers appear to have assumed that forms of worship and

[41] C. Taylor, 'British churches and Jamaican migration: a study of religion and identities, 1948–65', unpubl. PhD diss. Anglia 2002, p. vii.
[42] Sutcliffe and Smith, *Birmingham, 1939–1970*, iii. 365.
[43] Wilkinson, *Church in black and white*, 114.
[44] BCA, MC9/3, Dec. 1954.
[45] IJ39GB.
[46] BCA, MC9/4, May 1960.

fellowship familiar to Caribbean Christians were supplementary to normal patterns of church life, although the same report contained the first hint to long-standing white members that full integration would demand compromise: 'one wonders whether or not we ought to be more flexible and accommodating in the arrangements of our services so that we might, by all means, serve some!'[47] Anecdotally, in conversation with long-standing members of Moseley Road, some found this difficult to accept. In general, however, the congregation appears to have been more successful than many in integrating Black and White. By 1961 the Circuit superintendent was confident enough to believe that Moseley Road was now 'regarded as a centre for many of the West Indian people who live in that area'.[48] Furthermore, the experience of this and other inner-ring churches appears to have partially conscientised the Circuit as a whole to racial issues: in 1961 disgust at the restrictions imposed by the Commonwealth Immigrants Bill led the Circuit meeting to send a strongly-worded resolution to the *Birmingham Post* (in which a long-running debate on the issue was taking place) deploring the idea that immigration might be settled by unilateral legislation and not by mutual agreement with Commonwealth countries.[49]

Whilst the welcome given to Black Christians at Moseley Road was generally positive, not all congregations were similarly hospitable. In 1957 the Birmingham Christian Social Council issued guidelines on welcoming newcomers 'for the serious consideration of church people' after discussions with a number of Black worshippers. The advice (*see* figure 3) illustrates some of the problems experienced by new arrivals to some Birmingham congregations. Whilst certainly more comprehensive than previous advice, there remained little consideration of the systemic discrimination experienced by many Black and Asian newcomers to the city, the assumption being that 'good manners' were sufficient. However, what passed for good manners amongst English-born worshippers could often appear cold and unwelcoming to Afro-Caribbean migrants; not least because of the very different expectations of how one behaved in church. This impression is corroborated by Claire Taylor's research on Jamaican migrants to London in the same period: whilst clergy and churchgoers could certainly exhibit outright hostility on occasion, much of the rejection experienced by Black Christians in English churches came as a result of cold or distant behaviour, and a fundamental thoughtlessness (shared by most of the population at the time) as to the needs of newcomers from overseas.[50] Of course, whatever the causes, the offence to Caribbean people was often the same. Even by 1971 one study of Birmingham congregations suggested that churchgoers still too often showed only passive toleration towards Black Christians, and frequently

47 Ibid. Sept. 1962.
48 Ibid. June 1961.
49 Ibid. Dec. 1961.
50 Taylor, 'British churches and Jamaican migration', 43, 77.

Figure 3
Birmingham Christian Social Council guidelines on welcoming immigrants, 'for the serious consideration of church people', 1957

1.	The attitude of Christians should be one of simple friendliness, being neither frigid, fussy nor hearty. Extremes are barriers.
2.	Coloured people feel the need to be invited to the homes of Christians on a basis of continuing friendship (not one visit only).
3.	They appreciate being invited (*and brought*) to church groups and organisations.
4.	Those doing the inviting should not be put off or disappointed by failures on the part of their guests to turn up.
5.	It would help if churches could provide facilities for coloured people to meet in their own groups, in addition to taking their full part in the life of the churches.
6.	Coloured members of the congregation value invitations to help in church life, e.g., as steward, sideman, or in the choir.
7.	Christians should consciously exercise good manners in day to day contacts with coloured people, e.g., on buses, in shop queues, etc.
8.	We should remember that our coloured friends are often disillusioned with England as they find it. We should use every opportunity to help them see the good side.

Source: GBCN (Sept. 1957)

much worse.[51] The main exceptions here were Evangelical or Pentecostal congregations, whose chief criterion for group membership was the believer's baptism, regardless of race or other social distinctions.[52]

Re-educating churchgoers about race and immigration was a long process, but clergy letters uniformly warned against the claims of racist organisations. In 1961 for example, George Browning of St George's, Edgbaston, reminded parishioners 'how easily and freely we talk about this problem and make our criticisms and condemnations without knowing many of the facts.... There are thirty-eight thousand vacant jobs in the West Midlands alone and ... immigrants come here because there is such poverty at home and the jobs need filling'.[53] However, whilst changing attitudes was a vital first step, local church action seldom went further at this stage, with few attempts made to tackle specific social problems faced by the city's Black and Asian communities. A real shift in attitudes only occurred over a longer period of time. Younger age groups of churchgoers appeared to mix naturally across ethnic groups, having grown up together in a multi-cultural society. Indeed, one

[51] Jarvis and Fielding, 'The church, clergy and community relations', 85–98.
[52] Rex and Moore, *Race, community and conflict*.
[53] *SGEPM* (Oct. 1961).

national study of urban young people published in 2005 found those who self-identified as Christians more likely to display positive attitudes to other ethnic groups than their non-faith peers.[54] A particular shift appears to have occurred in the late 1970s and early 1980s, as churches began to appreciate the domestic implications of campaigning against apartheid in South Africa, and became more aware of serious racial flare-ups at home (in Birmingham, notoriously, the Lozells disturbances of 1985). At the 1979 general election, the Revd Peter Chave of Kings Norton URC reminded his congregation that whilst there was no 'Christian' voting pattern as such, a vote for the National Front was completely unacceptable.[55]

Besides the increasingly robust stance against racism, a quieter but equally significant process of integration was also taking place. For older churchgoers who had grown up in a largely white community, there was a particularly marked sense of triumph in having overcome previous divisions. One interviewee remembered how thirty years previously, shortly after the first Afro-Caribbean worshippers had begun to attend her church:

> I was coming down the ... road, saw Mrs. ---- and she saw me, and we said hello to one another – that was the first time and I felt so pleased that I was able to identify a person and not just see a coloured lady. Now whoever I see – they're just May or Florence or Grace or whoever – they're people now, but before, they were just brown-skinned.[56]

Though precise figures are elusive, one study (the first survey of its kind in the UK) estimated that by 1983 Black Anglicans constituted 10 per cent of all regular churchgoers in the diocese of Birmingham.[57] There is every reason to suppose a similar percentage amongst the Free Churches. But whilst some credit is due to white churchgoers who overcame their hesitations and prejudices as did the speaker above, the significant part played by Black Christians in the life of the mainstream Churches in Birmingham by the end of the twentieth century is primarily testimony to the staying power of African and Caribbean people themselves, who persisted with the Church they loved despite the varied reception that they first encountered.

Community and anomie in the outer ring: St Bede's, Brandwood

Just as statistics of religious affiliation pressed upon the minds of many church leaders by the mid-twentieth century, so too did the belief that

---

[54] L. J. Francis and M. Robbins, *Urban hope and spiritual health: the adolescent voice*, Peterborough 2005, 159–60.
[55] *Kings Norton URC Monthly News* (May 1979).
[56] Reference withheld to preserve speaker's identity.
[57] Wilkinson, *Church in black and white*, 34.

urban living was not naturally conducive to religious observance.[58] Keeping pace with urban expansion had constituted a persistent challenge for the English Churches since at least the late eighteenth century. Though the early nineteenth century has often been portrayed as the great age of church extension, Rex Walford's careful documentation of the diocese of London's 'Forty-Five Churches' campaign suggests considerable initial success in establishing places of worship in the new suburbs of the interwar period.[59] Nor was London exceptional. Despite a particularly acute shortage and uneven distribution of resources, Terry Slater has argued that the Anglican diocese of Birmingham coped remarkably well with the massive house-building programmes undertaken in the city between the wars, resulting in more than 100,000 new dwellings in vast estates to the south, east and north. Two large church extension appeals in 1926 and 1935 met with a quick and generous response, resulting in fifteen new churches by 1939 – several of which continue to flourish today.[60] By the early 1940s the city council had again begun to draw up plans for further housing expansion – not for new satellite towns as the then bishop of Birmingham E. W. Barnes had hoped, but more estates for the city's outer ring.[61]

As with previous church extension schemes, postwar efforts were strongly motivated by the conviction that if the Church did not respond satisfactorily to the growth of the new suburbs tens of thousands of people would lose touch with Christianity, to the detriment of neighbourhood and society as well as the Churches themselves. The postwar period thus saw most local denominational bodies engaged upon extensive programmes to establish an institutional Christian presence in the new suburbs. The Roman Catholic archdiocese of Birmingham prioritised the building of schools, in due course following these with church buildings (St Mary's Pitt Heath amongst them) on neighbouring sites.[62] The Anglican and Free Churches by contrast prioritised church building – often initially functional, multi-use constructions designed to be replaced by a more obviously ecclesiastical structure when sufficient funds were raised. The Anglican diocese of Birmingham ran three major appeals, the first two in 1946 and 1953 as part of its 'Ten Year Forward Movement' (which became a model for other diocesan appeals elsewhere) and the third in 1956 as part of the diocesan golden jubilee.[63] The experience of organising and developing congregational life and witness in new

---

[58] For an influential example of this view see E. R. Wickham, *Church and people in an industrial city*, Cambridge 1957.

[59] Walford, *Growth of 'New London'*.

[60] T. Slater, *A century of celebrating Christ: the diocese of Birmingham, 1905–2005*, Chichester 2005, 123–5.

[61] Machin, *The Church and social issues*, 126–7.

[62] Sutcliffe and Smith, *Birmingham, 1939–1970*, iii. 260

[63] Slater, *A century of celebrating Christ*, 128.

outer ring estates is explored through the story of a church established in the third of these appeals: St Bede's, Brandwood.

For Leonard Wilson, bishop of Birmingham during much of the 1950s and 1960s, new neighbourhoods without a church of their own risked being little more than 'circles without centres' – a phrase which became the title of the diocesan church extension campaign which ran from 1953 to 1969.[64] Announcing the Bishop's Jubilee Appeal to parishioners in 1956, Edward Ashford of Kings Norton reminded them that merely providing community centres for new estates was not enough: 'I am sure that if the prime object of every citizen of Birmingham were to see established in every community a lovely House of God, the zeal which inspired such an effort would carry them forward in ease to find homes for the people.'[65] Promoting the same appeal to St George's, Edgbaston, that same year, George Browning warned, in stronger terms:

> If in twenty years' time any one of us is heard to comment on the subject of juvenile delinquency or falling moral standards or the increase in broken homes as features of our national life, then it is hoped that our consciences will … say 'what did you do to provide churches and Christian teaching for the vast housing estates created in 1956?'[66]

Such hopes and fears were not significantly out of step with those of many planners and social researchers in the 1950s. A succession of postwar studies, though optimistic about the potential of the new suburbans estates, nevertheless remained realistic about the scale of the challenge ahead.[67] Health experts frequently talked of 'new town blues' – the stress of being uprooted from closely-knit inner city neighbourhoods and deposited in isolating and characterless outer-ring developments with few amenities. Whilst emphasising both the positive and negative aspects of new estate life, social investigators similarly noted widespread complaints of a lack of neighbourliness.[68] The study of family churchgoing undertaken by the Christian Social and Economic Research Foundation in 1957, which focused heavily on families from new estates, likewise reported stresses on family life and a decline in religious observance as a result of social isolation.[69] Focusing solely on the assumptions of clergy and policy experts, it is easy to suppose that community

---

[64] R. McKay, *John Leonard Wilson: confessor for the faith*, London 1973, 161.

[65] *KNPM* (Oct 1960). Here was the pastoral and missionary dimension of the emphasis on the 'House of God' discussed in chapter 4 above.

[66] *SGEPM* (June 1956).

[67] M. Clapson, 'Working–class women's experiences of moving to new housing estates in England since 1919', *TCBH* x (1999), 345–65.

[68] Amongst influential examples see M. Young and P. Wilmot: *Family and kinship in east London*, London 1957, and *Family and class in a London suburb*, London 1960, and P. Wilmot, *The evolution of a community: a study of Dagenham after forty years*, London 1963.

[69] Christian Economic and Social Research Foundation, *Aspects of the problem facing the*

spirit had almost vanished from new estates, relying upon incoming 'authorities' for its cultivation. However, if with hindsight some new developments were terrible planning failures, the actual experience of estate life varied greatly during the immediate postwar decades. Richard Sykes has noted how slum clearances and rehousing tended to undermine the importance placed upon neighbourliness except in the minority of cases where slum populations were rehoused *en masse* to the same estate.[70] Even where this did not occur, Mark Clapson has argued that much 'manifest neighbourliness' was shown, particularly in the early years of life on new estates, and especially between women at home with young children during the week.[71]

It was from precisely these beginnings that organised church activity first began on the south Birmingham estate of Brandwood. Beryl Taylor, a longstanding member of St Bede's, had moved into one of the first Brandwood roads with her husband just before World War Two, and they had subsequently welcomed the first families into the newer roads which sprang up around theirs in the late 1940s and early '50s. Many residents came together to celebrate Queen Elizabeth's coronation in 1953 and early on a Girls' Club was established by local mothers (including Mrs Taylor). In the late 1950s, some of these women petitioned Edward Ashford (in whose massive Kings Norton parish Brandwood fell) to begin a regular Sunday school on the estate. Significantly, Beryl Taylor remembered, many of these women were not themselves churchgoers, but remained keen to ensure that their children received a proper religious upbringing.[72] Having already established new churches in Longbridge and West Heath, Ashford and his colleagues at King's Norton now turned their attention to Brandwood. Besides the new Sunday school, another important outreach strategy to large new estate populations was the parish magazine. Parish magazines were popularised in the last third of the nineteenth century as a way of keeping congregation and wider community in touch with their church, as general literacy rose and urban populations continued to grow. The mid-twentieth century in some respects marked the heyday of the genre, with magazines not only providing basic information about services and church activities but also an opportunity for the clergy to speak directly to non-churchgoers.[73] At one point in the 1950s the *Kings Norton Parish Magazine* had more than 3,000 active subscribers – equating very approximately to one in seven house-

Churches: an analysis of certain findings of the survey of factors affecting Setting up a Home, made in Birmingham, Leeds and London in January 1957, London 1960, 32.

[70] R. P. M. Sykes, 'Popular religion in Dudley and the Gornals, c. 1914–1965', unpubl. PhD diss. Wolverhampton 1999, 323–40.

[71] Clapson, 'Working-class women's experiences', 349–54. See also L. Hanley, *Estates: an intimate history*, London 2007.

[72] IJ27SB.

[73] See, for example, A. Webster, 'Parish magazines', *Theology* xlvii (July 1943), 156–9; C. R. Forder, *The parish priest at work: introduction to systematic 'pastoralia'*, London 1947, ch. xviii; and N. Stacey, 'The parish newspaper', *Theology* lix (Dec. 1956), 487–91.

holds in the area.[74] The monthly delivery of the magazine (by hand, usually by regular churchgoers) was itself a helpful component of pastoral strategy, with Ashford thanking magazine distributors in 1950 for 'the important role they were playing in bringing people into contact with the church'.[75] When the young St Bede's congregation first published its own magazine in 1962, Bishop Leonard Wilson's foreword similarly emphasised how 'a good parish magazine can be a valuable means of keeping us alive to the joys and sorrows of the community'.[76]

The new dual-purpose hall housing the fledgling St Bede's congregation was dedicated by the bishop of Aston on 17 September 1960 amidst considerable local interest. The congregation worked hard to foster a sense of belonging among estate residents. Alongside services and the Sunday school, St Bede's also hosted cubs and scouts, a young wives' fellowship and a weekly adult social night organised by church members. The latter appear to have been popular and, according to the church magazine, 'had a tremendous effect on promoting community spirit in Brandwood'.[77] The Sunday congregation also reaped rewards, with healthy attendances and a strong youth club. As Beryl Taylor remembered, these early years were 'very exciting times'.[78] However, early success appears to have been short-lived. With hindsight Mrs Taylor believed that regular churchgoers had become so busy organising activities that they neglected to build lasting relationships with those outside the church.[79] Certain local factors were also influential, including personality issues, a lack of diocesan resources and a frosty response from local residents to a proposed purpose-built vicarage, which was seen as an unnecessary expense. By the late 1960s the congregation also appears to have become increasingly reluctant to support purely social organisations when they failed to add worshippers to the Sunday congregation. However, there also existed a more general perception that the early community spirit on the Brandwood estate was beginning to cool. This is certainly implied by the growing number of clergy letters encouraging parishioners to take greater interest in each other. In 1966 the first issue of a relaunched parish magazine saw the new curate, Trevor Hextall, explain how the publication was intended for everyone in the parish – 'we – you and I – make the news; don't imagine that our own little worlds are the only things that

---

[74] Based on the number of households in the Brandwood and Kings Norton wards in 1961: BCL, TS '1961 Census – small area statistics, ward totals, city of Birmingham – extracts relating to population and housing'. The true proportion is probably higher, given that the two wards would also have included parts of other parishes.

[75] *KNPM* (Feb. 1950).

[76] *Progress: the magazine of St Bede's Church, Brandwood* 1 (Christmas 1962), BCA, EP110/7/1/2.

[77] Ibid.

[78] IJ27SB.

[79] Ibid.

count'. Conversely, he warned of the 'depressing picture' which would result if Brandwood residents remained inside the three thousand 'self-interested little groups we call families'.[80]

Hextall's comments invite interesting comparisons with the otherwise exalted views of family life expressed in church circles in the 1950s and '60s.[81] Great expectations for the family still remained, but were mingled with an increasing sense of disappointment that – rather than pulling together – family concerns and community concerns were fast diverging, leading to an atomisation of neighbourhood life. Several wider social trends appeared to corroborate this assertion.[82] First, the postwar period saw families spend a greater proportion of leisure time at home. Wider access to mortgages and hire-purchase brought the prospects of owning – and beautifying – one's own home within the means of many working-class families. Television and radio offered continuous and varied entertainment without stepping beyond the front door.[83] Women often found themselves channelled towards servicing the new suburban 'cult of the home', but the growing popularity of DIY amongst men suggests that they, too, were drawn in. The trend towards home-based leisure was strengthened by the popularisation of ideals of companionate marriage which (if not exactly universal) nevertheless became more common amongst both working and middle classes, particularly on new estates. This partly dissolved the once-rigid demarcation of male and female leisure pursuits, the latter centred around home, shops and street, the former centred around work, pub, club or society.[84] Third, while neighbours frequently remained on friendly terms, an expectation of privacy once mainly characteristic of middle-class neighbourhoods was increasingly asserted in working-class communities.[85] With respectability increasingly located in the private home, many parents correspondingly become less inclined to allow their children to play in the street.[86] Fourth, an increased tendency for parents to consider the discipline of children as solely their prerogative weakened the power of what Elizabeth Roberts has called an 'interlocking chain of authoritarian figures: neighbours, teachers, clergymen and policemen' in local neighbourhoods which had together enforced the ground-rules for the behaviour of the young.[87] Maureen Wall of St Bede's (b. 1944) was the youngest interviewee to remember being taken to task by

---

[80] SBBPM (Jan. 1966).

[81] See chapter 3 above.

[82] This paragraph owes a particular debt to Roberts, Women, and H. McLeod, 'Why were the 1960s to religiously explosive?', Nederlands Tijdscrift voor Teologie lx/2 (2006), 109–30

[83] McLeod, 'Why were the 1960s so religiously explosive?', 113–15, 121–2.

[84] McKibbin, Classes and cultures, 165.

[85] Tebbutt, Women's talk?, 173, 177. The wider dimensions of this renegotiation of 'public' and 'private' are considered in chapter 6 below.

[86] Roberts, Women, 41.

[87] Ibid. 162.

neighbours (and then punished again by her father) for childhood trans-gressions.[88]

The anomie of suburbia became a familiar late twentieth-century trope, but it is important not to overstate the case. Oral histories of community life by Mark Clapson, Elizabeth Roberts and Melanie Tebbutt all suggest that the decline in neighbourliness and community ties on new estates should not be exaggerated, at least amongst women, and at least before the 1970s.[89] In Brandwood itself, evidence collected in 1973 by a team of missionaries on sabbatical at nearby Cranmer Hall (the Church Missionary Society training college in Selly Oak) paints a similar picture. Commissioned by the vicar of St Bede's to undertake a church and community profile, the team found that far from living socially atomised lives, 72 per cent of Brandwood residents felt that they knew their neighbours well, and 43 per cent had relatives within a mile.[90] Nor did estate life seem unusually detrimental to church-going: despite a sharp decline in the previous decade, church attendance in Brandwood still compared favourably to the national average. Nevertheless, while a majority of those surveyed regarded Brandwood as a decent place to live, few felt any sense of real community (indeed, only 8 per cent even identified themselves as 'Brandwood' residents).[91] On such a new estate, this was arguably unsurprising. However, there were also other factors: local social amenities were comparatively few (a common problem in postwar housing) and only 6 per cent of residents belonged to a club or society within the parish. Increased mobility was both cause and effect here: half of those surveyed regularly travelled further afield to spend their free time.[92] Though concern at the effects of population mobility on church and Sunday school attendance was not new, growing car use in working-class communities from the mid-1950s meant the churches were now competing with a much wider selection of alternative leisure opportunities.[93] In the Brandwood of 1973, 69 per cent of residents had use of a car – some way above the 1979 national average of 52 per cent.[94] In this respect, Brandwood's experience reflected (albeit slightly more acutely) that of many new postwar housing estates,

[88] IJ28SB.

[89] Clapson, 'Working-class women's experiences', 354–5; Roberts, Women, 229; Tebbutt, Women's talk?, 154.

[90] 'Crowther Hall report: a study of St. Bede's Parish, Brandwood, Oct. 1972–Mar. 1973', BCA, EP110/17/5, 37, 39.

[91] Ibid. 13, 24, 52.

[92] Ibid. 28, 41.

[93] On growing car use see P. Thompson, 'Imagination and passivity in leisure: Coventry car workers and their families from the 1920s to the 1970s', in D. Thomas, L. Holden and T. Claydon (eds), The motor car and popular culture in the 20th century, Aldershot 1998, 244–74 at p. 260. On population mobility and churchgoing see W. S. F. Pickering, 'The secularised Sabbath: formerly Sunday, now the weekend', Sociological Yearbook of Religion in Britain v (1972), 33–47.

[94] 'Crowther Hall report', 34; Marwick, British society since 1945, 238.

whereby initial enthusiasm for estate-wide sociability was gradually super-seded by more associative networks (many beyond the estate) and a more conditional cordiality between residents.[95]

To describe a partial withdrawal from geographical community is not to imagine a previous 'golden age' of spare time spent exclusively with near neighbours. Amongst 'respectable' working-class populations such as lived in Brandwood, associational leisure habits had a long history. Even in the early days of the estate, St Bede's curate Trevor Hextall noted that 'there are roads in the parish where twenty families have practising beliefs but each is not aware of the other'.[96] Even so, the Crowther Hall evidence suggests that, by the 1970s, most Brandwood residents spent their leisure time neither with religious and voluntary organisations nor with immediate neighbours without further reason than proximity. In this context, pastoral strategy had to shift from seeking to establish the church at the centre of its local community to working from the margins, often seeking first to foster a sense of community within which the church could then thrive and engage. Though the task could be most difficult in newer housing estates such as Brandwood, it seems that most congregations experienced similar challenges. In February 1973 the vicar of St George's, Edgbaston, Donald Bradley, reminded parishioners that the local church could no longer lay claim to be the 'spiritual Mount Olympus' of its neighbourhood.[97] This was a far cry from the Liturgical Move-ment's vision of the 'House of God' as central to its locality, and the recog-nised spiritual home of the community. Likewise, rather than presuming to occupy the Brandwood centre-stage, St Bede's, it was more modestly said, contributed to the wider building of neighbourliness through the 'unique privilege' of being 'a worshipping community'.[98] In reality, the congregation did much more than this, even with limited resources. Church-run commu-nity activities numbered among the very few such activities existing on the estate in the 1970s and 1980s. From these, some new members were drawn into the Sunday congregation. Many interviewees who were young parents at this time remembered joining the church through the personal support of the vicar or through a vibrant mother and toddler group. Of less long-term success but some medium-term significance were neighbourhood 'contact groups' established by the church. A revival of the 'street stewards' scheme tried by many churches in the 1960s,[99] groups of churchgoers living close by served as initial contacts for local residents seeking prayer, pastoral support or rites of passage.

---

[95] M. Clapson, *Invincible green suburbs, brave new towns: social change and urban dispersal in postwar England*, Manchester 1998, 166–7.

[96] Newspaper cutting (n.d. [1963?]), miscellaneous newspaper cuttings relating to St Bede's, Brandwood, BCA, EP110/17/1.

[97] SGEPM (Feb. 1973).

[98] SBBPM (Jan./Feb. 1980).

[99] See Busia, *Urban churches in Britain*, 87.

Attempting to foster a wider sense of community frequently meant seeking to dismantle many of the barriers between the 'religious' and the 'secular'. All the congregations featured in this study attempted lay pastoral visiting schemes at some time during the 1970s and 1980s, partly on the theological grounds that mission was the task of the whole people of God; partly from a pragmatic recognition that fostering Christian community was beyond the means of the clergy alone. Several interviewees related occasions when the church had helped local people through visiting schemes, albeit that many older interviewees continued to prefer pastoral visits from their clergy 'as in the olden days' (as Betty Foreman of Cotteridge Church remarked).[100] Even those who had enthusiastically embraced the potential of lay visiting were aware that the wider non-churchgoing public felt short-changed by anything less than a dog-collar: Beryl Taylor noted the occasional remark in the local shop that 'we don't see your vicar around much these days'.[101]

A second key way in which many churches sought to overcome the growing distance between congregation and community was to invite community use of church buildings for non-religious activities. This shift was exemplified in the many church buildings constructed from the 1960s onwards to include flexible or multi-purpose spaces. At one pioneering construction, St Philip & St James, Hodge Hill, in east Birmingham, congregational seating could be moved aside to provide space for badminton, youth clubs and other community arts and social activities.[102] In 1969 the Kings Norton Discussion Group paid a visit to Hodge Hill to see this experimental approach for themselves. Their impressions were almost wholly positive: 'do people mind carrying on secular activities in front of the altar? ... No – if you can't do it in front of the altar it shouldn't be done at all!'[103] St Bede's itself was typical of many of the new temporary mission churches of the postwar period: a multi-purpose space with flexible seating and only a curtain to close off the communion table from the rest of the hall. Although many regulars hoped in time to build a permanent replacement with a more 'religious' aesthetic, the St Bede's which arose from the ashes of a 1991 arson attack retained its multi-purpose character. The notion of bringing 'sacred' and 'secular' together was also fundamental to the vision of nearby Cotteridge Church, created out of the local Anglican, Methodist and URC congregations in 1985. As its vicar Michael Blood reflected four years later, 'we did not want a building where different groups just hired rooms and kept themselves to themselves, but we envisaged a place where there was real inter-dependence in a united body which made up the church. We went to great trouble to give all the rooms

100 IJ12CT.
101 IJ27SB.
102 C. R. Hinings, 'The Hodge Hill sociological survey – preliminary analysis', in J. G. Davies (ed.), UBISWRA: research bulletin, 1966, Birmingham 1966, 37–40.
103 KNPM (June 1969).

different names so that no one part of the building became "the church" – it was all the church, a place where barriers were broken down'.[104]

One should not underestimate the conceptual leap required from church-goers to accept social and leisure activities in a space where children had once been hushed into 'reverent dignity' and reminders of the outside world could arouse irritation. Yet most interviewees who expressed a view seemed positive about the change. For Keith Bradbury of the Cotteridge Church (b. 1942) the advantages were clear:

> there was a sort of difficulty for people who didn't go to church just crossing the doorstep to get into the church, which is why the Cotteridge Church and the way it is at the moment is just such a wonderful place, cos people go to the coffee bar and they go to keep fit classes, other things, which are on church premises, and they don't realise they're there.[105]

Ironically, it appears to have been non-churchgoers who initially found this blurring of the boundaries most difficult to accept. In a 1965 survey of Balsall Heath residents for the University of Birmingham's Institute for the Study of Worship and Religious Architecture, Robin Hinings found that in most respects churchgoers were more likely to accept the use of church buildings for 'secular' purposes whilst non-churchgoers were more inclined to expect a church building to look obviously 'religious'.[106] Nevertheless, though traditional religious architecture continued to exert a significant aesthetic 'pull', many congregations succeeded in establishing their buildings as local centres for community welfare and leisure activities. This did not amount to religious revival: an active programme of community work rarely translated into significant increases in Sunday attendance and many projects lived a precarious existence with scarce material resources. Moreover, public funding was increasingly dependent upon a strict demarcation between pros-elytism and community service. Nevertheless, when shops and amenities on housing estates closed and public-sector employees frequently lived outside the communities in which they worked, estate churches could take conso-lation from knowing that, despite the huge challenges facing institutional Christianity, they were sometimes amongst the last organisations rooted in the communities that they sought to serve.

In the post-Second World War period many active Christians in Birmingham became increasingly aware that their local church could no longer automati-cally be considered a focal point for their local community. This was often most acutely felt by churches in depopulating neighbourhoods, forced to find new patterns of ministry without any residential community *per se*. However,

---

104 *Together: the Cotteridge Church* (Sept. 1989), Cotteridge Church, Birmingham.
105 IJ14CT.
106 C. R. Hinings, 'The Balsall Heath survey: a report', in J. G. Davies (ed.), *UBSWRA: research bulletin, 1967*, Birmingham 1967, 56–72 at p. 69.

even in populous residential districts there was no guarantee that inhabitants would identify with their local community at all, let alone with a local church. A sense of perspective is important here: many urban churches had never been focal points in their communities, and yet many also continued to exercise a more effective presence in their neighbourhoods than other organisations. It is also easy to overstate the degree to which cohesive neighbourhood life existed at the beginning of the postwar period and the degree to which it had evaporated by the end of the century. Even so, it seems indisputable that a fragmentation and privatisation of neighbourhood life took place over the postwar period, resulting in a distancing of many Christian congregations from their local communities, with major challenges for both evangelistic mission and socially-based community engagement. In response, the period witnessed many new initiatives designed to enable churches to reconnect with their localities, many concerned first to contribute towards a wider building of community and only then to begin to speak about the Christian faith. If there was a generational pattern to the church experience of this process, it was that prewar birth cohorts of churchgoers felt the loss of close community connections most acutely, in some cases cleaving to long-standing patterns of local ministry and mission, in other cases experimenting with new forms, sometimes with limited expectations. However, to a significant extent churchgoers of all ages found themselves needing to learn to adapt, recognising that mission and ministry now began not from the centre, but from the margins.

6

Towards the Margins:
Being Christian in a Pluralist Society

Reviewing in her sixties, the changes that she had seen during her lifetime, Sheila Robertson of St George's, Edgbaston, reflected that

> An awful lot of earth-shattering things have happened on an awful scale – it's a very different world from the one we were born into – even got married into.
>
> *Interviewer: What do you think are the big … [changes]?*
>
> The moral certainties. We grew up in a world where whether or not you went to church, there was still the basic framework – the Ten Commandments, I suppose … You knew where people came from, whereas now you haven't a clue with their attitudes and beliefs … it's endlessly making allowances for other people without really knowing what allowances have to be made.[1]

Few historians and sociologists would deny that the increasingly religiously and culturally pluralistic turn of postwar society posed major challenges to Christianity's historic influence. In part, pluralism was the consequence of a long-term tendency for social and political elites to take an increasingly 'permissive' stance on questions of personal morality and the growing reluctance of these elites to endorse Christian norms and values above others. A social and political ideal of 'Christian nationhood' progressively gave way to one of 'civilised society', a concept with a variety of intellectual and cultural inspirations, and less conscious debt to Christianity.[2] However, increased cultural pluralism was also underpinned by growing individual self-assertion which, if it did not exactly result in the pure individualism predicted by some classical sociologists, nevertheless reflected the triumph of an 'ethic of authenticity' which understood the 'self' as the ultimate source of authority.[3] The general impact on the Churches of their increased cultural marginalisation, and of an increasingly permissive moral climate, has been increasingly well-documented in recent historical accounts.[4] This chapter, however, seeks to explore the particular consequences of these changes for local church life

---

[1] IJ37SG.
[2] McLeod, *1960s*, 262–5.
[3] Taylor, *Ethics*. See also Garnett, Harris, Grimley, Whyte and Williams, *Redefining Christian Britain*, particularly part I.
[4] Parsons, 'Between law and licence', 231–6; Brown, *Religion and society in twentieth-*

and the problems and possibilities that they generated for grass-roots Christians. In so doing, it also begins to draw together some key points. Centrally, it suggests that a significant postwar renegotiation of the boundaries between 'public' and 'private' spheres had profound implications for Christian witness, practice and engagement with moral and ethical questions. First, the chapter explores local church attitudes to the place of Christianity in society in the late 1940s and 1950s, evaluating the claim that the Churches were overly complacent about their importance in society and unprepared for the displacement of Christianity amidst the cultural revolutions of the 'long 1960s'. Second, it considers local church leaders' responses to these revolutions, particularly through changing attitudes to sexual behaviour and to the new popular medium of television. Yet the challenges of being a Christian within a pluralistic, post-Christendom society related not simply to responding appropriately to particular ethical issues but also to how far one could speak of God in public at all. The chapter thus concludes with a brief exploration of churchgoers' experiences of sharing their faith with others.

Church, society and nation in the 1940s and 1950s

In hindsight, the Churches of the immediate postwar decades have often been characterised as complacent, more inclined to consolidate than innovate, assuming themselves and Christian values to be central to English society and therefore failing to anticipate the extent of social change. For Grace Davie, though the Churches managed the task of postwar reconstruction 'pretty well', their continued attachment to prewar assumptions seemed 'perilously close to complacency'.[5] Similarly, Adrian Hastings concludes that despite many new church initiatives in the 1940s and '50s, ecclesiastical life was, ultimately, characterised by a 'deep, collective refusal to face up fully to what was happening, a resolve to restore and celebrate the past before it was finally too late'.[6] Contemporary published accounts sometimes confirm this picture: writing in 1950 the Anglican historian Roger Lloyd ventured that 'whilst the Church of England is not yet without spot or wrinkle ... it is a glorious church, and for his membership no one need be apologetic'.[7] But how far was such confidence evident at local church level? In 1940s and 1950s Birmingham at least, local churches often did appear comparatively assured that existing forms of institutional Christianity remained appropriate. Nevertheless, this confidence was heavily tempered

---

century Britain, 224–52; McLeod, 1960s; N. Yates, Love now, pay later? Sex and religion in the fifties and sixties, London 2010; Green, Passing, 135–79.

5 Davie, Religion in Britain since 1945, 32.

6 Hastings, English Christianity, 3rd edn, 1991, 424.

7 Lloyd, Church of England, 315.

by more pessimistic assessments of Christianity's place in society as a whole. If clerical calls for a return to religion have seemed with hindsight miscalculated, a genuine (if short–lived) religious renewal in the early to mid-1950s appeared to bring reassurance that Britain's Christian foundations remained intact. Moreover, if this surge of religious sentiment was partly attributable to a certain synchronicity between mid-century Christian culture and the aspirations of 'austerity Britain',[8] the Birmingham evidence suggests that it would be wrong therefore to ignore the strenuous efforts made by many local churches to encourage those generally sympathetic to Christianity into more regular attendance.

The immediate postwar decades saw widespread agreement within and beyond the Churches that reconstruction was as much a spiritual as a material task. In the summer of 1945 the Revd Thomas Tunstall of St Agnes, Cotteridge, warned parishioners of the need to stem a serious decline in moral standards which, he believed, was 'undoubtedly a direct result of the sad neglect of religion in this country during the last forty years'.[9] Tunstall's comments mirrored the sentiments of the Archbishops' Commission on Evangelism report *Towards the conversion of England*, published the same year, which warned that missionary activity was needed as much at home as overseas.[10] Other denominational leaders concurred, Birmingham's Roman Catholic archbishop Joseph Masterson writing in 1947 of 'these days when the religion of the country is at such a low ebb'.[11]

The fight against Nazi Germany had widely been conceptualised as a 'struggle against the powers of evil' on behalf of 'western civilisation and Christianity'.[12] In this context, a variety of religious commentators and public figures saw neglect of moral or religious duty as socially and politically, as well as spiritually, dangerous. Claims of widespread apostasy were hardly new, but arguably acquired renewed significance in the late 1940s amidst increased scrutiny of the national spiritual temperature – engendered partly by the growing international threat of Communism and also a more general determination to win the peace as well as the war.[13] Whilst largely eschewing the virulent anti-Communism of their American counterparts, many Birmingham clergy nevertheless appeared wary of both the atheistical implications of Communism's materialist ideology, and of the potential threat to individual conscience (one of the foundation stones of the modern

8 Hastings, *English Christianity*, ch. xxxii; Brown, *Religion and society in twentieth century Britain*, ch. v.
9 *SACPM* xxxi/306 (July–Aug. 1945).
10 Archbishops' Commission on Evangelism, *Towards the conversion of England*.
11 BAA, AC (Advent 1947).
12 A. Wilkinson, *Dissent or conform? War, peace and the English Churches, 1900–1945*, London 1986, 264; K. Robbins, 'Britain, 1940 and "Christian civilisation"', in K. Robbins (ed.), *History, religion and identity in modern Britain*, London 1993, 195–213.
13 D. Kirby, 'The archbishop of York and Anglo-American relations during the Second World War and early Cold War, 1942–55', *JRH* xxiii (Oct. 1999), 327–45 at p. 340.

English religious settlement) by an extreme statist method of government.[14] Indeed, the spectre of Communist power abroad led some to become suspicious of collectivist activity at home. Whilst most clergy (at least in the Anglican and Free Churches) seem to have shared Archbishop William Temple's cautious enthusiasm for greater state intervention in health, education and housing, by the early 1950s some had begun to fear that excessive government planning was unintentionally breeding a subdued and spoonfed citizenry, potentially prey to either totalitarian control or material self-interest.[15] Of course, clerical attitudes could vary markedly: in south-west Birmingham for example, the Longbridge parish of the left-leaning John Morris bordered the Kings Norton parish of the combatively anti-Communist Edward Ashford. However, across party political lines most clergy of the time appear to have shared a belief in personal freedom (albeit within certain moral limits) as a support to religious vitality against the twin evils of totalitarianism and materialism. As a lecturer to the Carr's Lane 70 Club suggested in 1953, if 'society becomes the only thing of importance ... no room is left to realise a Christian relationship with God'.[16] This qualified support for personal conscience in matters moral and religious is notable given how often subsequent historians have focused upon the more disciplinary aspects of the Church's influence in this period.[17]

Local church leaders in Birmingham also appeared united regardless of politics in urging a renewed public-spiritedness in the face of national challenges. A dual advocacy of individual liberty and civic duty was in strong continuity with much Christian social thought[18] since the late nineteenth century, though it also acquired a distinctively mid twentieth-century character in the light of international instability on one hand and perceived national complacency on the other. Parish and congregation were urged to 'pull together' in the face of contemporary problems. Whilst a generalised (and rarely dissected) concern for 'declining morality' was frequently expressed, clergy letters in church magazines show equal concern over the growth of a 'materialist' mindset – particularly after the mid-1950s, as a national consumer boom began to gather pace.[19] Many clergy believed that

---

[14] S. J. Whitfield, *The culture of the Cold War*, Baltimore 1991, 77–100; I. Jones, 'The clergy, the Cold War and the mission of the local church: England, c. 1945–60', in D. Kirby (ed.), *Religion and the Cold War*, Basingstoke 2003, 188–99.

[15] G. Parsons, 'From consensus to confrontation: religion and politics in Britain since 1945', in Parsons, *Growth of religious diversity*, ii. 123–60 at pp. 126–8; S. Fielding, P. Thompson and N. Tiratsoo, *England arise! The Labour party and popular politics in 1940s Britain*, Manchester 1995, 135.

[16] *CLJ* li/3 (Apr. 1953).

[17] For example Brown, *Religion and society in twentieth century Britain*, 177–87.

[18] J. Harris, *Private lives, public spirit: a social history of Britain, 1870–1914*, Oxford 1993, especially ch. vi. See also, for the interwar period, Green, *Passing*, 149.

[19] On affluence see D. Sandbrook, *Never had it so good: a history of Britain from Suez to the Beatles*, London 2005, 97–137. For its impact on religion see McLeod, *1960s*, 102–12

a return to religious duty offered a powerful antidote to a perceived increase
in individual selfishness, which they feared would in turn breed social division as sectional interests took precedence over national unity. Such was the
case during the long-running Austin car-workers' strike of 1951, which occa-
sioned a vigorous spat in the pages of the Kings Norton parish magazine. In
April of that year Edward Ashford, whose massive parish then encompassed
Austin's Longbridge plant, described the dispute as exemplifying a contemporary lack of concern for service and common purpose. Insisting that he
did not oppose Trades Unions *per se*, Ashford none the less argued that they
had departed their noble origins to become 'prisons for men's spirits'. In May
a local union member, Frank Ludford, a non-churchgoer but regular parish
magazine reader, wrote complaining about Ashford's attack, asserting that
any current lack of purpose or selflessness owed less to industrial dispute and
more to the spectre of a third world war. 'What then is the Church doing to
prevent this threatened catastrophe?' asked Ludford, 'What, one might ask,
can it do?' In reply, Ashford reminded critics

> That they are part of the church, and that if they were doing their duty to
> God and the church, we should be able to cope with present evils ... Let them
> come back to the House of God, where they know perfectly well they belong,
> and the church would be able to cope. Meanwhile with all her faults and
> weaknesses, the church is ... the last stronghold of Godliness and worship
> and service and selflessness.[20]

Whilst by no means all churchgoing Christians would have agreed with
Ashford's conservative politics, his words nevertheless reflected some widely-
held assumptions amongst church leaders about the relationship between
Church and society. The health of Church and nation were perceived to be
closely intertwined. Although official discourse on Christian 'duty' encompassed far more than churchgoing, weekly attendance at the 'House of God'
was held to be a significant factor in holding society on a true moral and spiritual course. If (as for Ashford) there was widespread clerical disappointment
at the lack of Christian commitment displayed in society, this was based
on an assumption that the populace retained an underlying attachment to
Christian norms and values which the Church was therefore entitled to
ask them to observe. Moreover, if 'Church' and 'society' were increasingly
following different paths, Ashford was by no means alone amongst clergy in
ascribing blame to society, rather than the Church.

Not only in retrospect, but also to many contemporary observers, these
seemed like arrogant assumptions. Even critics without a specific ideological
axe to grind complained that the Churches too seldom practised what they
preached to expect unqualified loyalty. However, arrogant or not, views such
as Ashford's also need to be regarded in the light of considerable evidence of

---

[20] *KNPM* (May 1951).

Christianity's continued cultural currency in the immediate postwar period. Until the mid-1950s at least Christianity arguably not only remained deeply influential on English cultural norms and values, but also continued to benefit from the support of the many influential political and cultural figures who considered it of sufficient importance (whether for principled or pragmatic reasons) to commend its active support and propagation. Even the agnostic Clement Attlee was heard during his premiership to remark that 'there is no more urgent need today than the reaffirmation of the moral values on which our Christian civilisation is based'.[21] Indeed, as Matthew Grimley has argued, Christianity (and in particular Anglicanism) seemed, if anything, more central to conceptions of national community in the 1940s than fifty years earlier.[22] For many contemporary observers the renewed harmonisation of Church and public culture was epitomised in the coronation of 1953, which for sociologists Edward Shils and Michael Young 'provided at one time and for practically the entire society such an intensive contact with the sacred that we believe we are justified in interpreting it … as a national act of communion'.[23] Clerical calls for increased religious commitment, far from being cries in the wilderness, were thus echoed in a variety of quarters.

At grassroots level, and for all their talk of 'declining morality', Christian clergy frequently agreed with this relatively up-beat assessment. At Kings Norton in 1953 Ashford expressed his certainty that 'the coronation has brought a movement, however imperceptible, towards God'.[24] The following year expectation was heightened further by the apparent success of Billy Graham's Haringey Crusade: for the Revd Arthur Burrell at St George's, Edgbaston (himself no 'hot-gospeller'), the ripple effect from the mission was 'something that I do not think would have happened even a year or two ago'.[25] As S. J. D. Green has noted, such heightened expectations were widely expressed amongst Christian church leaders.[26] National opinion poll data was more ambivalent, though not entirely gloomy: Mass Observation's 1947 survey of religious and social attitudes in a London borough portrayed a 'puzzled people', critical of religious hypocrisy and sceptical about certain articles of Christian belief.[27] However, data from Geoffrey Gorer's *Exploring English character*, collected in the early 1950s, suggested that 29 per cent of women and 18 per cent of men attended church once a month or more. The same survey suggested that three-quarters of English people identified themselves with a religion or denomination (although fewer – 69 per cent – in

[21] This is quoted approvingly in GBCN (July 1952).
[22] Grimley, *Citizenship*, 203.
[23] E. Shils and M. Young, 'The meaning of the coronation', *Sociological Review* i (1953), 63–81 at p. 80.
[24] KNPM (July 1953).
[25] SGEPM (July 1954).
[26] Green, *Passing*, 254–5.
[27] Mass Observation, *Puzzled people*, 14–17, 156–9.

large cities).[28] There appeared to be a temporary growth in the 1950s in the numbers of people who felt that this diffusive Christian allegiance should be expressed in church affiliation and in at least occasional church attendance.

Certainly, therefore, Christianity appears to have benefited from a fairly favourable cultural climate, in which the reassertion of Christian values was welcomed in at least some significant quarters. However, comparatively few historians have seriously considered the degree to which local churches may themselves have been active agents in any gains in membership or attendance that they enjoyed.[29] Despite the suggestion that many Christians in the 1940s and 1950s understood mission primarily in terms of overseas work or large rallies, many congregations nevertheless expended considerable energy in seeking to strengthen local residents' connections with their church. In part these efforts were inspired by a plethora of postwar denominational development campaigns, so-named to evoke the spirit of collective wartime endeavour, such as the national Methodist 'Commando Campaigns' or the diocese of Birmingham's 'Ten Year Forward Movement', begun in 1946 (an ironically Stalinist-sounding title, given the political views of clergy like Edward Ashford).[30] Of course many went to church purely for reasons of personal piety, regarding outreach as a matter for the clergy. One minister in the Moseley Road and Sparkhill Circuit complained in June 1953 that 'our members generally are willing to approve schemes which do not call for a great deal of personal activity' and perceived a widespread 'unwillingness on the part of many to commit time and energy for specifically Christian work'.[31] However, if true for some, many other lay Christians responded to the call and expended considerable effort in visiting lapsed church members, publicising church activities in the community, or supporting outreach initiatives. For example, as slums were cleared and new estates built in the immediate postwar decade, the Moseley Road and Sparkhill Methodist Circuit developed a 'Methodist Migration Scheme', designed to link church members moving out of the inner city to a chapel in their new suburban neighbourhood.[32] Most of the churches included in the present study ran stewardship and pastoral visiting campaigns in the 1950s and several reported growth in attendance as a direct result of these. Young people and church-based youth activities appear to have offered a particularly effective path into church for

---

[28] Gorer, *English character*, 451, 449.

[29] One of the few sustained explorations of this theme is M. Smith, 'The roots of resurgence: Evangelical parish ministry in the mid-twentieth century', in K. Cooper and J. Gregory (eds), *Revival and resurgence in Christian history* (SCH xliv, 2008), 318–28. The agency of the Churches is also noted in Sykes, 'Popular religion in decline', 287–307 at p. 292.

[30] Parsons, 'Contrasts and continuities', 23–93 at p. 47; Slater, *A century of celebrating Christ*, 127.

[31] Moseley Road and Sparkhill Methodist Circuit quarterly meeting, minutes, June 1953, BCA, MC9/3.

[32] Ibid. Sept. 1947.

both youth and their parents. At the newly-built Grenfell Baptist Church in 1957, young people from the church had themselves gone out to the nearby park to invite their peers to an evangelistic rally.[33] Of course, being busy was one thing; making a significant impact was another. Further research is needed into the extent to which local church outreach efforts in the 1940s and 1950s contributed to the temporary revival of churchgoing. However, regarding the charge of postwar complacency at least two observations can be made from the Birmingham evidence: first, that at least some local clergy and committed church members were aware that a domestic missionary challenge lay before them and were prepared to respond; and second, that clergy nevertheless continued to assume their right to recall a self-proclaimed 'Christian nation' to be more attentive to its religious duty.[34]

The 1950s were remembered by the oldest cohort of people interviewed for this study as a decade in which Christian norms, values and practices were still central to many aspects of life (albeit perhaps partly in the light of the quite different world of the 1960s and 1970s). Whilst many of this cohort often recognised and enthusiastically embraced changing times, many also reflected with some sadness on Christianity's declining social significance since. Many also retained an instinctive attachment to the importance of religious 'duty': Philip Masterman (b. 1904), of St Mary's Pitt Heath, claimed never to have derived anything much from attending daily mass, but nevertheless continued to go because, he believed, Christian faith was an act of duty and willpower.[35] By contrast, interviewees born in mid-century and brought up during the 1950s were in retrospect more likely to be critical of the church of their youth. Much of what constituted 'Christian society' to their elders was remembered by younger interviewees as stifling formality with little necessary connection to the Christianity that they subsequently practised or rediscovered. This group was also noticeably less inclined to speak of faith as 'duty': Julia Poole (b. 1938) of Carrs Lane had moved in and out of church in young adulthood according to whether she found a congregation which suited her. When interviewed in 1998 she continued to question whether 'I still want to continue doing my spiritual searching through a church and its services, because I find myself exploring my spirituality in lots of different ways'.[36] Those whose spiritual journeys took a wholly different direction – towards Charismatic renewal – likewise frequently spoke of turning away from 'religion' (understood as hollow convention) to a living faith founded upon a free and loving response to God. Heather Francis of St Bede's, Brandwood, had attended church for a period as a young adult, but only after a particularly profound experience of God and a warm welcome from the St Bede's congregation 'realized that he was a living Lord ... I knew

---

[33] GBCN (June 1957).
[34] See also Green, *Passing*, 252–3.
[35] IJ68SM.
[36] IJ56CL.

him as a living person, that he was real'.[37] These contrasting attitudes to Christian observance reflect the characterisation of late 1930s–1950s birth cohorts as a 'generation of seekers' (to use Wade Clark Roof's phrase) in contrast to the greater attachment to duty and convention shown by their elders.[38]

Christianity, the public and the private

One inescapable feature of assessments of the 1940s and '50s in both oral testimony and scholarly analysis is the shadow cast over them by 'the Sixties' and all that that decade has come to represent. For some, the 1960s witnessed the decisive eclipse of 'Victorian values' or, in Arthur Marwick's words, a 'retreat from the social controls imposed in the Victorian era [a period he describes as one of 'dullness and conformity'] by evangelicalism and non-conformity'.[39] Callum Brown likewise argues that a decade and a half of 'moral austerity' partly inspired by religious revival was followed by the widespread rejection of a 'Puritan' mindset.[40] Christie Davies has even controversially suggested that the late '50s and early '60s marked 'a clear and definite turning point' during which 'respectable Britain decayed steadily' and the nation 'embarked upon the final leg of a U-curve of deviance' – in large part, Davies argues, because of waning commitment to Christianity.[41] The idea of the Sixties as a period of reaction against 'Puritanism' and 'Victorianism' is not unproblematic, particularly if these terms are adopted uncritically and taken to have their own explanatory power. Both labels have also suffered from being deployed more polemically than analytically, to stigmatise a particular political, religious or cultural orthodoxy. The suggestion that the Sixties marked a neat 'turning point' away from Christian-based morality and towards personal liberation also requires nuancing: critiques of 'Puritanism' and 'Victorianism' were already being heard in the 1880s[42] and not everyone in the 1960s experienced 'liberation' to the same extent. Most recently, Simon Green has argued that both educated and popular opinion was already moving decisively away from some of the chief tenets of the Victorian 'puritan' mindset (strict Sabbath observance, temperance and restraint in personal behaviour) in the 1920s and 1930s, placing the 1960s

---

[37] IJ25SB.
[38] Clark Roof, *Spiritual marketplace*, 12–15.
[39] Marwick, *British society since 1945*, 3rd edn, 1994, 141–53.
[40] Brown, *Religious and society in twentieth century Britain*, ch. v.
[41] C. Davies, *The strange death of moral Britain*, New Brunswick, NJ 2004, 28. Davies seeks to use 'respectable' and 'deviant' as shorthand for the moral norms and heterodoxies of twentieth-century Britain, rather than as pejorative terms (although as with Marwick's 'Victorian' and Brown's 'Puritan' labels, arguably does not entirely succeed in avoiding polemic).
[42] McLeod, *Secularisation*, 201.

towards the end, rather than the beginning, of this historical shift.[43] Christian attitudes themselves varied, with some decrying and others celebrating the erosion of 'Puritan' and 'Victorian' social attitudes.[44] Nevertheless, we cannot abandon the terms entirely: the idea of a struggle between the 'conservative' forces of 'Victorianism and Puritanism' and the 'progressive' forces of the 'permissive society' was a powerful and widely recognised (if not entirely unprecedented) distinction at the time and tells us much about how contemporaries viewed the social changes of the day.

However, rather than taking the opposition between 'Puritanism' and 'permissiveness' as a cultural given, the historian's task is to understand what the terms signified and how they were reckoned to be related. Debates over ideals and behaviour adopted a variety of contours – some theological, some more political or cultural; some along long-term fault-lines, others creating new divisions. Whilst age and generation could be important, elders were not always more 'conservative' than the young. However, the sense of what was morally or behaviourally 'normal' for each cohort during an individual's formative years (and the degree of societal change subsequently experienced) did give to successive age cohorts distinct 'generational' stories about the shifting moral climate of postwar Britain. If the idea of the 1960s as a sudden 'turning point' away from 'Victorian' or 'Puritan' paradigms is an over-simplification, the cohort of interviewees born in the 1940s and growing up through the exciting and sometimes confusing years of the 'long 1960s' may none the less be regarded as a 'hinge' generation, standing between their elders (formed in a world where duty, obligation and respectability were powerful social forces) and their descendants (for whom these values often sounded strange and old-fashioned, given the increased acceptance of personal authenticity as the guiding norm of conscience and action).

Before returning to the Birmingham evidence, a short detour into the history of moral attitudes may be worthwhile. Most historians writing about the moral and cultural climate of the immediate postwar decades characterise the late 1940s and early 1950s as a period of deference, convention and (in Frank Mort's words) a tendency to 'live according to the rule'.[45] Put simply, whatever individuals believed in private on a particular moral matter, there was general acceptance of the existence of an 'agreed public standard' of thought and behaviour which was morally normative if not universally observed. Acknowledging the existence of such a 'rule' is crucial to understanding not only the continued influence of the Churches and a wider, more diffusive Christian ethic in 1940s and early 1950s society, but

[43] Green, *Passing*, 135–79.
[44] Parsons, 'Introduction: deciding how far you can go', 5–21; McLeod, *1960s*, 220–34; M. Roodhouse, 'Lady Chatterley and the monk: Anglican radicals and the Lady Chatterley trial of 1960', *JEH* lix (2008), 475–500.
[45] Mort, 'Fathers and sons', 353–84 at p. 364.

also the strength of the backlash against organised Christianity when public consensus on virtue began to crumble. This 'agreed public standard' drew heavily on mid twentieth-century Christian teaching for its currency, but the Churches themselves also drew strength from being able to assert that Christian teaching concurred with what most of the population considered normal, decent behaviour – or at least with 'the done thing' (a concept Elizabeth Roberts notes appears frequently in oral testimony from the period[46]). Key to the acceptance of this 'agreed public standard' was a particular conception of the relationship between 'public' and 'private' spheres. The heuristic distinction between 'public' and 'private' life is well-known to cultural historians and is important for understanding the cultural landscape of mid twentieth-century England. On one hand, a strong demarcation of 'public' and 'private' could lead to convictions that certain aspects of life belonged more firmly in one sphere than the other. Regarding sexual behaviour, for example, the dominant assumption in early twentieth-century England (including amongst most Christian church leaders) was that sex belonged within the sphere of private life.[47] On the other hand, a clear distinction between 'public' and 'private' spheres could also lead to a different inference: that what counted as acceptable behaviour in one sphere did not always translate into the other. Again, such a 'double standard' frequently operated with regard to sexuality, in that private lapses of conduct were frequently overlooked (at least amongst men) provided this was not seen to corrode the public ideal of marital fidelity.[48] A 'double standard' arguably also operated with regard to ideals of social respectability. Whilst in theory behaviour was expected to be 'respectable' in both public and private life, 'respectability' frequently narrowed into a concern to keep up public appearances regardless of what occurred within the home.

If the 'double standard' (in all its forms) remained part of the moral landscape of mid twentieth-century Britain, the discrepancy between 'public' and 'private' behaviour was becoming increasingly unacceptable to a growing number both within and outside the Churches. However, the method of resolving this discrepancy was a matter of considerable disagreement – a disagreement which is arguably fundamental to the tensions which existed between mid-century Christian values and behaviour and the more 'permissive' turn of the long 1960s. On one hand, the moral orthodoxy of mid-century Britain, to which many Christian clergy and laity and other public bodies and interest groups subscribed, was heavily predicated on the notion

---

46 Roberts, *Women*, 14.
47 S. Szreter and K. Fisher, *Sex before the sexual revolution: intimate life in England, 1918–1963*, Cambridge 2010, 351.
48 K. Thomas, 'The double standard', *JHI* xx (1959), 195–216; J. Weeks, *Sex, politics and society: the regulation of sexuality since 1800*, 2nd edn, London 1989, 22.

of 'character'.[49] The precise ingredients of 'good character' were debated,[50] but since the late nineteenth century it had been underpinned by an assumption that 'virtue was an essentially public characteristic', a rejection of 'ego in favour of altruism', championing 'not simply ... private rationality or piety but ... the best interests of society as a whole'.[51] Individuals acquired 'good character' not primarily through their own inner resources, but by seeking to practise and internalise the best norms and virtues – the 'agreed public standard' – of society as a whole. Though not a specifically Christian concept, Christians of all types nevertheless found 'character' a highly potent idea. And although in the 1940s some Liberal Protestant writers (including Leslie Weatherhead and Carrs Lane's own Leslie Tizard) were increasingly interested in the interior realm of 'personality' as the wellspring of human identity,[52] 'character' still exercised considerable influence. The prioritisation of 'character' made 'double standards' unacceptable because they implied that private behaviour was resistant to the correcting influence of the 'agreed public standard'. Though not a new argument,[53] clerical critiques of 'double standards' in both personal morality and religious observance were becoming more numerous in the mid-twentieth century; partly in response to accusations of hypocrisy from non-churchgoers, and partly since many clergy saw spiritual renewal as central to postwar reconstruction.

However, for a growing number of intellectuals and ordinary women and men in the long 1960s, the problematic element in the discrepancy between 'public' and 'private' behaviour was not a shortfall in private morality, but the stifling effects of an 'agreed public standard' on individual self-determination. The roots of this more individualised conception of personhood date back at least to the eighteenth century, in the Enlightenment's emphasis on the bounded, autonomous individual and the Romantic movement's understanding of the inner being as the ultimate fount of creativity. The idea that what was believed or practised in private should not be constrained by public mores informed much of the critique of 'deference' and 'convention' aimed at the 'establishment' (including the Churches) in the long 1960s. In simple terms, 'doing your own thing' became more desirable than doing 'the done

---

[49] M. Freeman, '"Britain's spiritul life: how can it be deepened?" Seebohm Rowntree, Russell Lavers and the "crisis of belief", ca. 1946–54', *JRH* xxix (Feb. 2005), 25–42; Wills, 'Delinquency', 157–85.

[50] H. McLeod, 'The privatisation of religion in modern England', in F. Young (ed.), *Dare we speak of God in public?*, London 1995, 4–21 at p. 9.

[51] Harris, *Private lives, public spirit*, 249.

[52] This is explored with reference to the USA in H. A. Warren, 'The shift from character to personality in mainline Protestant thought, 1935–1945', *Church History* xlvii (1998), 537–55.

[53] See, for example, S. Morgan, 'Knights of God: Ellice Hopkins and the White Cross Army, 1883–95', in R. N. Swanson (ed.), *Gender and Christian religion* (SCH xlii, 1998), 431–45.

thing'.[54] Whilst the impact of this shift in moral authority from the public to the private sphere could be traced through a variety of aspects of life, here just two are considered: attitudes to television and to sexual behaviour.

In the postwar period, it is likely that churchgoing Christians were as fascinated and repelled by TV as were their non-churchgoing neighbours. That said, a sense of moral and spiritual purpose frequently inclined clergy and reflective laity to evaluate the content and social impact of television more intentionally than those who regarded it merely as entertainment. In the mid-1950s clergy letters in parish magazines portrayed television more as a novelty than as morally problematic. Where criticisms were made, these chiefly related to its counter-attractive appeal, tempting worshippers to contentment with broadcast services or some other recreation altogether. Such expectations may well have derived from past experience of radio: in 1938 one Gallup survey had reported that 25 per cent of respondents had at some point stayed away from church because they could hear a service on the wireless.[55] However, initially at least, evidence of the counter-attractive power of the mass media was ambiguous: a preference for broadcast services over the real thing was (and continued to be) largely confined to older adults, who were more likely to tune into religious broadcasts anyway. One 1954 survey found no clear evidence that religious programming encouraged churchgoers to stay at home.[56] However, with the spread of TV ownership (by 1961, 75 per cent of families owned a set[57]) this may have changed. In 1965 the Revd Robert Aitken of Grenfell Baptist Church cited market research suggesting that 'in homes where there is no television churchgoing is more frequent'.[58] Several older interviewees also noted the power of television: for Keith Bradbury (b. 1942), TV's fast pace and ability to cut quickly from scene to scene had immediately left even the most engaging oratorical preacher at a clear disadvantage.[59] Brenda James of St Bede's, Brandwood (born mid–1930s) remembered how the popularity of the BBC's *The Forsyte Saga* in 1967 had hit evening attendances so badly that many churches cancelled or rescheduled their services.[60]

From the late 1950s alarm over television's influence, where it existed, increasingly focused upon programming – particularly where this challenged the 'agreed public standards' that institutional Christianity generally endorsed as the norm. Television constituted the fastest means for the transmission

---

54 Roberts, *Women*, 159–60.
55 A. Briggs, *The history of broadcasting in the United Kingdom*, IV: *Sound and vision*, Oxford 1979, 763–6, 796–9.
56 Gallup, *Great Britain, 1937–1975*, I: *1937–74*, 8. For further evidence on the ambiguous effects of religious broadcasting on churchgoing in the middle third of the twentieth century see Green, *Passing*, 81–2.
57 Marwick, *British society since 1945*, 117
58 GBCN (Nov. 1965)
59 IJ14CT.
60 IJ26SB.

of new ideas and enjoyed unique access to the increasingly private world of home and family (a privacy which television arguably helped to embed). As a result it became regarded as an important influence on the moral and spiritual climate of the nation, and particularly upon the young. The arrival of commercial television in 1955 prompted particular unease amongst those who regarded broadcasting as a public service. In 1957 the Moseley Road and Sparkhill Methodist Circuit meeting complained to the ITA about the broadcast of an advertisement for alcohol immediately after *Children's Hour*.[61] Greater controversy followed a more liberal attitude towards programming at the BBC under the directorship of Sir Hugh Greene (1960–9).[62] Most objections concerned the transmission of material perceived to fit poorly with the Corporation's historic civilising mission. One evening in 1963 Edward Ashford, vicar of Kings Norton, tuned into *That was the week that was* to see what the fuss was about, but quickly turned off in disgust: '"Just the thing to do", say the so-called broad–minded', he wrote, '"If you do not like it, switch it off".' However, Ashford retorted, 'he is a poor citizen or neighbour who, knowing that there is a leaking drain in the street, pouring out a deadly stench and disease, seals up his own doors and windows and leaves the rest to die of fever'.[63]

In time Ashford's public excoriation of *TW3* and its successors would earn him a passing reference in the autobiography of the programme's presenter-in-chief, David Frost.[64] Yet his arguments also offer an insight into common criticisms of television made by moral conservatives in general in the 1950s and 1960s, and more widely into some Christians' difficulties with the new moral and social currents of those decades. Though more conservative than many of his clerical colleagues, Ashford nevertheless shared a wider assumption that public life should be characterised by an agreed ideal which then informed behaviour in the private sphere. To broadcast anything short of these standards threatened either to undermine the public ideal or to subordinate it to audience preference so that the 'private' ultimately came to dictate the 'public'. Precisely this point was made in a parish magazine article in 1973 by the St Bede's vicar, Bob Jackson, who commented that whilst television could be a force for good, its unchallenged hegemony could generate problems: just as 'a gas explosion may maim a householder … equally injured is the alcoholic, the drug or sex addict, whose condition has been aggravated by the flaunting of these things'.[65]

---

[61] Moseley Road and Sparkhill Methodist Circuit quarterly meeting, minutes, Sept. 1957, BCA, MC9/4.
[62] Parsons, 'Between law and licence', 237.
[63] *KNPM* (Jan. 1965).
[64] D. Frost, *An autobiography*, I: *From congregations to audiences*, London 1993, 143. My thanks to Hugh McLeod for pointing this out to me.
[65] *SBBPM* (Feb.–Mar. 1973).

Christian concern over 'permissive' programming appears to have reached the first of several peaks in the mid-1960s. The Midlands briefly took centre stage as the birthplace of the 'Clean up TV' campaign, started by the Wolverhampton housewife and former schoolteacher Mary Whitehouse. A former member of the Oxford Group, she had become concerned at the BBC's apparent endorsement of the 'new morality' after watching the 1963 programme *A kind of loving*, in which certain interviewees had defended the acceptability of sex amongst young couples once engaged. Two thousand people attended the campaign's first major meeting in Birmingham Town Hall on 5 May 1964.[66] For Callum Brown, 'Clean up TV' and its successor the National Viewers' and Listeners' Association 'unite[d] Protestant Evangelicals and Roman Catholic priests in condemnation of "immoral" broadcasting'.[67] However, whilst churchgoers numbered heavily amongst the audience, opinions amongst those present were divided, as archive correspondence with the Catholic archbishop of Birmingham suggests. One representative of the Birmingham Archdiocesan Board of Catholic Women, present at an earlier 'Clean up TV' meeting, wrote explaining how 'a number of Catholic women afterwards asked me to approach the Archbishop for his official permission to back the scheme ... It is felt that if this fails, no other large protest will ever be made'.[68] Others, however (notably amongst the more highly educated) seemed more sceptical: 'the whole tone of the movement is simply anti-sex', wrote one local Catholic laywoman to the archbishop, 'I feel that in this sense it is radically one-sided, and gives the impression that in order to be a Christian, one must be a prude'.[69]

It is difficult to say which view was more representative of Christian opinion of the time. Nigel Yates suggests that whilst there were many (particularly grass-roots) churchgoers and some church leaders in sympathy with 'Clean up TV', the campaign attracted little 'corporate, institutional support' from the major denominations.[70] Some were also further alienated by the campaign's associations with Moral Rearmament, whilst the Catholic Church was at this stage wary of participation in umbrella groups, preferring to develop distinctively Catholic equivalents (the archbishop's secretary responded to one enthusiast for 'Clean up TV' that they would be better to join the 'Look, Listen' groups of Fr Agnellus Andrew; 'quiet work' of 'great value ... heeded by the BBC and, with support, could be more effective than "campaigns"'[71]). The debate followed a similar trajectory within the Methodist Church: the national Methodist Conference voted to establish a

[66] For the most comprehensive discussion see Yates, *Love now, pay later?*, 142–50.
[67] Brown, *Religion and society in twentieth century Britain*, 250.
[68] Agnes Lambert to Fr. O'Brien, 22 Mar. 1964, papers concerning 'Clean Up TV' campaign, 1964–5, BAA, box 2, folder 20.
[69] Theresa Wicker to archbishop of Birmingham, 7 May 1964, ibid.
[70] Yates, *Love now, pay later?*, 143.
[71] David Cousins to Agnes Lambert (copy), n.d. but 1964–5, BAA, box 2, folder 20.

Methodist working group on standards in television rather than affiliate to 'Clean up TV', although there was evidence that this decision was regretted by some Birmingham Methodists, including a past president of Conference, E. Benson Perkins.[72] This tendency to take the moral middle ground echoes the 'measured judgement' that Arthur Marwick sees as more widely typical of authority figures during the long 1960s.[73] However, more eirenic forms of engagement rarely hit the headlines, and whatever the true picture, stridently critical voices (of which there were plenty) came to characterise the Churches' reaction to permissive programming in the minds of external observers. As one correspondent to the *Birmingham Mail* wrote in May 1964,

> that evils of repression and censorship and Puritanism are greater than those they set out to cure is evident throughout history. The present group of women [the 'Clean up TV' campaign] share with the inquisition, the followers of Cromwell and the advocates of Prohibition in America one common feature: an intolerance of any views other than their own.[74]

The suggestion that 'Clean up TV' belonged to a past, more repressive age, reflected a growing tendency to regard Christian-based morality as irrelevant to modern society.

Characterising opinions as 'up to date' or 'out of touch' is so much part of contemporary political rhetoric that it is easy to forget how many people in the 1960s viewed their times as historically pivotal. Each generation feels itself to be 'modern', but talk of a 'world come of age' (implying the assumption of full adult freedoms) was particularly widespread in the Sixties. This is clearly illustrated by the debates over sexual ethics which blew up in Church and society during the decade. Gerald Parsons has helpfully identified a tension between 'law and licence' running through many church debates over the 'permissive' legislation of the period.[75] As with debates over broadcasting standards, Christian voices could be heard on both sides of the argument. The controversy over Bishop John Robinson's *Honest to God* (1963) provides an early illustration. On the one hand Robinson himself advocated a more liberal 'situational ethics' which depended not upon 'guiding rules', but upon awareness of one's own internal moral compass and openness to 'the cumulative experience of one's own and other people's obedience'.[76] Implied here was a teleological conviction that external regulation was problematic since modern people could think for themselves. Responding to *Honest to God* in his parish magazine in 1963, Edward Ashford recognised the currency of the idea that 'in this generation, man has "come of age"

---

[72] Moseley Road and Sparkhill Methodist Circuit quarterly meeting, minutes, Sept. 1965, BCA, MC9/4.

[73] Marwick, *The Sixties*, 13–14.

[74] *Birmingham Mail*, 9 May 1964 (copy in BAA, box 2, folder 20).

[75] Parsons, 'Between law and licence'.

[76] J. A. T. Robinson, *Honest to God*, London 1963, 119 and ch. vi.

without God' even in repudiating it: 'anything more adolescent than man in our generation it would be hard to imagine', he wrote. 'We have never in our history been so generally filthy-minded, and obsessed with sex, as witness radio plays, films, books, hoardings and placards, selling this, that and the other.'[77] The metaphor of adolescence was significant given the concurrent cultural prominence of youth and the generation gap. All sides of the debate could agree that English society was currently experiencing growing pains. However, for advocates of the 'new morality' adolescence represented awakening independence from the regulatory environment of childhood, whilst its critics meant quite the opposite: a phase of wilful self-centredness blind to the value of behavioural limits.

More than regarding television, Christian debates on sexual ethics appear to have acquired a strongly generational character, although the precise relationship between attitudes and age cohorts was complex. Certainly new currents of sexual morality were closely identified with the young: the Catholic Mary Mason (b. 1953) of St Mary's Pitt Heath remembered how for many of her contemporaries disregarding Church teaching on contraception was 'like the first rebellion against the church … all of a sudden people were saying "you can't dictate to us" – in this day and age you should be able to choose how many children you want, and why'.[78] (Again here dogmatic conservatism was associated with a disappearing past.) An identification between youth and sexual liberation was also made in Anglican and Free Church circles: in a series of talks to Carrs Lane adults by members of the church's youth group in 1965, one teenager explained how his classmates 'admit that the teachings of Jesus did contain ideas of permanent value' but 'as a whole fail to give adequate moral guidance for our time … conditions have changed fundamentally in many ways, entirely new problems have arisen and therefore a radical readjustment of belief and behaviour is needed'.[79] Similarly, in a critical review of the 1973 Festival of Light rally in London, the Revd Eric Forshaw, an industrial chaplain attached to St George's, Edgbaston, felt that the speeches must have seemed 'slightly comic … to a generation well-stimulated by commercial erotica and well-cautioned against sexual repression'.[80] Larger surveys of the time appear to corroborate this impression of a generational dimension to changes in ethics: Geoffrey Gorer's 1971 *Sex and marriage in England today* found clear evidence that the under-35s were more liberal on questions of contraception, premarital sex and homosexuality than was the cohort aged 35–45.[81] More recently, Simon Szreter and Kate Fisher's oral history research on sexual attitudes within marriage amongst the 1906–24 birth cohort suggests that a majority of their

---

[77] *KNPM* (June 1963).
[78] IJ66SM.
[79] *CLJ* lxiii/11 (Nov. 1965).
[80] *SGEPM* (Sept. 1973).
[81] G. Gorer, *Sex and marriage in England today*, London 1971, 276–7, 300–1, 312.

interviewees remained ambivalent about the effects of the sexual revolution, defending 'a version of personal sexual fulfilment based on sexual creativity and mutual self-realisation behind closed doors'.[82]

Yet if certain clear differences in sexual attitudes emerge between age cohorts, a growing body of evidence also suggests that the sexual revolution of the long 1960s was not quite the watershed its champions supposed. For example, regarding pre-marital sex, an opinion poll cited in the *Carrs Lane Journal* in 1965 suggested that only 25 per cent of young people claimed to have had sex before marriage,[83] a figure which is unlikely to have been much lower amongst older cohorts. (Using a slightly different measure, Joanna Bourke suggests figures of 30 per cent for the cohort born 1904–14, 39 per cent for the cohort born 1914–24, and 43 per cent for the cohort born 1924–34,[84] denoting a steady rather than sudden rise across the century.) Moreover, Hera Cook argues that large-scale change in sexual practices really only took place later, in the 1970s and 1980s, arguing that if the 1960s were significant, it was for changes in attitudes and a greater individual willingness to be open about one's sexual habits.[85] Moreover, if advocates of sexual liberation suggested that the confinement of sex to the private sphere in the nineteenth and early twentieth century had bred ignorance and sexual repression, a majority of Szreter and Fisher's oral history interviewees (b. 1906–24) saw sexual pleasure within marriage as closely related to the innocence and privacy of the experience.[86] In more general terms one *Daily Express* survey in 1969 found that 87 per cent of the population believed that 'the permissive society' had gone too far.[87] If broadly correct, this left little room for significant variation between age groups. Moreover, if young and old frequently differed over points of personal moral behaviour, there were other areas of large-scale moral agreement: certainly Birmingham churchgoers increasingly found themselves able to unite across denominational, theological and generational lines on a number of prominent social issues and campaigns (for example, global debt, homelessness or racism) which could mitigate differences over personal morality.

A second reason for rejecting an overly simplistic account of age and moral/sexual attitudes was that (just as with religious socialisation), changing attitudes amongst the young were partly influenced by the more *laissez-faire* stance of older adults. Examining a variety of indicators of social behaviour, Christie Davies suggests that significant change had already begun to take place in the late 1930s/early 1940s, albeit with a partial and temporary

---

82 Szreter and Fisher, *Sex before the sexual revolution*, 58.
83 *CLJ* lxiii/8 (Aug. 1965).
84 Bourke, *Working class cultures in Britain*, 30.
85 H. Cook, *The long sexual revolution: English women, sex and contraception, 1800–1975*, Oxford 2004, 283, 338.
86 Szreter and Fisher, *Sex before the sexual revolution*, 364–83.
87 *KNPM* (Nov. 1969).

reversal in the 1950s.[88] If attitudes began to change before the 1960s this is scarcely surprising, given that the chief ecclesiastical popularisers of the 'new morality' were themselves interwar rather than postwar children.[89] In a sermon on sexual ethics in 1965, Carrs Lane's Revd Michael Hubbard correspondingly noted how

> In a very real way those of us who are older, those of us who even in a very small way have helped to make the world in which we live by being adult citizens, get what we deserve; our standard, our patterns of behaviour, the tensions which we have helped to create are all reflected in the young people growing up in our midst.[90]

Admittedly, it was characteristic of Carrs Lane's dominant theological Liberalism to seek to understand the spirit of the age. However, it seems that across many of the case-study churches, older churchgoers found that their views had changed further than they might have expected. June Knight (b. 1930s) of Cotteridge Church remembered feeling initial disapproval when her son began living with his partner outside marriage. However, she admitted that

> your views change to circumstances.... Thinking about it, if I wanted to live together with someone and wasn't married, I think I would do it ... in our day you didn't do it because of what people thought and said ... we weren't allowed to go on holiday together which would have been very nice, but we weren't – a few people were starting to do that sort of thing but I know I wouldn't get away with it – not to say I wouldn't have liked to have done it though, and I don't think anybody'd be any different.[91]

June Knight's experience parallels the 'relearning' process that Richard Sykes suggests older cohorts frequently underwent in the latter part of the twentieth century in response to changing religious and social trends.[92] However, such a 'relearning' with regard to sexual ethics may – if wider research is correct – have occurred more often amongst individuals born from the 1930s than those born earlier in the century.[93] By contrast, those living their formative years after the 1960s did so amidst a general social expectation that (regardless of personal preference) sexual morality was a matter of personal choice.

A second age-related consideration for local churches was that, given the widespread identification of youth with personal autonomy, defending cherished moral precepts could risk alienating young members. Denise Penney (b. 1979) of St George's, Edgbaston, felt that discouragements to cohabita-

---

88 Davies, *Strange death of moral Britain*, 19.
89 McLeod, 'Privatisation of religion', 15–16.
90 *CLJ* lxiii/8 (Aug. 1965).
91 IJ6CT.
92 Sykes, 'Popular religion in Dudley and the Gornals', 321.
93 Szreter and Fisher, *Sex before the sexual revolution*, 54.

tion outside marriage was 'one major thing to put people off' church.[94] Wider surveys suggest that whilst young adult Christians still frequently responded differently from their non-churchgoing peers on many questions of personal morals and ethics, they have sometimes (particularly amongst non-Evangelicals) shown greater parity of opinion with their own cohort than with older churchgoers.[95] Many younger interviewees preferred a more open, exploratory ethical approach: Katie Ellis (b. 1980) of Cotteridge Church, characterised the 'Christian way' on drugs as being wholly negative, whereas at school 'they give you the facts and say it's up to you … and if you treat people in a more adult way, they're going to react in a more adult way'.[96]

As this example suggests, exposure to changing pedagogical orthodoxies at school and sometimes in church may have been significant. For Julia Poole (b. 1938), a Carrs Lane's Junior Church leader over many years, the children of the 1960s and 1970s were 'a questioning generation … they were being encouraged to ask questions in school, well past the stage of donating facts and information to youngsters … it was a different way of viewing the world'. Responding to this trend, and guided by educationalist John Hull (at that time a member of the congregation), Carrs Lane radically overhauled its children's provision with the intention (in Mrs Poole's words) 'to encourage [children] to explore their faith in lots of different ways, not just accept what Mummy and Daddy, Nanny and Grandpa, had decided'.[97] Broadly speaking, this shift to a more interactive, questioning approach to the teaching of faith and values was welcomed by most interviewees who discussed it, from a variety of theological traditions. For Jan Hughes (b. 1949), a Charismatic Evangelical from Grenfell Baptist Church,

> it seemed to be quite regimented in the old days … but we live in a different day and age and I think everything has evolved to suit the culture … we can't carry on as though we're in the 1940s or 1950s … Kids see through sham; they know if you're real or not … But if you're coming across as a real, genuine person who actually believes this, and your life, and your attitude to them … that will speak volumes.[98]

'How far one could go' in placing personal authenticity above *a priori* rules in questions of morals and ethics became a key marker of theological and ecclesiastical difference in the late twentieth century (as witnessed by debates on

---

[94] IJ33SG.
[95] Such a conclusion is suggested by triangulating a number of quantitative studies by Leslie Francis, for example L. J. Francis and W. K. Kay, *Teenage religion and values*, Leominster 1995; Francis and Robbins, *Urban hope*; and A. Village and L. J. Francis, 'An anatomy of change: profiling cohort differences in beliefs and attitudes amongst Anglicans in England', *Journal of Anglican Studies* viii (2009), 59–81.
[96] IJ5CT.
[97] IJ56CL.
[98] IJ49GB.

women's ordination and homosexuality, to name but two).[99] However, as the above two testimonies suggest, the predominant shift occurred towards an ethic of personal authenticity rather than away from it.[100]

Public theology at the grassroots: coming out as Christian

Although historians have rightly seen shifts in personal morality as an important engine of cultural change, these were not the only dilemmas raised for churchgoers by the changing relationship between 'public' and 'private'. For many late twentieth-century Christians one of the most significant (and frequently discussed) challenges of inhabiting an increasingly pluralistic society was the greater difficulty of sharing one's faith with others. The notion that religion was a private matter was by no means new, having become deeply embedded in the religious and political culture of the nineteenth and early twentieth centuries. For Hugh McLeod, the balance was already tipping decisively towards religious pluralism by the late nineteenth century.[101] Nevertheless, until at least the 1950s the pluralisation and privatisation of English religion took place within an overarching Christian national discourse.[102] If evangelists could still encounter derision and criticism, this was more often for their alleged vulgarity, emotionalism or hypocrisy than because proselytism was considered unacceptable in itself. However from the 1960s or thereabouts, though proselytism continued in myriad secular forms (not least mass advertising and 'outreach' by arts organisations), missionary religion was widely regarded as at least morally problematic and at worst socially subversive.

Exploring this development requires some wider contextualisation before turning explicitly to the Birmingham evidence. Besides the longer-term factors, some specifically postwar trends may have helped to cement social suspicion of proselytism. A succession of totalitarian enemies may have led many Britons to prize individual freedom and distrust institutional ideology. For political progressives, Britain's imperial past may also have provided an object lesson in the dangers of imposing one's beliefs on others. Rising affluence and a culture of consumption undoubtedly widened the scope of everyday personal choice, gradually raising it to an article of faith. The late 1950s satire boom fed suspicion of self-proclaimed 'authorities', whilst new youth cultures encouraged teenagers to 'do their own thing'. A similar feeling that belief was a private matter seems to have widely pervaded the mainstream Churches and by the 1960s confidence to undertake evange-

---

99 Parsons, 'Between law and licence', 247.
100 Garnett, Harris, Grimley, Whyte and Williams, *Redefining Christian Britain*, 12.
101 McLeod, *Secularisation*, 28.
102 Grimley, *Citizenship*, 223–6.

listic mission was being sorely tested.[103] Keenly aware of accusations of irrelevance and hypocrisy, 'deeds'-based witness became the order of the day in
many mainstream churches, particularly where the new liberal theology had
prompted questioning about Christianity's truth or uniqueness, and thus of
the value of making converts.

This acute crisis of confidence did not last, however, and the early 1970s
witnessed a partial recovery of confidence in the distinctiveness and relevance of the Christian Gospel. The mood was captured by an article entitled
'The end of appeasement' in the monthly church magazine insert *The Sign*
in January 1971. Echoing Austin Farrer's contention that too many recent
theologians had been 'appeasers' of the spirit of the age, the article called
on Christians to be 'light-bearers, carriers of a message which, always true,
needs now to have its truth underlined by personal conviction and commitment ... a time of appeasement is over and a time for fighting has come'.[104]
Though the tone was not unexpected for a publication with Evangelical
roots, similar convictions were expressed across the theological spectrum.
(At Carrs Lane, where proselytism had been an uncomfortable topic for
much of the preceding decade, ministers now reminded members to 'stop
apologising for the faith but to offer it as a glorious and joyful faith by which
all can live'.[105]) For some Christians in the 1970s and 1980s Charismatic
renewal and its often intimate and dramatic personal encounters with the
divine gave a further spur to speaking out with confidence. By the mid-
1980s the Churches were again more vigorously asserting their voice in the
public sphere. The 1985 Church of England report *Faith in the city* (and
its self-defeating excoriation by the Conservative party) greatly enhanced
the Churches' public profile if not their actual political influence.[106] In a
different way the annual 'Make Way' marches (spearheaded by the Evangelical singer-songwriter Graham Kendrick) also exemplified the new mood,
with thousands of Christians (not solely of an Evangelical persuasion) gathering together in walks of worship, witness and celebration in towns and
cities throughout the country. However, this renewed public confidence was
frequently not paralleled in the lives of individual Christians, who continued
to express nervousness at sharing their faith – a situation which had both a
generational dimension and impact.

Interviews with Carrs Lane members offer a good starting-point for
exploring why many found talking about faith so difficult. For some, the
evangelistic techniques of the past were a significant obstacle. As Richard
Collins (b. 1948) explained,

---

[103] A. Chapman, 'Secularisation and the ministry of John R.W. Stott at All Souls,
Langham Place, 1950–1970', *JEH* lvi (2005), 496–513 at pp. 505–6.
[104] *The Sign* (Jan. 1971).
[105] *CLJ* lxx/3 (Mar. 1972).
[106] H. Clark, *The Church under Thatcher*, London 1993, 105–6; Hastings, *English Christianity*, pp. xxv–xxvi.

> I think there's a perception ... I think evangelism is a bit of a dirty word, perhaps in the URC more generally – I think people have a very narrow view of evangelism – it's either people on street corners, or rallies, or going round knocking on doors...[107]

Mr Collins expressed frustration that newer, more relational and culturally-sensitive approaches to communicating the Gospel were now tarred with the same brush. The higher incidence of interviewees in young and mid-adulthood touched by Charismatic Evangelicalism (Mr Collins among them) tended to accentuate the contrast with an older generation particularly scarred by experience of sharply declining attendance in the 1960s and 1970s, and by the more liberal critiques of proselytism popular in those decades.

Such reservations concerned the morality of intruding on the (private) beliefs of others. Those expressing this view were well aware of the implications for the future transmission of faith of not actively seeking to make converts, but personal integrity was frequently prized more highly. As John Chandler (b. 1929) of Carrs Lane explained:

> I've got less and less enthusiastic about any sort of proselytism ... I accept the word 'mission' in general – doing something for somebody ... but I wouldn't have much place in the narrower sense for trying to change people's views ... in a sense I can see the weakness of my position ... I recognise that it's ... much more difficult to present it in a parcel which you then hand on to the next generation.[108]

For some, hesitation about what they themselves believed undoubtedly played a part in their reluctance to participate in evangelistic activity. However, even those of firm Evangelical faith could admit to trepidation about sharing their faith with non-believers. Kath Priestley (b. mid-1930s) of Grenfell Baptist Church recalled watching a television programme on ancient Egypt and had described it so enthusiastically to work colleagues next day that one had promptly borrowed a library book on the subject. 'If you can talk about something like Tutankhamen with such enthusiasm that someone else wants to find out about it', she reflected, 'why can't you talk about your faith that other people are so interested that they want to go and find out about it?'[109]

Part of the answer may have been that ancient history did not attract the same social stigma as religious belief. Interviewees of all ages who remained faithful Christians were nevertheless keen to avoid being labelled 'religious' by family or friends, the word having become synonymous with convention or empty ritual. However, the meaning of the stereotype varied between

---

[107] IJ46CL.
[108] IJ54CL.
[109] IJ44GB.

age groups, suggesting some interesting possible changes in the nature of hostility to Christianity in the period. For teenagers, being 'religious' meant being labelled 'weird', as Katie Ellis (b. 1980) implied:

> [People] say 'oh you're a Christian' – I say 'well I go to church', cos there's always a label attached to it – 'oh you're really religious then', they say, 'do your mum and dad go to church?' I say 'yeah but they're not religious' – that's what I always say. Why do I say that? I dunno – guess I don't want to give the impression that they sit at home and pray every night – they should do I suppose … I don't know![110]

Adolescent peer-pressure was hardly new, but younger interviewees' fear of being labelled cultural deviants contrasts strikingly with the perspectives of older interviewees. For the latter being labelled 'religious' in a negative sense more often implied a kind of dull saintliness. Frequently in history, the 'true believer' has found her/himself expected to uphold a higher standard of behaviour than others, and the twentieth century was no exception in this respect.[111] To counter accusations that churchgoers were goody-goodies, Bill Hobbs of St George's, Edgbaston, stressed how he liked to drink and smoke in moderation as much as anyone else.[112] For Keith Bradbury, faith was most effectively shared by 'demonstrating that we who go to church are just ordinary people – we're no better than you are'.[113] Older church-goers also distanced themselves from the opposite (but equally common) stereotype – that of the religious hypocrite. Several recalled occasions when a colleague neighbour or they themselves had used the words: 'my wife/husband/mother/etc. doesn't go to church, but she's a far better person than those who do'. Most interviewees felt that Christians should be discernibly better people as a result of their faith. However, in interviewees' general experience, non-churchgoers seemed equally uninterested in Christianity regardless of whether the Christians whom they encountered manifested either unusual selflessness or common frailty.

Even so, the tendency of interviewees to feel themselves judged according to their actions rather than their words may have contributed to a preference for 'deeds'-based witness over proclamation. Interviewees from prewar birth cohorts were particularly likely to talk about 'practical Christianity' – an idea in wide circulation in the mid twentieth century (the formative years of these age groups). In 1944, for example, a contributor to the *Heneage Street Baptist Church Newsletter* expressed relief that 'for those of us who are not eloquent … theological frills, dogma and creeds are not essential for us to display our religion … Every Christian's daily motto should be "to do good

---

110 IJ5CT.
111 Williams, *Southwark*, 105–25.
112 IJ29SG.
113 IJ14CT.

is my religion"'.[114] However, having set that standard, failure could bring criticism. As K. A. Busia found in his 1966 study of 'Brookton', 'all those interviewed ... based their criticisms of the church on the acknowledgement ... that the teachings of Christ had provided a new basis for human rela- tions', yet 'the church should give a more effective and dynamic expression of the active compassion and love of neighbour which Jesus Christ taught'.[115]

A further barrier to confidence in evangelism was the difficulty of knowing the personal views of others in a pluralistic society.[116] Keith Bradbury remembered one occasion when he had made passing reference to church in a business meeting, expecting to be laughed at by his two long-standing colleagues, only to discover that both were also practising Christians.[117] Sharing faith with others was also made more complex by the increasingly multicultural character of Birmingham in the last decades of the twentieth century. However, the difficulty here related not so much to the presence of people of other faiths *per se*, but to the conclusions drawn by secular-minded authorities about how questions of faith should be handled in a multi-faith context. Interviewees mostly spoke positively about people of other faiths. For example, Heather Francis, an Evangelical member of St Bede's, Brand- wood, felt that 'from the Christian point of view I think each culture has so much to give and so much to learn from each other'.[118] For Susan Williams of St Mary's Pitt Heath, the presence of different faiths actually widened the scope for discussion of beliefs:

you talk more about your faith at work – people ask you questions, which I can't remember happening ten or more years ago ...

[Interviewer: 'Do you think that's because people are more hostile, or ...?'

No, more interested I think. And I mean there are more people – Sikhs who practise their faith or Muslims who practise their faith – and of course they have the same worries about their children not practising, so there's a lot that you share than perhaps with people who've got no faith.[119]

The religious possibilities of a multicultural society were most keenly noted by the youngest interviewees. Joanna McGrath (b. 1980/1, also of St Mary's) seemed comfortable in her own Catholicism whilst appreciating the oppor- tunity to learn about others through Religious Education and friendship with Jewish and Muslim classmates.[120] At the end of the twentieth century it was arguably too early to assess the long-term impact of a multicultural

---

114 *HSBCN*, 167 (Dec. 1944).
115 Busia, *Urban churches in Britain*, 96.
116 S. Bruce, *Religion in modern Britain*, Oxford 1995, 129.
117 IJ14CT.
118 IJ25SB.
119 IJ65SM.
120 IJ64SM.

upbringing, but there is some evidence that people of faith were well-placed to flourish: one large-scale survey of fourteen- and fifteen-year-old pupils across urban Britain surveyed in the late 1990s and early 2000s found that young people who self-identified as members of the major faith communities were on average better-disposed towards those of other ethnic groups than young people professing no faith.[121]

A greater challenge for interviewees came through what they perceived to be increased pressure from employers, colleagues or public authorities to forbid overt expressions of faith in the workplace or public sphere for fear of offending others. Whilst in theory such pressure applied equally to all faiths, some interviewees felt that in practice greater allowance was made for other world faiths than for Christianity, either as an affirmation of multi-culturalism or (more pragmatically) to avoid accusations of racism. Paul and Philippa Harris (b. 1963 and 1965 respectively), Christians of broadly, though not conservative, Evangelical convictions, spoke scathingly of some media commentators who had questioned the appropriateness of a Christian church funeral for Princess Diana in September 1997 (only a few months prior to our interview):

> [Mrs H]: It's discrimination against Christians as well, isn't it? If it had been a Muslim leader, people wouldn't have said that. They wouldn't ask why there wasn't any Christianity in their [service].
> ...
> [Mr. H]: This country is in some senses religiously ignorant – no jokes about other religions cos that's racism, but you can slag off Christians as much as you like – it smacks to me of dual values and political correctness gone out of hand.[122]

This feeling of marginalisation was exacerbated by a perception of growing ignorance of both Christianity in particular and religion in general at the end of the twentieth century. Heather Francis, for instance, remembered how recently at the school at which she worked

> one teacher stood up at Easter and said to the children 'what is Easter?' you know ... and the children were calling out all sorts of things – 'it's sweets, it's chocolate, no school', you know – all sorts of things, and he said 'it's for Easter eggs and bunny rabbits'...
>
> ['And that was it?']
>
> That was it. He was a senior teacher and I'm afraid I went to him afterwards and said 'it's just not on, you know' – I can't understand the way it is.[123]

---

[121] Francis and Robbins, *Urban hope*, 159–60.
[122] IJ16CT.
[123] IJ25SB.

Whilst successive cohorts of interviewees showed an increasing sensitivity to the criticisms of the Churches made in wider society, they also appeared increasingly impatient with the failures of the more secular-minded or religiously indifferent who failed to make a corresponding effort to understand Christianity. For Jo Grayson (b, 1966, of Cotteridge Church) such lazy presumptions were exemplified in the inaccuracy of the portrayal of Christians in TV comedy shows,[124] whilst Katie Ellis (b. 1980, also of Cotteridge) expressed irritation at a film on baptism featured in a recent Religious Education lesson, in which a non-churchgoing woman had protested at a vicar's refusal to baptise her child without attending baptism preparation, when 'you know just why they're doing it – cos they've had a baby and it's nice to do it and have all the photos ... it really bugs me!'[125] Intriguingly, observations on the religious illiteracy or insensitivity of wider society came disproportionately from the youngest interviewees, born between the 1960s and 1980s. Whilst on one level this reflected the less religiously observant character of the late twentieth century, it may also reflect a growing inclination within the Churches to question the marginalisation of faith by a culture apparently increasingly disinclined to seek to understand Christianity or make allowances for it.

Negotiating the problems and possibilities of communicating faith to others was just one aspect of the challenges that postwar Christians faced in learning to be a minority within an increasingly multicultural and culturally pluralistic society; a society, moreover, in which the dividing line between the professedly religious and the religiously uninterested was increasingly sharply drawn.[126] Though the development of such a society was founded partly upon long-term trends, the growing turn from Christianity as the basis of English society in the period from the 1960s onwards appeared a particularly shocking reversal of fortunes to those clergy and laity who had lived through the immediate postwar decades in which Christianity had seemed – if anything – more central to cultural life than in the previous generation. Exploring a local congregational perspective has highlighted some significant dimensions of this upheaval which have often been overlooked in more general accounts. Notably it has argued that whilst the Churches of the 1940s and early 1950s have been portrayed as socially repressive forces, Anglican and Free Church clergy frequently employed a rhetoric of personal freedom alongside an emphasis on religious duty, regarding a renewal of personal religious seriousness as crucial to the postwar peace. Although more realistic about the scale of the challenge than some historians have imagined, local church leaders became increasingly confident that they could call

---

[124] IJ11CT.
[125] IJ5CT.
[126] For Simon Green this was one – if not the – key characteristic of religious change in twentieth-century England: *Passing*, 87.

upon the population to fulfil their religious duty precisely because so many wider cultural signals appeared to indicate (until the mid-1950s at least) a wider resurgence of interest in Christianity. If this resurgence partly related to a hospitable cultural climate, the Birmingham evidence suggests that the initiative of local churches in fostering renewed affiliation should not be discounted. Having said that, the resurgence of interest in Christianity and the Churches was temporary, and by the mid-1950s a more questioning, sceptical attitude prevailed, which related in part to a growing cultural emphasis on personal authenticity and the rejection of notions of duty to external authorities. If such a turn has been widely noted, this chapter has highlighted a dimension of it which has been less commonly recognised: the effects of a far-reaching renegotiation of the relationship between public and private values and behaviour. As suggested by the discussions of attitudes to television and sexual behaviour, a strong cultural trend prevailed towards regarding the public sphere as the aggregation of private desires. The Churches, by continuing to assert that society should continue to seek agreed common values which shaped individual character, found themselves acting contrary to the predominant direction of travel of society at large. If this bequeathed different cohorts of churchgoers distinctive life experiences, age and life transition also arguably became important metaphors for social change as a whole: were the revolutions in moral behaviour taking place from the 1960s evidence of an 'adolescent' phase in English society, or the attainment of moral and behavioural 'maturity', in which the precepts of Christianity belonged to a past, more 'childish' phase of life?

Conclusion

Amidst the flurry of recent debate about secularisation and religious change in postwar Britain, comparatively little attention has been paid to the experience of those who swam against the cultural tide and continued to belong to local churches. This study, rooted in both documentary and original oral history research has sought to redress that imbalance through an exploration of church-based Christianity in postwar Birmingham. In exploring how churchgoers interpreted and responded to the changes that they saw in family, congregation, neighbourhood and wider society, an attempt has been made to begin to provide for the post Second World War period the kind of in-depth historical investigation of grass-roots Christian belief and practice that has so enriched our understanding of other historical periods. Admittedly, any foray into new historical territory raises as many questions as it answers. The history of the relationship between Christianity and English culture in the late twentieth century is growing up fast but is yet to attain its majority. However, this local church perspective has confirmed the potential significance to our understanding of religious change of major shifts in family life and religious socialisation, changing assumptions about public duty and the regulation of personal behaviour and new patterns of leisure. The Birmingham evidence has also highlighted some potentially significant issues which have thus far received much less attention from current historians: the large-scale postwar reconstruction of urban areas and the resulting major population movements; the spiritual and psychological impact of declining numbers in local churches; the challenges posed by evolving conceptions of beauty and taste for Christian worship; and the greater difficulty of individual faith-sharing in a society more sharply divided between the professedly Christian and the professedly non-religious. Centrally, the book has offered a rare case study in the place of age and generation in history, arguing that an exploration of age and generational identity helps to make sense of the far-reaching changes in the religious character of English society and the place of the institutional Churches within it – and indeed that in some significant respects, these changes cannot be understood without reference to generational change.

In the period from 1945 to 2000, age and generational identity became increasingly urgent (if not entirely unprecedented) issues within local church life. The experience of 'mainstream' congregations in Birmingham confirms a significant age-related dimension to changing patterns of churchgoing, becoming more noticeable in the late 1950s and 1960s, as youth and Sunday school membership and attendance embarked upon a sharper downward curve than adult church affiliation. There was some local evidence that this trend was particularly associated with a cohort born from the early 1940s onwards, given that a drop in Sunday school and youth membership in the mid-1950s appeared to precede a similar trajectory in adult church membership in the 1960s. Overall, there was a discernible ageing in the church-going population over the period, and though a minority of congregations continued to work comparatively successfully with children, teenagers and young adults, most churches across the last quarter of the twentieth century were disproportionately middle-aged or elderly – a significant reversal of the situation in the early twentieth century, when a higher percentage of young people than adults had some regular church connection.

One notable result was that the age profile of church members became an increasingly important barometer of spiritual health for many congregations, with local churches acquiring or losing members and reputations as a result. Others consciously sought to build distinctive ministries with particular age groups, even whilst the church's potential as a meeting place for all generations widely remained a valued ideal. The salience of generational identity to postwar Christianity should not be assessed purely with regard to birth cohort (for example, where a significant event in a congregation's history could shape the perspectives of those who lived through it – for example, the union of three congregations at the Cotteridge Church or the advent of Charismatic renewal at Grenfell Baptist). However, the preponderance of one or more birth cohorts within a congregation could also have profound consequences for congregational life and mission as one group's formative assumptions and prior experiences frequently (though not necessarily) reshaped their church in their own image, often weakening the congregation's potential appeal to other age-groups (for example, at Carrs Lane where a strong cohort of young adults who had joined the church in the middle of the century continued to constitute the majority of the congregation in the 1990s). At very least such findings should encourage historians to be more attentive to the significance of age and generation in local church life, and (conversely) justify an engagement with questions of personal and collective story and history amongst those who study contemporary religious congregations and communities.

Engagement with questions of age, generation and religion in history nevertheless requires considerable methodological care. Generational labels are at best convenient shorthand: historical 'generations' are not pre-given entities moving through time intact and monolithic, but rather are fluid, multi-layered and dialogically constructed. Many of the key differences between age groups emerging in the present study related not so much to divergences of opinion as to the different cultural inheritances and life-historical circumstances of different cohorts according to their location in time. Exploring this developmental dimension of generational identity can add considerable depth to otherwise two-dimensional studies of age-cohort difference. At the heart of this more multi-layered approach is an ongoing dialogue between remembered past and problematised present. If this dialogue presents its own interpretational challenges, it can also become a source of meaning, much as contemporary oral historians are increasingly interested in the 'feedback loop' between memory and present experience.[1] Experience suggests that generational identity is best approached obliquely in interviews: when, rarely, generational language was introduced, answers mostly revealed very little, leading to well-worn clichés (being 'a child of the Sixties') which interviewees frequently found difficult to unpack. Indeed the most productive way of exploring generational identity was not to raise it at all but simply to listen to what was said. (A similar point is made by Sarah Williams in relation to the oral history of popular religion as a whole.[2])

Nevertheless, and accepting the need to avoid 'the excessive reification of collective identities and ... the naïve presumption of their continuity',[3] a snapshot of local church life at the turn of the millennium suggests three rough, but reasonably distinct social generational groupings, sharing broad affinities which transcended more local identities and which had coalesced through the intersection of many individual life histories and shared experiences. The first of these was a 'prewar generation' (born roughly late-1920s or before), who remembered growing up in a society where church was – if not universally respected – at least a generally accepted part of the cultural landscape. In their formative years religious observance had been 'the done thing' – in wider cultural expectation if not in terms of universal practice. Whilst the attitudes of this group were partly reminiscent of the 'settled accommodation' that social psychologists see as fairly typical of older adulthood, they were also marked by a more historically contingent emphasis on loyalty, duty and perseverance – key cultural values of their formative years probably embedded more deeply by the experience of enduring six years of world war. This 'prewar' grouping was also distinguished through having grown up in a society in which there were 'agreed public standards', the subsequent demise of which was celebrated by some and mourned by others. Whilst the legacy of 'living according to the rule' was felt most obviously in matters of moral and social behaviour, it also affected perceptions of worship (for example, in a common preference for liturgical order which, if it was typical of older adulthood in general, may particularly have reflected their Christian formation in a worshipping culture which prized 'reverence' and 'dignity').

Besides the experience of world war, this older generation was also marked by a second significant shared experience: the sweeping away of many familiar religious and cultural landmarks, particularly between the late 1950s (when a renewed downturn in Christian affiliation became evident) and the early

---

[1] P. Summerfield, *Reconstructing women's wartime lives: discourse and subjectivity in oral histories of the Second World War*, Manchester 1998, 12–15.

[2] S. C. Williams, 'The problem of belief: the place of oral history in the study of popular religion', *OH* xxiv/2 (1996), 27–34 at p. 29.

[3] G. Cubitt, *History and memory*, Manchester 2007, 16.

1980s (by which time many of the new theological, liturgical, cultural and missiological responses to secularisation had begun to lose their novelty and establish themselves firmly within the ecclesiastical landscape). Some of this older generation regarded change as inevitable and in places greatly welcome. But there was also disappointment that much had been lost along the way. A desire to encourage younger generations in faith and practice mingled with regret that the kind of church culture which had nourished them no longer seemed to have wide appeal. However, this 'prewar generation' had also themselves changed and been part of these changes. In particular, many welcomed what they saw as a shift away from the more sombre styles of church and behaviour they had remembered from their youth (which some identified as the last vestiges of a 'Victorian' pattern of religion), sometimes overcoming previously strong expectations or barriers to do so. Many had themselves sought to be less strict with their own children than their parents had been with them. This did not generally entail a revolt against tradition; more a softening of it. For many of them, change was perhaps necessary, but if it had to come, it should be evolutionary; not revolutionary.

Amongst a 'postwar generation' born roughly from the mid-1930s to the early 1950s and entering adolescence between the mid-1940s and the mid-1960s, this conception of social and religious change generated less sympathy, although not complete rejection. For many in this grouping, church and congregational involvement could remain important, but primarily on the grounds of personal value and integrity rather than because of 'the rule'. A significant number of this middle grouping had themselves spoken of reacting against the conventions of their elders during a formative period in their lives, and some noted their distinctive status as the first 'teenagers'. In this respect, they constitute a kind of 'hinge' generation between their elders and those younger, in the same way as Hugh McLeod identified the 1960s as a 'hinge' decade in wider patterns of religious change.[4] Subsequently as parents themselves, several had allowed their children greater autonomy in spiritual exploration than they themselves had been permitted. Unlike their elders, members of this group often sensed a wider gulf between Church and society, and that the Church was 'lagging behind'. They could differ considerably over the appropriate spiritual response (notably in their attitudes to Charismatic Christianity), though most emphasised the importance of practical service and of the Church 'earning the right to be heard'. However, this was not necessarily a more secular outlook. Indeed, a disproportionately large number of interviewees in this group had left church in teenage or young adulthood, returned to church in later life, sometimes through quite profound spiritual experience, and had progressively assumed greater responsibility within their congregations (something seemingly quite characteristic of mid-adulthood in many historical periods). In this respect, a rejection of

4   McLeod, 1960s, 258.

'the rule' in favour of personal authenticity had by a circuitous route led them back to a renewal of personal faith and practice.

It was somewhat more difficult to generalise about the final broad grouping; what might be termed a 'post-1960s' generation. This is perhaps scarcely surprising given the tendency for identity to be in greater flux in adolescence and young adulthood, but also given the absence (at least before 2001) of any inescapably era-defining historical experience such as the war. Nevertheless, a number of observations can be made from the Birmingham evidence. Whereas for the 'postwar' generation the ideal of 'living according to the rule' was at least a memory, those growing up since the 1960s encountered it only as a shadowy presence in the attitudes of some of their elders. By contrast, this youngest generational grouping had been nurtured in a society in which questioning and personal choice were highly valued (in popular culture, education and the broadcast media if not necessarily within family life). Their cultural landscape offered a wide variety of ethical, behavioural and ecclesiastical options. For some, this was reflected in more eclectic spirituality or a plural, 'portfolio'-style approach to Christian affiliation which somewhat challenged the hegemony of the congregational form. This generational grouping frequently found speaking about faith to others a sensitive topic and were most keenly aware of the gap between their own faith and practice and that of the majority of their peers. Nevertheless, younger Christians (even those of settled religious commitments) were also the most consistently positive about the possibilities of a multi-cultural and multi-faith society, even whilst being frequently critical of the marginalisation of Christianity within it. This perhaps reflects the fact that, for this generation, pluralised, post-Christendom Britain was the *status quo*, rather than a traumatic retreat from a prior position of cultural significance (as it was for some older interviewees).

That these were the three main social generational groupings to emerge from the oral evidence suggests that the classic 'builder/baby-boomer/baby-buster' typology widely used by sociologists and practical theologians has at least some general salience to the history of Church-based Christianity in the twentieth century, albeit with qualifications. For one thing, as the pen-portraits have sought to show, formative life experience was at least as important as difference of opinion in the creation of different social generational identities. Second, even where attitudes and opinions mattered, the Birmingham evidence suggested some subtle but important differences in generational contours: for example, the differences in outlook between those born before and after 1945 (the classic 'baby-boom') were probably less significant than those born before the mid-1930s and those born subsequently and growing up in the immediate postwar years. A second *caveat* is that a larger-scale study might well highlight more subtle gradations of generational identity only partially glimpsed here. At the older end, there would be considerable value in exploring similarities and differences in outlook and formative experiences between those growing up in the 1920s and 1930s and becoming parents in the immediate postwar years, and those born around the turn of the twentieth century, given some potentially significant differences in attitudes to worship and personal religious practice. Likewise whilst younger interviewees were more sparsely represented in the Birmingham sample, the wider research literature suggests significant differences in experience and outlook between those born between the early 1960s and early 1980s and those born subsequently (the so-called 'Generation Y'), which could benefit from more sustained historical contextualisation. Notably there is a need to explore the experience of the renewed Evangelical Churches (both within and outside the historic 'mainstream') into which young adults were disproportionately concentrated, and against which some were reacting by the 1990s.

A third qualification is that the three generational portraits above derive from a snapshot in time at the end of the period of study, that is in 1998. Whilst in the succeeding decade many aspects of grass-roots Christian experience have remained similar (for example, an overall decline in attendance, increased consciousness of being a more distinct minority community within society as a whole – both of which date at least to the first half of the twentieth century[5]), much has also happened which doubtless profoundly affected the constitution of generational identities in 2012. At national and international level the first decade of the twenty-first century saw the re-emergence of religion into public debate (underway since the 1970s) acquire a noisier, more anxious tone – partly due to fears over global religious extremism and partly due to renewed government overtures to Britain's faith communities to become partners in regeneration or public-service delivery. For local churches this renewed public prominence was double-edged: a welcome opportunity for renewed community engagement, but generating renewed hostility from increasing numbers of the population who believed religion's influence to be socially harmful (42 per cent of respondents to a 2004 YouGov poll commissioned by the broadcaster John Humphrys[6]). In the Churches, new alignments have emerged as old ones have faded: homosexuality, such a polarising question within the mainstream Churches in 2012, was only beginning to re-emerge as a contentious issue in the late 1990s. By contrast the Charismatic movement, which so divided the postwar generation of Christians in particular, burned less brightly by 2011, many of its insights absorbed within Churches otherwise eschewing a 'Charismatic' label. Individual congregations have also seen both change and continuity. A member of one case-study church, on reading the draft pen-portrait of their congregation, commented how remarkably little had changed since 1998. Elsewhere, however, churches have merged with ecumenical partners, started new community projects and outreach initiatives, seen neighbour-

5 Green, *Passing*, 61–87.
6 Only 17% felt that it was beneficial: http://www.yougov.co.uk/extranets/ygarchives/content/pdf/Humphrys%20Religion%20Questions.pdf, accessed 06.12.2010.

hoods change and clergy come and go. One case study church – Moseley Road Methodist – closed in 2011. Life has also moved on for each of the 1998 interviewees, in work, family circumstances, church membership and personal spiritual journeying. Nevertheless, by an ongoing process of cultural sedimentation, the generational contours of the late twentieth century continue to exert their influence.

This portrait of changing generational identity in turn raises the question of what might be meant by 'generational change' in Christianity and culture more widely, and its relationship to secularisation (as understood in Hugh McLeod's definition of the term). There is much in the Birmingham evidence to suggest that secularisation and religious change in postwar England were intimately related to age and generational factors. Regarding the relative significance of 'age', 'cohort' and 'period' effects, this study largely concurs with David Voas's view that cohort effects (discernible differences in belief and practice between age cohorts) were most significant, although unlike Voas (who suggests that religious belief and practice changes little over adulthood)[7] just under a third of the Birmingham interviewees over 18 at the time had moved either into or out of church for a period as adults. In particular, the study to a significant extent supports Callum Brown's suggestion that a 'break in the cycle of intergenerational renewal' had profound consequences for Christian norms, values and institutions (albeit with some qualifications). In this respect, it also echoes Danièle Hervieu-Léger's description of secularisation as a form of 'social amnesia' – a break in the chain of collective memory.[8]

That said, as Jane Garnett, Matthew Grimley, Alana Harris, William Whyte and Sarah Williams rightly note in their book *Redefining Christian Britain: post-1945 perspectives*, the 'generational disjuncture' theory of religious change need not in every case imply secularisation, or even a disregard for cultural memory.[9] If this observation is here applied specifically to Christianity (recognising that it originally related to religion as a whole), a key question for this study is what enabled the 'remembrance' and successful reappropriation of Christian faith by the churchgoing minority, given the growing lack of interest in Christianity amongst the non-churchgoing majority. Acknowledging the importance for many interviewees of personal experience of God, and recognising the salience of individual personality type to personal religiosity,[10] this study has none the less focused chiefly on the social, cultural and ecclesiastical factors at play. Home circumstances were certainly often significant: from the mid-1950s the churches empha-

---

[7] D. Voas, 'Explaining change over time in religious involvement', in Collins-Mayo and Dandelion, *Religion and youth*, 26–32.

[8] D. Hervieu-Léger (trans. S. Lee), *Religion as a chain of memory*, New Brunswick, NJ 2000.

[9] Garnett, Harris, Grimley, Whyte and Williams, *Redefining Christian Britain*, 119.

[10] L. J. Francis, *Faith and psychology: personality, religion and the individual*, London 2005.

sised the importance of two churchgoing parents in the religious nurture of children (with good reason, according to some recent research[11]), and whilst this was progressively less common amongst the population as a whole, it was increasingly the case for successive cohorts of interviewees. However, interviewees' home and family were particularly significant where parents exhibited a 'living faith' (one which seemed real to both them and their children, and was consistently lived out). Interviewees often remembered this as a benign influence in their formative years at a later point of spiritual searching. Where no parental Christian influence was present, another significant Christian adult role model could perform a similar function.[12] For those who fell away from active churchgoing in adolescence, but returned later in life, significant life events (marriage to a Christian partner, childbirth or reflection on their own children's upbringing) could reignite active faith – again a particularly common experience for the 'postwar generation'. In particular, the number of Christians married to non-Christians decreased with each successive cohort, which may reflect the growing importance of companionate marriage based on shared values, or may equally reflect a longstanding tendency for 'mixed' marriages to default to the dominant cultural norm (Christianity in the mid-twentieth century, but a non-observant agnosticism in the early twenty-first).

In terms of wider influences, it was potentially significant that from the early 1950s many congregations made strenuous efforts to deepen their common life and welcome newcomers and young members. If 'community' did not exactly disappear from postwar English society, it became more plural, more associational, more complex to negotiate and less reliant on geographical proximity. In such a context the sense of welcome and belonging experienced by many interviewees may have been significant to their continued practice. Moreover, though this study has focused primarily on the congregation, the late twentieth-century Churches also discovered a plethora of alternative associational forms through which shared identity could be practised. These extra-congregational sites of energy (some quite novel, others long-standing) appear to have been particularly significant for those growing up in the 1970s and after. Further research in this area could be valuable, especially as some have even suggested that these forms – rather than the congregational milieu – are likely to be most resistant to decline.[13] The perception that Christianity was increasingly a counter-cultural choice may also have been a significant spur to continued participation, even despite the stresses and strains caused by swimming against the tide. Though in many ways the 'counter-culture' of the long 1960s was distrustful of organised religion, the Christian Churches also discovered their own counter-cultural forms (for example, the Charismatic movement), which appear to have been important in enabling many

---

[11] Crockett and Voas, 'Generations of decline', 567–84.
[12] See also Hirst, 'Social networks and personal beliefs', 86–94.
[13] Hervieu-Léger, *Religion as a chain of memory*; P. Ward, *Liquid Church*, Carlisle 2002.

interviewees to renew or rediscover active Christian faith. The renewal of Christian commitment through the rejection of dominant cultural norms also had an important generational dimension. In his study of popular religion in the Black Country, Richard Sykes notes that whilst in the 1940s and 1950s conversion to Christianity remained a 'profoundly conservative act', younger interviewees increasingly appeared to understand it as 'a vital part of the process by which the individual broke with the religiosity of an older generation'.[14] Such a pattern was also evident in the faith journeys of the Birmingham interviewees. Though such a break did not mean the wholesale abandonment of historic forms of Christian belief and practice, it did reflect a wider cultural renegotiation of relations between elders and youth based upon the assertion of the autonomy of each generation in evaluating and re-appropriating, rather than merely handing on, the norms and values that they had inherited. In this respect, the 'generation gap' was a wide but nevertheless bridgeable divide. Of course, there remained much about early twenty-first-century church life which would have been recognisable to the worshipper of 1945, and for a significant number of church members this was part of its appeal. However, if the Christian Churches retained a presence within postwar Britain partly because of important continuities in culture, belief and practice, it was also because enough Christians and enough local churches successfully managed to disentangle Christian faith from late nineteenth- and early twentieth-century norms and values and re-express it in contemporary cultural terms. Arguably therefore, the Churches survived not merely because the 'chain of memory' was maintained, but because faith was made present again, and not (unlike a more nominal or diffusive Christian identity) primarily dependent upon memory for its vitality.

If these observations offer some interpretation of the continued appeal of organised Christianity for a minority of the postwar population, what conversely might be suggested about the 'loss of Christian memory' amongst the majority? Here, greater circumspection is necessary, since the sources used in this study offer only a specific, churchgoing Christian, set of perspectives on such questions. Nevertheless, some possibly significant factors contributing to the turn from organised Christianity can be noted. Here, the notion of secularisation as 'social amnesia' only takes us so far. At the risk of over-stretching the metaphor, forgetting can have various causes and take diverse forms. It may be deliberate (such as in the desire to push a traumatic incident out of mind); it may be accidental (perhaps due to the lapse of time or the crowding in of other priorities); and it may even be involuntary (such as occurs through dementia or brainwashing). Likewise, the explanations offered for the emergence of post-Christendom within English culture may be said to relate to different forms of memory loss. Some of these factors involve a quite deliberate rejection of the Church and mid-century

---

[14] Sykes, 'Popular religion in Dudley and the Gornals', 257.

Christian norms and values. Others have highlighted factors in which a waning connection with Christianity was more incidental than intended (a kind of forgetfulness rather than a pushing out of mind). Others have noted factors which reduced the public significance of Christianity whether individuals wished it or not (a kind of involuntary forgetting). Of course, 'amnesia' was never total: strident critics of religion continued to speak out precisely because religion seemed all too resilient to be quietly consigned to memory. However, the impression gained is (unsurprisingly) of a combination of all three forms of collective amnesia, albeit that the consignment of religion to the realm of social memory seemed from the perspective of the Birmingham sources to become more deliberate/involuntary towards the close of the period.

To begin with the more 'accidental', the Birmingham evidence supports Hugh McLeod's assertion that collective religious amnesia was in part a by-product of affluence.[15] If greater personal wealth and security was a fairly long-standing aspiration, it only came within the grasp of the majority of the population from the 1950s onwards. Certainly Birmingham clergy in the 1950s were arguably as much concerned by the anaesthetic effects of prosperity as with moral or intellectual challenges to Christianity. In particular, affluence brought access to new technological innovations (which opened up a greater range of possibilities and influences upon which to base one's life). As the discussions of home life and television suggest, local churches found themselves working harder to attract interest in the face of the opportunities that technology brought. Affluence and new technology also contributed to greater population mobility. Here, the evidence is somewhat ambiguous: on one hand, new churches planted on postwar housing estates initially thrived, and their subsequent difficulty in holding members may relate as much to a wider decline in the importance of socialising with neighbours and the increasingly home-centred nature of family life as to the experience of transplantation *per se*. However, increased population mobility was certainly significant with regard to the postwar expansion of higher education. Discussions of the religious impact of higher education have thus far mainly concentrated on changing levels of belief and practice. However, this study has noted an important consequence for the local church: the departure of large numbers of young adults from their home congregations. Even for the many who continued in Christian belief and practice, reconnecting with church in a new town or city became even more a matter of conscious choice, and that choice frequently took them to churches which already attracted large numbers of young people. However, in this study the evidence base is relatively small-scale, highlighting the need for further research into the relationship between religiosity and university experience. Questions of affluence and the expansion of higher education also raise the question

---

[15] McLeod, *1960s*, 102–23.

of the continued relevance of social class to patterns of religious change (discussion of which was intriguingly absent from the oral and documentary sources considered, but clearly still relevant to local patterns of churchgoing from neighbourhood to neighbourhood). More work is needed to understand what is going on here.

Besides such wider considerations, this study has also argued for the importance of changing patterns of religious socialisation – a factor central to the interpretations offered by Brown, McLeod and Sykes. This too had its 'accidental' dimensions. Whilst some postwar parents were certainly keen to distance themselves and their children from Christian influence, many others simply enforced their children's church or Sunday school attendance less strongly. Indeed, clergy in the 1950s and 1960s seem to have been less preoccupied with the family conventions of die-hard atheists than with the practices of this large, nominally Christian penumbra of the 'occasionally and conditionally conforming' whose attachment to church appeared to be weakening. However, if in general terms this was a drift which the Churches were ultimately powerless to reverse during the period, the study also suggests that some decisions made by local churches themselves may unwittingly have contributed to it. For example, what began as a concern for reverence and propriety of behaviour in church appears to have created a Sunday morning atmosphere which many non-churchgoers (and quite a few regulars) found dull, boring or oppressive. Notably, mid twentieth-century assumptions that the presence of children intruded onto the hushed and 'reverent' atmosphere of worship seems to have fostered a wide (if not universal) expectation that church was an inappropriate place for the young, thus potentially alienating their parents as well. Though from the mid-1950s concerted attempts were made to make congregations more welcoming (particularly to young people), this was arguably too late for many. As Hugh McLeod has written, many young people growing up at the end of the twentieth century had 'so little exposure to the Bible or Christian language and ritual that all these things seemed strange and were not so much rejected as unconsidered'.[16]

Nevertheless, changing attitudes towards the socialisation of children and young people also suggested a widespread, more deliberate step back from religion and Christianity in particular. In this respect, Callum Brown has argued for the particular significance of women's increasing reluctance to construct their identities in terms of mid-century Christian norms and values. On one level, this study has suggested that surprisingly little discussion of women's relationships with the Churches took place in local church records and sometimes as much discussion of the influence of men as fathers. However, where women's religious choices were undeniably significant was in an increased reluctance to act as agents in the transmission of Christianity from one generation to the next. In this respect, the critical importance of

[16] Ibid. 262.

the religious socialisation of the postwar generation of children and teenagers begs significant questions about the motivations and life experiences
of their parents, growing up between the First and Second World Wars.
Compared to the pre-1914 and post-1945 periods, the interwar period has
been comparatively neglected by church historians, but the evidence of this
study suggests that Simon Green (amongst others)[17] is right to insist that
historians of religion neglect the interwar period at their peril, since it may
yet tell us much about the ways in which attitudes to religion and religious
socialisation were changing well before the more obvious upheavals of the
long 1960s.

Regarding Brown's parallel assertion that sexual liberation was a crucial
factor in the rejection of Christianity, there was insufficient direct evidence in
the material gathered for this study to comment either way. However, to the
extent that it may have been significant, it was arguably as one manifestation
of a more wholesale renegotiation of the relationship between 'public' and
'private' behaviour in the period (little discussed thus far in precisely these
terms by historians of religion), in which there was increasing resistance to
the notion that 'agreed public standards' should regulate personal behaviour.
This cultural turn proved particularly challenging in the Churches, in which
attachment to the concept of common ideals ran deep. This privileging of the
'private' over the 'public' was in turn one aspect of the elevation of personal
authenticity as the yardstick for individual behaviour. That people should be
free to 'decide for themselves' without undue interference from 'authorities'
became increasingly established both within church life and beyond it, even
as this posed challenging questions about intergenerational transmission.
This was evident in the increased nervousness of postwar parents and youth
leaders to be directive in matters of beliefs and values and the increased
delicacy of personal evangelism or faith-sharing.

Though the study offers further evidence of the importance of changing
parental attitudes, it nevertheless also admits a role for adolescent rebellion. Whilst in general, intellectual crises of faith seemed of less concern to
clergy than a number of other challenges, and figured only occasionally in
oral testimony, those interviewees entering teenage in the long 1960s were
considerably more likely than their elders to have taken a conscious decision
to cease churchgoing. Amongst the variety of factors in such decisions noted
by McLeod and Sykes (amongst others), the emergence of new, exciting
youth-specific cultures also appears to have played a part in the opening up
of a 'generation gap' both within and outside church, as suggested by debates
over church music and sexual ethics. The rejection of church by many teenagers in the long 1960s was, on this evidence, often bigger than any single
issue, and part of a wider distrust of *a priori* authorities of which institutional
Christianity was just one. However, this study has also highlighted the degree

[17] Green, *Passing*, 29. See also Sykes, 'Popular religion in Dudley and the Gornals'.

to which the local churches still exerted a degree of control over their attractiveness or otherwise to young people. Worship style, welcome and fellowship and messages about personal and ethical behaviour could still matter. For example, if Arthur Marwick is right to describe rock music as 'the central component' of the 'new participatory and uninhibited culture' emerging in those decades,[18] it is surely a matter of some historical significance whether churches chose to reflect or ignore this in their weekly worship. This study thus supports Hugh McLeod's assertion that 'theological ferment' within the Churches was a contributory factor to the religious crises of the long 1960s, but underlines that such ferment related not only to ideas but also to cultural change within the churches.

Having said that a search for personal authenticity in matters of belief and behaviour could result in a turn away from organised Christianity, it should be acknowledged that this study also suggests that the so-called 'subjectivisation' thesis also has its limits. Concern for 'personal authenticity' did not necessarily result in a rejection of Christian faith and practice. It is also striking that of the many postwar parents who believed that it was important for their children to 'decide for themselves', increasingly few appeared to feel that this was best achieved by encouraging their attendance at church or Sunday school in order to make their own informed decision. Indeed, more concluded that 'deciding for oneself' required little religious input (or indeed sometimes distancing their children from religious influence altogether). The implication is that secularisation cannot adequately be explained by reference to a kind of objective, neutral concern for personal authenticity. If so, what additional factors encouraged successive cohorts to discontinue their association with the Churches and helped to entrench the view that religion and personal authenticity were inimical? Further research is needed here. However, one partial answer is offered by those historians who have noted an increasing disinclination amongst key social and cultural institutions (for example, parliament, the courts, schools and the media) to privilege the Churches and Christian norms and values – and on occasion to seek more actively to reduce their influence. In this sense, quite apart from any 'accidental' waning of religious commitment or deliberate rejection of it, individuals involuntarily experienced a loss of Christian memory as influential public institutions reduced officially-sanctioned opportunities to express or practise it. Of course, there were still many ways in which Christianity and the Churches remained visible in public, educational or media culture, a presence which at times generated considerable debate. Even by the end of the twentieth century Christianity was not 'merely' a memory in English society. Nevertheless, the present study suggests that Christian clergy and laity were well aware of the power of the media, the law and education to spread powerful positive or negative messages about Christianity, or at

---

[18] Marwick, *The Sixties*, 19.

times to ignore it altogether. Moreover, the oral testimony suggested that by the end of the century, many Christians believed that Christianity was not receiving a fair hearing within wider society. In exploring changing attitudes to Christianity in public discourse, scholars have frequently and understandably focused on the most contentious flashpoints (for example, controversial legislation, books or broadcasts). However, more subtle changes in the norm may have been equally influential in changing attitudes – and certainly were for the Birmingham interviewees. If so, the messages about God, the Church, the purpose of existence and the nature of the good life which were projected within the largely uncontroversial everyday cultures of the media and education system should be a key area for further research.[19]

Running alongside this variety of factors were two further ways in which questions of age and generation were related to religious change. First, there was a far-reaching renegotiation of relationships between old and young in the postwar period and of the place of successive generations in history. The dominant understanding of change expressed by older interviewees and by local church and national church leaders in the forties and fifties was one of evolutionary rather than revolutionary change. Each generation, it was held, was entitled to develop cherished norms but within limits set by elders. However, for the anthropologist Margaret Mead, this 'co-figurative' paradigm of intergenerational relations, dominant in the modern west up to the mid-twentieth century, was progressively challenged by a new paradigm (which Mead calls 'pre-figurative') in which 'today, everyone born and bred before World War Two is … an immigrant in time … struggling to grapple with the unfamiliar conditions of life in a new era'.[20] Through technological change, vastly increased social and cognitive mobility and the development of age-specific subcultures, the young were increasingly able to by-pass expectations placed upon them by their elders:

> Even very recently, the elders could say: 'You know, I have been young and you have never been old'. But today's young people can reply: 'You have never been young in the world I am in, and you never can be.'[21]

The degree of change should not be overstated: Mead was writing at a time when intergenerational tension was arguably unusually high and the Birmingham evidence suggests a lessening of such tension towards the end of the century. Moreover, the 'prefigurative' paradigm that Mead expected to emerge has largely failed to materialise: even in the early twenty-first century, contemporary society remains highly selective in its privileging of youth, with power and wealth in many respects continuing to lie with the baby-boomers,

---

[19] See also, however, Yates, *Love now, pay later?*, and W. Whyte, 'The *Jackie* generation: girls' magazines, pop music and the discourse revolution', in Garnett, Harris, Grimley, Whyte and Williams, *Redefining Christian Britain*, 128–37.

[20] M. Mead, *Culture and commitment: a study of the generation gap*, London 1970, 72.

[21] Ibid. 61.

rather than with the young.[22] However, a certain cultural fascination with youth, and belief in the freedom of each generation to create its own future, has stuck. In the words of interviewee Martin Hargreaves of St George's, 'people [started] thinking that youth had actually got the answers in a way which I don't think was thought in 40s and 50s at all'.[23] This conception of historical change, in which generations were not so much links in a chain as autonomous units, proved a hard (if not insurmountable) challenge for the Church as a 'communion of saints' or 'imagined community' for whom a degree of historical continuity was essential.

Second, and regardless of the actual generational mechanics of change, it was significant how frequently the language of age and generation itself came to be used to describe the cultural and religious shifts occurring in Britain and the west during the 'long 1960s'. In the late nineteenth and early twentieth centuries a wide variety of philosophers, sociologists and theologians from Nietzsche to Bonhoeffer began to talk of a 'world come of age'. The Birmingham evidence has offered tantalising glimpses of the extent to which a similar vocabulary of life-course transition was also used by churchgoers and non-churchgoers to interpret the religious and social changes that they experienced. If at one level people in every age feel themselves to be living at a critical point in history, this was particularly so during the cultural revolutions of the long 1960s. That the nation was experiencing growing pains was widely accepted. Where opinions differed sharply was on the question of which new life stage was being embarked upon, and which was being left behind? Was society, as some argued, emerging from civilisational childhood (characterised by deference to elders and to quasi-parental legal, political and ecclesiastical authorities) and maturing into cultural adulthood (marked by personal responsibility for one's own actions)? Or, as others asserted, was English society not so much entering maturity as becoming adolescent, over-assertively individualistic and neglectful of personal responsibility? Christians could be found on both sides of the debate, but at grass-roots level the 'adolescent' analysis of social change perhaps slightly predominated over that of the 'world come of age'.[24] By contrast, it seems that a larger majority of the population viewed organised religion as part of that past, childish phase, to be revisited primarily to discredit or to transcend it.[25] Whether in reality early twenty-first-century society was entering full civilisational adulthood or merely going through an adolescent 'phase' is an intriguing question, but one best left to another kind of book.

[22] For example E. Howker and S. Malik, *Jilted generation: how Britain has bankrupted its youth*, London 2010.
[23] IJ37SG.
[24] Nigel Yates has drawn similar conclusions in *Love now, pay later*, 102.
[25] A similar point about the fate of 'tradition' in innovating societies is made in Cubitt, *History and memory*, 201–2.

APPENDIX

Oral History

In the following list of interviews, biographical details have been left deliberately basic in order to avoid identification of individuals and preserve the
anonymity originally guaranteed to interviewees at the time of the research.
Having experimented with giving the birth date and occupation of each
interviewee, I tested (in confidence) a long-standing member of one of
the case-study congregations to see if they could identify the speakers – 50
per cent of her guesses were correct. As a result, I have preferred to give
a general socio-economic classification rather than specific job titles. This
level of anonymity is comparatively rare in oral history but in this study
the need to identify speakers with a particular congregation makes interviewees more easily identifiable than in most oral histories, where even full
biographical details rarely reveal a person's identity. Giving anonymity to
interviewees is quite standard practice in qualitative social research where
the interview sample is drawn from an identifiable community. Any genuine
researcher who wishes to know more about the sample for academic purposes
is welcome to contact me.

Where two or more names are listed under the same entry, this indicates that they were interviewed together. Otherwise, all interviews were
conducted on an individual basis. All names have been changed. In addition, interviews were conducted with five ordained clergy connected with
the case-study churches, although this material has only been used as background for the study.

All interviewees were born in England unless otherwise stated.

IJ1MR (14 Dec. 1997) Miss Lilian Rayner: b. early/mid-1920s, L3.2 'higher'
profession (retired). Two churchgoing parents.
IJ2MR (15 Dec. 1997) Miss May Gladding: b. 1917, L7.1 intermediate clerical/
administrative (retired). Two churchgoing parents.
IJ3CT (3 Feb. 1998) Mrs Carol Jenkins: b. 1934, retired housewife and mother.
Churchgoing mother.
IJ4CT (3 Feb. 1998) Mr Fred Knight: b. 1931, L7.4 'intermediate' technical
(retired).
IJ5CT (4 Feb. 1998) Ms Katie Ellis: b. 1980, L15 student. Two churchgoing
parents.
IJ6CT (10 Feb. 1998) Mrs June Knight: b. early–mid-1930s, L7.3 'intermediate'
technical and auxiliary (retired). Two churchgoing parents.
IJ7CT (10 Feb. 1998) Mr David Nicholson: b. 1964, L3.4 new self-employed
higher profession. Two non-churchgoing parents.

IJ8CT (11 Feb. 1998) Mr Robert Grant: b. 1950 (Scotland), L3.2 'higher' profession. Two churchgoing parents.

IJ9CT (11 Feb. 1998) Ms Claire Lewry: b. 1982, L15 student. Churchgoing mother.

IJ10CT (13 Feb. 1998) Mrs Janet Nicholson: b. 1954, L4.1 'lower' professional. Two churchgoing parents.

IJ11CT (15 Feb. 1998) Mr Tim Grayson and Mrs Jo Grayson: both b. 1966, respectively L3.1 and L3.2 'higher' professions. Both with two churchgoing parents.

IJ12CT (16 Feb. 1998) Mrs Betty Foreman: b. 1906, L12.7 'semi-routine' child-care, then housewife and mother (retired). Two non-churchgoing parents.

IJ13CT (16 Feb. 1998) Mr Bernard Scutt: b. 1917, L3.1 'higher' profession (retired). Two churchgoing parents.

IJ14CT (17 Feb. 1998) Mr Keith Bradbury: b. 1942, L3.1 'higher' professional managerial. Two churchgoing parents.

IJ15CT (17 Feb. 1998) Mrs Joy Bradbury: b. 1942, L7.3 'intermediate' technical and auxiliary. Two churchgoing parents.

IJ16CT (24 Feb. 1998) Mr Paul Harris and Mrs Philippa Harris: b. 1963 and 1965 respectively, L3.1 'higher' profession and L4.1 'lower' profession respectively. Both with two churchgoing parents.

IJ19SB (11 Mar. 1998) Mr Kevin Shepherd: b. 1977, L15 university student. Churchgoing father.

IJ20SB (18 Mar. 1998) Mr Bert Moseley: b. 1922, L12.4 'semi-routine' operative (retired). Two churchgoing parents.

IJ21SB (17 Mar. 1998) Mr David Wright: b. 1947, L4.2 'lower' profession. Two non-churchgoing parents.

IJ22SB (23 Mar. 1998) Mrs Sharon Parker: b. late 1940s, L7.1 'intermediate' clerical and administrative. Two non-churchgoing parents.

IJ23SB (24 Mar. 1998) Mrs Christine Wright: b. c. 1946, L4.2 'lower' profession (retired). Two non-churchgoing parents.

IJ24SB (30 Mar. 1998) Mrs Kathy Stubbs: b. 1949, housewife and mother. Two irregularly churchgoing parents.

IJ25SM (30 Mar. 1998) Mrs Heather Francis: b. 1940, L12.2 'semi-routine' sales and subsequently service. Two non-churchgoing parents.

IJ26SB (2 Apr. 1998) Mrs Brenda James: b. 1932, L3.2 'higher' profession (retired). Two churchgoing parents.

IJ27SB (7 Apr. 1998) Mrs Beryl Taylor: b. 1919, retired housewife and mother. Two churchgoing parents.

IJ29SB (8 Apr. 1998) Mrs Maureen Wall: b. 1944, L12.7 'semi-routine' child-care. Two non-churchgoing parents.

IJ30SG (15 May 1998) Mr Bill Hobbs: b. 1920, L7.1 'intermediate' clerical and administrative. Two churchgoing parents.

IJ31SG (20 May 1998) Mr Dennis Fricker: b. 1926, L9 'own account' worker – trade (retired). Two churchgoing parents.

IJ32SG (21 May 1998) Mr James Phillips: b. 1940, L3.1 'higher' profession. Two churchgoing parents.

IJ33SG (22 May 1998) Mrs Marjorie Norman: b. 1940s, L7.1 'intermediate' clerical and administrative. Two churchgoing parents.

IJ34SG (25 May 1998) Ms Denise Penney: b. 1979, L15 student. Two church-going parents.

IJ35SG (25 May 1998) Mr Bernard Cranbourne and Mrs Violet Cranbourne: b. 1920 and 1927 respectively, L3.1 'higher' profession (retired) and housewife and mother (retired) respectively. Both with two churchgoing parents.

IJ36SG (26 May 1998) Ms Catherine Thorpe: b. 1944, L3.1 'higher' profession. Two non-churchgoing parents.

IJ37SG (2 June 1998) Mr Martin Hargreaves: b. 1945, L3.1 'higher' profession. Two non-churchgoing parents.

IJ38SG (5 June 1998) Mr Harry Robertson and Mrs Sheila Robertson: both b. late 1930s/early 1940s, L3.1 'higher' profession (semi-retired) and L3.1 'higher' profession (retired) respectively. Mr Robertson had two churchgoing parents; Mrs Robertson a churchgoing mother.

IJ39SG (12 June 1998) Ms Joan Egan: b. 1923, L3.1 'higher' profession (retired). Churchgoing mother and irregularly churchgoing father.

IJ40GB (23 June 1998) Mrs Violet Best: b.1934 [?] (West Indies), L7.1 'inter-mediate' clerical and administrative (retired). Two churchgoing parents.

IJ41GB (23 June 1998) Ms Wilkins: b. 1951, L3.1 'higher' profession. Two churchgoing parents.

IJ42GB (30 June 1998) Mr Doug Hensman and Mrs Margaret Hensman: both b. 1920s, L11.1 'lower' technical craft occupation and L12.6 'semi-routine' clerical (both retired). Mr Hensman had two non-churchgoing parents; Mrs Hensman a churchgoing mother.

IJ43GB (1 July 1998) Ms Juliette McLean: b. 1969, formerly L4.1 'lower' profes-sion subsequently L15 student. Two churchgoing parents.

IJ44GB (1 July 1998) Mr Lawson: b. 1984[?], school pupil. Two churchgoing parents.

IJ45GB (2 July 1998) Miss Kath Priestley: born c. 1935, L7.1 'intermediate' clerical and administrative (retired). Two non-churchgoing parents.

IJ46GB (7 July 1998) Mrs Merlene Watson: b. 1930s (West Indies), L7.1 'inter-mediate' clerical and administrative (retired). Two churchgoing parents.

IJ46CL (13. Sept. 1998) Mr Richard Collins: b. 1948, L1 employer in large organisation. Churchgoing mother and non-churchgoing father.

IJ47GB (15 Sept. 1998) Ms Jeanette Andrews: b. 1969, L4.1 'lower' profession and mother. Churchgoing mother and irregularly churchgoing father.

IJ49GB (16 Sept. and 14 Oct. 1998) Mr Devon Weeks: b. 1920s (West Indies), L12.4 'semi-routine' operative (retired).

IJ50GB (17 Sept. 1998) Mrs Jan Hughes: b. 1949, L3.1 'higher' profession. Irregularly churchgoing mother and non-churchgoing father.

IJ51CL (30 Sept. 1998) Mrs Kathleen Norton: b. 1921, L3.2 'higher' profession (retired). Two churchgoing parents.

IJ52CL (1 Oct. 1998) Mr Jim West: b. 1924, L1 employer in large organisation (retired). Two non-churchgoing parents.

IJ53CL (6 Oct. 1998) Mrs Edna Haybury: b. 1909, L3.1 'higher' profession, housewife and mother (retired).

IJ54CL (7 Oct. 1998) Mr John Chandler: b. 1929, L3.1 'higher' profession (retired). Two non-churchgoing parents.

IJ55CL (13 Oct. 1998) Mr Brian Gregory: b. 1945 (Scotland), L2 'higher' management. Two non-churchgoing parents.

IJ56CL (19 Oct. 1998) Mrs Julia Poole: b. late 1930s/early 1940s, L3.1 'higher' profession. Two churchgoing parents.

IJ57CL (19 Oct. 1998) Mr Ken Poole: b. 1937[?], L3.1 'higher' profession (retired). Churchgoing mother.

IJ58CL (20 Oct. 1998) Mr Edmund Bridger and Mrs Isobel Bridger: b. 1912 and 1920s respectively, L3.1 'higher' profession' and L6/L7.1 'higher' supervisory or 'intermediate' clerical and administrative respectively (both retired). Both with two churchgoing parents.

IJ59CL (21 Oct. 1998) Miss Hilda Robbins: b. 1923, L3.1 'higher' profession (retired). Two churchgoing parents.

IJ61GB (29 Oct. 1998) Mr Andy Sadler and Mrs Becky Sadler: both b. late 1960s, L4.1 'lower' profession and housewife/mother respectively.

IJ62CL (3 Nov. 1998) Mr Phil Thomas: b. 1944, L5 'lower' managerial. Two irregularly churchgoing parents.

IJ63CL (3 Nov. 1998) Mrs Caroline Thomas: b. late 1940s, L3.1 'higher' profession. Two churchgoing parents.

IJ64SM (1 Nov. 1998) Ms Joanna McGrath: b. 1980/1, L15 student. Churchgoing family when younger.

IJ65SM (2 Nov. 1998) Mrs Susan Williams: b. 1943, L3.1 'higher' profession. Two churchgoing parents.

IJ66SM (9 Nov. 1998) Mrs Ida Garvey (b. 1927, L12.2 routine service occupation (retired), Mrs Mary Mason (b. 1951, L7.1 'intermediate' clerical and administrative) and Mrs Theresa Wilby (b. 1953, L13 'routine' operative). Mrs Garvey was mother of Mrs Mason and Mrs Wilby. All had two churchgoing parents.

IJ67SM (15 Nov. 1998) Ms Anna Carter: b. 1983, school pupil. Two churchgoing parents.

IJ68SM (23 Nov. 1998) Mr Philip Masterman: b. 1904, retired white collar manufacturing industry employee.

IJ69SM (27 Nov. 1998) Mr John Hardy and Mrs Sheila Hardy: both b. 1940s (Mr Hardy in Eire), respectively L1 employer in large organisation and L7.1 'intermediate' clerical and administrative and housewife/mother. Both with two churchgoing parents.

IJ70SM (7 Dec. 1998) Mr Pat Mannion: b. 1944 (Eire), L9.1 'own account' worker – construction.

IJ71SM (8 Dec. 1998) Mr Peter O'Rourke: b. 1960s, L5 'lower' managerial. Two non-churchgoing parents.

IJ72SM (10 Dec. 1998) Mr Dermot Leary: b. 1940s (N. Ireland), L5 'lower' managerial. Two churchgoing parents.

Bibliography

Unpublished primary sources

Birmingham, Archdiocesan Archives (BAA)
Ad clerums file: *Ad clerums* (1945–65)
Archbishop's papers: box 2, folder 7 (papers concerning Birmingham arch-diocesan guild of catechists, 1944–71), folder 20 (papers concerning 'Clean Up TV' campaign, 1964–5), folder 24 (papers concerning community relations, race relations and civil liberties, 1964–71); box 14, folder 13 (papers concerning youth organisations, 1942–60)
Diocesan papers, box 7, folder 2 (permissions to attend non-Catholic schools, 1944–5, 1957–61)

Birmingham, Birmingham Methodist District Offices, Amesbury Road, Moseley
Methodist returns 5: Birmingham, 1992–6

Birmingham, Carrs Lane Church
'Carrs Lane Review' (typescript, 26 Jan. 1996)
'The purpose and vision of Carrs Lane Church' (typescript, 26 Apr. 1996)

Birmingham, City Archives (BCA)
CC 20/3 'The Church: its future in Cotteridge' (report of a working party), 1980
EP110/5/4/1 St Bede's, Brandwood, church council minute book, 4 Sept. 1960–12 Dec. 1965
EP/110/5/4/2–3 St Bede's, Brandwood, PCC minutes, 1966–75, 1975–80
EP/110/5/7/1 Visitation/parish assessment form, 11 Nov. 1982
EP110/16/1/1 Brandwood church hall, Brandwood area committee, minutes and associated newscuttings and printed material, 1959–61
EP 110/16/2/1 Notes and minutes of meetings of the Brandwood Group, 1973
EP110/17/5 'Crowther Hall report: a study of St. Bede's parish, Brandwood', Oct.1972–Mar. 1973 (typescript, 1973)
MB4/81–8 Belmont Row Methodist Circuit, plans and directories, 1946–87
MB5/68–141 Birmingham Wesley Circuit, plans and directories, 1938–71
MB8/50–5 Bristol Road and St Paul's (later Birmingham South West) Circuit, plans and directories, 1946–76
MB10/157–67 Birmingham Mission Circuit, plans and directories, 1972–7
MB18/9–11 Small Heath and Washwood Heath Circuit, plans and directories, 1952–8
MB19B/10–11 Great Barr and Kingstanding Circuit, plans and directories, 1947–74
MB21/1–8 Asbury Circuit, plans and directories, 1974–6, 1981
MB24/1–5 Sutton Park Circuit, plans and directories, 1974–7

MC9/3–4 Moseley Road and Sparkhill Methodist Circuit quarterly meeting, minutes, 1937–56, 1957–68

MC72/40 Kings Norton Methodist Church, leaders' meetings, minutes, 1971–3

MC72/41 Kings Norton Methodist Church, church council meeting, minutes, 25 Feb. 1974–12 Nov. 1984

MC72/42 Kings Norton Methodist Church, annual society meetings, minutes, 1967–73

Birmingham, Diocese of Birmingham, Church House
Church of England CBF Stats: parish returns, 113–16: Birmingham

Birmingham, Grenfell Baptist Church (GBC)
Church Meeting minutes, 29 July 1977–24 May 1995 (in possession of church secretary)
Grace, D., R. Hey and others, 'Grenfell Baptist Church: the history of Grenfell Baptist Church and people's attitudes on the role of the church in society' (typescript, photocopy, 1990)

Birmingham, St Bede's Parish Church, Brandwood
Jenkins, R. F, 'St Bede's Church, Brandwood: "Now You Are the Body of Christ"' (typescript 1985)
Parish statement, 1997

Birmingham, St George's Parish Church, Edgbaston
Parish statement, 1997

Birmingham, 'St Mary's Pitt Heath' [pseudonym; at time of research, sources in possession of parish priest}
Church notices books, Aug. 1973–July 1974; Aug. 1975–Aug. 1977
Noticebooks, Aug. 1983–Aug. 1984; May 1987–Sept. 1988
Parish News Sheets, 13 Nov. 1988–20 July 1997

London, Church of England Records Centre, Bermondsey (CERC)
CBF Stats: confirmation statistics, 1955–64, 1972–89
CBF Stats: parish returns, 1956, box 3: Birmingham
CBF Stats: parish returns, 1960: Birmingham
CBF Stats: parish returns, 1976–87, box 2: Birmingham
CBF Stats: parish returns, 1980: Birmingham
CBF Stats: parish returns, 1985: Birmingham [incomplete]
CBF Stats: parish returns, 1986: Birmingham
CBF Stats: parish returns, 1990, box 2: Birmingham [incomplete]
CBF Stats: parish returns, 1991, box 2: Birmingham

Manchester, Methodist Archives, John Rylands University Library
Marc DDEY 1/11, 12 Methodist Youth Department Sunday School Committee, minutes, 3 Jan. 1944–28 Jan. 1953; 27 May 1953–25 May 1961

Published primary sources

Birmingham, Baptist Missionary Society, International Mission Centre, Selly Oak
West Midland Baptist Association, *Yearbooks*, 1945–96/7

Birmingham, City Archives (BCA)
CC20/1 R. A. Smith, *70 years at Watford Road* (Kings Norton United Reformed Church [Congregational–Presbyterian]) (1974)
CC20/2/1–8 *Kings Norton URC Monthly News*, Oct. 1975–Sept. 1982
DRO 50/26 'Forward Movement' brochure (1948)
EP4/7/1–20 *Kings Norton parish magazine*, Jan. 1950–June 1970
EP58/7/1/3/39 *St George's parish magazine*, 1940, 1953–66, 1971–96
EP110/7/1/2 *Progress: the parish magazine of St Bede's Church, Brandwood*, nos 1 (Christmas 1962), 6 (Easter 1964)
EP110/7/1/3 *Parish magazine of St Bede's, Brandwood*, 1966–8
EP110/7/2/2 *St Bede's Church, Brandwood, newsletter*, May 1970–Feb./Mar. 1985
EP110/7/2/3 *St Bede's fortnightly focus*, nos 1 (6–20 Jan. 1985), 25 (22 Dec. 1985–5 Jan. 1986)
EP110/7/5/1 *St Bede's Banner: the magazine of St Bede's youth organisations* (typescript June 1961)
EP110/7/5/2 'Stewardship campaign brochure', 1964
EP110/7/5/5/ Folder of miscellaneous leaflets, publicity materials related to St Bede's, Brandwood, 1964–84
EP110/17/1 Miscellaneous newspaper cuttings relating to St Bede's, Brandwood

Birmingham, City Library (BCL)
L13.04 *Birmingham diocesan leaflets*, 1954–74
L18.1 *Carrs Lane Journal* xxxviii/1 (Jan. 1940)–xcv/12 (Dec. 1997)
L18.2 *Grenfell Baptist Church newsletter*, Jan. 1952–Dec. 1969
L18.2 *Heneage Street Baptist Church newsletter*, nos 115 (Aug. 1940)–251 (Dec. 1951)
Lp10.06 *Birmingham Youth for Christ: ten thrilling years, 1946–57: tenth anniversary brochure*
TS 1961 census: small area statistics, ward totals, city of Birmingham: extracts relating to population and housing

Birmingham, The Cotteridge Church
St Agnes, Cotteridge, parish magazine, Jan. 1943–July 1958
'The Cotteridge Church: communion in diversity' [GCSE Study Pack] (n.d. [mid-1990s?])
Together: the Cotteridge Church [monthly magazine], 1986–98

Birmingham, University of Birmingham Library
Christian Economic and Social Research Foundation, *Aspects of the problem facing the Churches: an analysis of certain findings of the survey of factors affecting Setting up a Home, made in Birmingham, Leeds and London in January 1957*, London 1960

London, Church of England Records Centre, Bermondsey (CERC)
PB150 Church Assembly, Church of England Council for Education, *Operation Firm Faith for Christ and his Church*, London 1955

Other papers [at time of research in possession of Miss M. Bourne]
Moseley Road Methodist Church, Balsall Heath, *Yearbook*, 1953–4
Moseley Road Methodist Church Special Bulletin (Mar. 1953–Sept. 1954)

Official documents and publications

Archbishop of Canterbury's Commission on Urban Priority Areas, *Faith in the city*, London 1985
Archbishops' Commission on Evangelism, *Towards the conversion of England: a plan dedicated to the memory of Archbishop William Temple*, London 1945
Birmingham Baptist Inner City Project, *Baptists in the inner city of Birmingham*, Birmingham 1988
Birmingham City Council Strategic Policy and Planning Unit, *Ward Profiles*, Birmingham 1991
British Parliamentary Papers, *1851 census, Great Britain, population 10, reports and tables on religious worship in England and Wales*, Shannon 1970 edn
Challenge 2000, *Planting for a harvest: a report on the spiritual state of England, 1995*, London 1995
Christian Research/Challenge 2000, *Churchgoers in England, district by district*, London [1991?]
Church of England, *Facts and figures about the Church of England 3*, London 1965
Church of England, *In tune with heaven: the report of the Archbishops' Commission on Church Music*, London 1992
Church of England Yearbook, 1997
Commission of the bishop's council for the diocese of Birmingham, *Faith in the city of Birmingham: an examination of the problems and opportunities facing a city*, Exeter 1988
Congregational Yearbooks, 1945–73
Flannery, A. (ed.), *Vatican Council II: The conciliar and post–conciliar documents*, 7th edn, New York 1984
HMSO, *2001 census: key statistics for local authorities, census area statistics*, London 2003 (www.Birmingham.gov.uk/Media?MEDIA_ID–116879)
—— *2001 population census in Birmingham: ethnic and religious groups, country of birth*, London 2001
Mass Observation, *Puzzled people: a study in attitudes to religion, ethics, progress and politics in a London borough*, London 1947
The official Catholic directory of the archdiocese of Birmingham, 1945–98
OPCS, *Census; census report no. 2: first results for the wards of the Birmingham Partnership*, West Midlands County Council 1982
OPCS, *1991 LBS/SAS Statistics* (CD ROM)
Roman Catholic hierarchy of England and Wales, *Joint pastoral letters of the hierarchy of England and Wales: the general mission*, London 1949
—— *Marriage and divorce*, London 1952

—— *The persecuted Church*, West Bromwich 1956

—— *Statement of the hierarchy of England and Wales: decree on ecumenism*, n.p. 1964

Sansbury, K., R. Latham and P. Webb, *Agenda for the Churches: a report on the People Next Door programme*, London 1968

URC Birmingham District Yearbook, 1997

URC Handbooks, 1981–97

Newspapers and periodicals

Birmingham Post

Church News

Home Words

Quadrant [Bulletin of Christian Research]

The Sign

Secondary sources

Addison, P., *Now the war is over: a social history of Britain, 1945–51*, London 1985

Adey, L. *Class and idol in the English hymn*, Vancouver 1988

Ainslie, J., 'English liturgical music since the Council', in J. D. Crichton (ed.), *English Catholic worship: liturgical renewal in England since 1900*, London 1979, 93–109

Altholz, J. L., 'The warfare of conscience with theology', in G. Parsons (ed.), *Religion in Victorian Britain, IV: Interpretations*, Manchester 1988, 150–69

Ammerman, N. T. and W. Clark Roof (eds), *Work, family and religion in contemporary society*, London–New York 1995

—— with A. E. Farnsley and others, *Congregation and community*, New Brunswick, NJ 1997

Anderson, M., 'What's new about the modern family?', in Drake, *Time, family and community*, 67–87

Archer, A., *The two Catholic Churches: a study in oppression*, London 1986

Ashworth, J. and I. Farthing, *Churchgoing in the UK: a research report from Tearfund on church attendance in the UK*, Teddington 2007

Astley, J., 'Faith development: an overview', in Astley and Francis, *Christian perspectives*, pp. xviii–xxii

—— and L. J. Francis (eds.), *Christian perspectives on faith development: a reader*, Leominster 1992

Badham, P. (ed.), *Religion, state and society in modern Britain*, Lampeter 1989

Bailey, P., *Leisure and class in Victorian England: rational recreation and the contest for control, 1830–1885*, London 1987 edn

Barker, E., 'The postwar generation and establishment religion in England', in Clark Roof, Carroll and Roozen, *Post-war generation*, 1–26

Barnes, J., *Ahead of his age: Bishop Barnes of Birmingham*, London 1979

Barrett, J. C. A., *Family worship*, London 1982

Baudrillard, J. (trans. J. Benedict), *The transparency of evil: essays on extreme phenomena*, London 1993

Bebbington, D. W., *Evangelicalism in modern Britain: a history from the 1730s to the 1980s*, London 1989

___ 'The secularisation of British universities since the mid-nineteenth century', in G. M. Marsden and B. J. Longfield (eds), *The secularisation of the Academy*, New York 1991, 259–77

—— 'The decline and resurgence of Evangelical social concern, 1918–1980', in Wolffe, *Evangelical faith and public zeal*, 175–97

Beit-Hallahmi, B. and M. Argyle, *The psychology of religious behaviour, belief and experience*, London–New York 1997

Bengtson, V. L., 'Is the "contract across generations" changing? Effects of population ageing on obligations and expectations across different age groups', in Bengtson and Achenbaum, *Changing contract*, 3–24

—— and W. A. Achenbaum (eds), *The changing contract across generations*, New York 1993

Bennett, O., *Cultural pessimism: narratives of decline in the postmodern world*, Edinburgh 2001

Benson, J., *Prime time: a history of the middle-aged in twentieth century Britain*, London 1997

Berger, P. and T. Luckmann, *The social construction of reality*, London 1966

Bîcat, A., 'Fifties children: sixties people', in Bogdanor and Skidelsky, *Age of affluence*, 321–38

Binfield, C., 'The Purley way for children', in D. Wood (ed.), *The Church and childhood* (SCH xxxi, 1994), 461–76

Bogdanor, V. and R. Skidelsky (eds), *The age of affluence, 1951–64*, London 1970

Bourke, J., *Working-class cultures in Britain, 1890–1960: gender, class and ethnicity*, London–New York 1994

Bowlby, J. (ed. M. Fry), *Child care and the growth of love*, London 1953 edn

Brake, M., *Comparative youth culture: the sociology of youth culture and youth subcultures in America, Britain and Canada*, London 1985

Brierley, P. W., *English church census 1989* [Computer File], The Data Archive [Distributor], Colchester 5 Nov. 1991, SN: 2842

—— *Youth and today's Church*, London 1999

—— *The tide is running out: what the English church attendance survey reveals*, London 2000

—— *Pulling out of the nosedive: a contemporary picture of churchgoing: what the 2005 English church census reveals*, London 2006

—— (ed.), *Prospects for the nineties: trends and tables from the English church census*, London 1991

—— (ed.), *Religious trends 6*, London 2006

—— and V. Hiscock (eds), *UK Christian handbook 1994/5*, London 1993

—— and H. Wraight (eds), 'Percentage population (adults and children) not attending church', *CRA Factfile 3* (Mar. 1997)

Brigden, S., 'Youth and the English Reformation', *P&P* xcv (1982), 37–67

Briggs, A., *The history of broadcasting in the United Kingdom*, IV: *Sound and vision*, Oxford 1979

Briggs, J. H. Y., 'The last hundred years: whither dissent?', in Nuttall and Briggs, *Dissent in Birmingham*, 10–21

Brivati, B. and H. Jones (eds), *What difference did the war make?*, London–New York 1995 edn

Brown, C. G., 'Did urbanisation secularise Britain?', *Urban History Yearbook* (1988), 1–15

—— *Religion and society in Scotland since 1707*, Edinburgh 1997

—— *The death of Christian Britain: understanding secularisation, 1800–2000*, London 2001, 2009 edns

—— 'The secularisation decade: what the 1960s have done to the study of religious history', in McLeod and Ustorf, *Decline of Christendom*, 29–46

—— *Religion and society in twentieth century Britain*, Harlow 2006

Bruce, S. *Religion in modern Britain*, Oxford 1995

—— *Religion in the modern world: from cathedrals to cults*, Oxford 1996

Bryman, A. (ed.), *Religion in the Birmingham area: essays in the sociology of religion*, Birmingham 1975

Burk, K. (ed.), *The British Isles since 1945*, Oxford 2003

Busia, K.A., *Urban churches in Britain: a question of relevance*, London 1966

Butterfield, H., *Discontinuities between generations in history: their effect on the transmission of political experience*, Cambridge 1972

Cameron, H., P. Richter, D. Davies and F. Ward (eds), *Studying local churches: a handbook*, London 2005

Carroll, J. W. and W. Clark Roof, *Bridging divided worlds: generational cultures in congregations*, San Francisco 2002

Carstairs, G. M., *This island now: the BBC Reith Lectures 1962*, London 1963

Casanova, J., *Public religions in the modern world*, Chicago 1994

Chandler, S., 'Oral history across generations: age, generational identity and interview testimony', *OH* xxxiii/2 (2005), 48–56

Chapman, A., 'Secularisation and the ministry of John R. W. Stott at All Souls, Langham Place, 1950–1970', *JEH* lvi (2005), 496–513

Cherry, G. E., *Birmingham: a study in geography, history and planning*, Chichester 1994

Chinn, C., *Birmingham: the great working city*, Birmingham 1994

Clapson, M., *Invincible green suburbs, brave new towns: social change and urban dispersal in post-war England*, Manchester 1998

—— 'Working class women's experiences of moving to new housing estates in England since 1919', *TCBH* x (1999), 345–65

Clark, D., *Between pulpit and pew: folk religion in a North Yorkshire fishing village*, Cambridge 1982

Clark, D. B., 'Local and cosmopolitan aspects of religious activity in a northern suburb', *Sociological Yearbook of Religion in Britain* iii (1970), 45–63

—— 'Local and cosmopolitan aspects of religious activity in a northern suburb: processes of change', *Sociological Yearbook of Religion in Britain* iv (1971), 141–59

Clark, H., *The Church under Thatcher*, London 1993

Clarke, P., *Hope and glory: Britain, 1900–1990*, London 1996

Clements, K.W. (ed.), *Baptists in the twentieth century*, London 1983

Cliff, P. B., *The rise and development of the Sunday school movement in England, 1780–1980*, Redhill 1986

Cloonan, M., *Banned! Censorship of popular music in Britain, 1967–92*, Aldershot 1996

Collingwood, R. G., *The idea of history*, Oxford 1946

Collins, S., 'The sociological context', in B. Mayo with S. Savage and S. Collins, *Ambiguous evangelism*, London 2004, 13–29

Collins-Mayo, S., B. Mayo, S. Nash and C. Cocksworth, *The faith of Generation Y*, London 2010

Collins-Mayo, S. and P. Dandelion (eds), *Religion and youth*, Farnham 2010

Collyer, D., *Double Zero: five years with Rockers and Hell's Angels in an English city*, Evesham 1983 edn

Connerton, P., *How societies remember*, Cambridge 1989

Cook, H., *The long sexual revolution: English women, sex and contraception, 1800–1975*, Oxford 2004

Corsten, M., 'The time of generations', *Time and Society* viii (1999), 249–72

Cox, J., *The English Churches in a secular society: Lambeth, 1870–1930*, Oxford 1982

—— 'Master-narratives of long-term religious change', in McLeod and Ustorf, *Decline of Christendom*, 201–17

Crawford, P., *Women and religion in England, 1500–1720*, London 1993

Crockett, A., 'Rural-urban churchgoing in Victorian England', *Rural History* xvi (2005), 53–82

—— and D. Voas, 'Generations of decline: religious change in 20th century Britain', *JSSR* xlv (2006), 567–84

Cubitt, G., *History and memory*, Manchester 2007

Cullen, M. J., *The statistical movement in 19th-century Britain: the functions of empirical social research*, Brighton 1975

Cuming, G., 'Liturgical change in the Church of England', in R. Davies (ed.), *The testing of the Churches, 1932–1982*, London 1982, 119–31

Currie, R., *Methodism divided: a study in the sociology of ecumenicalism*, London 1968

—— A. D. Gilbert and L. Horsley, *Churches and churchgoers: patterns of church growth in the British Isles since 1700*, Oxford 1977

Dakers, L., *Beauty beyond words: enriching worship through music*, Norwich 2000

Davidoff, L. and C. Hall, *Family fortunes: men and women of the English middle class, 1780–1850*, London 1987

Davie, G., *Religion in Britain since 1945*, Oxford 1994

—— *Europe: the exceptional case: parameters of faith in the modern world*, London 2002

Davies, C., *Permissive Britain: social change in the sixties and seventies*, London 1975

—— *The strange death of moral Britain*, New Brunswick, NJ 2004

Davies, R. (ed.), *The testing of the Churches, 1932–1982*, London 1982

—— and G. Rupp (eds), *A history of the Methodist Church in Great Britain*, London 1983

Davis, J., *Youth and the condition of Britain: images of adolescent conflict*, London 1990

de Certeau, M., 'History: science and fiction', in M. de Certeau (trans. B. Massumi), *Heterologies: discourse on the other*, Manchester 1986, 199–224

Dennison, P., 'The Roman Catholic Church', in N. Tiptaft (ed.), *Religion in Birmingham*, Warley 1972, 136–51

Drake, M. (ed.), *Time, family and community: perspectives on family and community history*, Oxford 1994

Driver, A. H. (with a contribution by H. W. Gosling), *Carrs Lane, 1748–1948*, Northampton 1948

Dyas, D. (ed.), *The English parish church through the centuries: daily life & spirituality, art & architecture, literature & music* (DVD–Rom), York 2010

Edmunds, J. and B. S. Turner, *Generations, culture and society*, Buckingham 2002

Edwards, D. L., *Religion and change*, London 1974

Elliott, B., 'Biography, family and the analysis of social change', in Drake, *Time, family and community*, 44–66

Elrington, C. R., 'Local government and public service', in Stephens, *The county of Warwick: Birmingham*, 331–41

___ 'Religious history: Church', in Stephens, *The county of Warwick: Birmingham*, 354–60

Erikson, E. H., *Identity and the life cycle* (1959), New York–London 1980

—— *Life history and the historical moment*, New York 1975

Evans, S., 'National service and the ordinand', *Theology* lx (1957), 443–6

Field, C. D., 'Adam and Eve: gender in the English Free Church constituency', *JEH* xliv (1993), 63–79

—— '"It's all chicks and going out": the observance of Easter in post-war Britain', *Theology* ci (1998), 82–9

Fielding, S., P. Thompson and N. Tiratsoo, *'England arise': the Labour party and popular politics in 1940s Britain*, Manchester 1995

Finch, J., 'Do families support each other more or less than in the past?', in Drake, *Time, family and community*, 67–90

Finney, J., *Finding faith today: how does it happen?*, Swindon 1992

Flory, R. W. and D. E. Miller, *Gen X religion*, New York–London 2000

Forder, C. W., *The parish priest at work: an introduction to systematic 'pastoralia'*, London 1947

Forster, P. G. (ed.), *Contemporary mainstream religion: studies from Humberside and Lincolnshire*, Aldershot 1995

Fowler, D., *Youth culture in modern Britain, c. 1920–c. 1970*, Basingstoke 2008

Fowler, J. W., *Stages of faith: the psychology of human development and the quest for meaning*, San Francisco 1981

Francis, L. J., *Teenagers and the Church: a profile of churchgoing youth in the 1980s*, London 1984

—— *Faith and psychology: personality, religion and the individual*, London 2005

—— and W. K. Kay, *Teenage religion and values*, Leominster 1995

—— and M. Robbins, *Urban hope and spiritual health: the adolescent voice*, Peterborough 2005

Freeman, M., '"Britain's spiritual life: how can it be deepened?" Seebohm Rowntree, Russell Lavers and the "crisis of belief", ca. 1946–54', *JRH* xxix (2005), 25–42

Frisch, M., *A shared authority: essays on the craft and meaning of oral and public history*, Albany 1990

Frost, D., *An autobiography*, I: *From congregations to audiences*, London 1993

Gallup, G. H. (ed.), *Gallup international public opinion polls: Great Britain 1937–1975*, I: *1937–74*, New York 1976

Garbett, C., *Watchman, what of the night? Eight addresses on the problems of the day* (1948), London 1949

Gardiner, J., *Wartime Britain, 1939–1945*, London 2004

Garnett, J., A. Harris, M. Grimley, W. Whyte and S. Williams (eds), *Redefining Christian Britain: post-1945 perspectives*, London 2007

Gerali, S., 'Paradigms in the contemporary Church that reflect generational values', in Ward, *Youth ministry*, 50–64

Gerloff, R. I. H., 'Black Christian communities in Birmingham: the problem of basic recognition', in Bryman, *Religion in the Birmingham area*, 61–84

—— *A plea for British Black theologies: the Black Church movement in its transatlantic cultural and theological interaction*, i, Frankfurt-am-Main 1992

Giddens, A., *Modernity and self-identity: self and society in the late modern age*, Oxford 1991

Gilbert, A. D., *Religion and society in industrial England, 1740–1914*, London 1976

—— *The making of post-Christian Britain*, London 1980

Gill, R., *Moral communities*, Exeter 1992

—— *The myth of the empty church*, London 1993

Gittins, D., *The family in question: changing households and familiar ideologies*, Basingstoke–London 1985

Gorer, G., *Exploring English character*, London 1955

—— *Sex and marriage in England today*, London 1971

Green, J., *All dressed up: the Sixties and the counter-culture*, London 1999

Green, S. J. D., *Religion in the age of decline: organisation and experience in industrial Yorkshire, 1870–1920*, Oxford 1996

—— *The passing of Protestant England: secularisation and social change, c. 1920–1960*, Cambridge 2011

Grimley, M., *Citizenship, community and the Church of England: Liberal Anglican theories of the state between the wars*, Oxford 2004

Grossberg, L., 'Another boring day in paradise: rock and roll and the empowerment of everyday life', *Popular Music* iv (1984), 225–56

Guest, M., *Evangelical identity and contemporary culture: a congregational study in innovation*, Carlisle 2007

—— L. Woodhead and K. Tusting (eds), *Congregational studies in the UK: Christianity in a post-Christian age*, Aldershot 2004

Halbwachs, M. (ed. and trans. with intro. by L. Coser), *On collective memory*, Chicago 1992 (first publ. as *The social frameworks of memory*, Paris 1952)

Halsey, A. H., *Change in British society*, 2nd edn, Oxford 1981

Hamilton, H. A., *The family church in principle and practice*, London 1943

Hanley, L., *Estates: an intimate history*, London 2007

Hareven, T. K., 'Recent research on the history of the family', in Drake, *Time, family and community*, 13–43

—— 'The search for generational memory', in D. K. Dunaway and W. K. Baum (eds), *Oral history: an interdisciplinary anthology*, 2nd edn, Walnut Creek 1996, 241–56

Harris, J., *Private lives, public spirit: a social history of Britain, 1870–1914*, Oxford 1993

—— 'Tradition and transformation: society and civil society in Britain, 1945–2001', in Burk, *British Isles*, 91–125

Hasegawa, J., 'The rise and fall of radical reconstruction in 1940s Britain', *TCBH* x (1999), 137–61

Hastings, A., *A history of English Christianity, 1920–1990*, London 1991 edn

—— 'All change: the presence of the past in English Christianity', in H. Wilmer (ed.), *20/20 visions: the futures of Christianity in Britain*, London 1992, 13–29

—— (ed.), *Modern Catholicism*, London 1991

Hebert, A. G., *Liturgy and society: the function of the Church in the modern world*, London 1935

Heelas, P. and L. Woodhead, *The spiritual revolution: why religion is giving way to spirituality*, Oxford 2005

Hennessy, P., *Never again: Britain, 1945–51* (1992), London 1993 edn

Herklots, H. G. G., *Operation Firm Faith for Christ and his Church: a practical handbook*, London 1957

Hervieu–Léger, D. (trans. S. Lee), *Religion as a chain of memory*, New Brunswick, NJ 2000

Hewison, R., *In anger: culture in the Cold War, 1945–1960*, London 1981

Hilborn, D. and M. Bird, *God and the generations: youth, age and the Church today*, Carlisle 2002

Hinings, C. R., 'The Hodge Hill sociological survey – preliminary analysis', in J. G. Davies (ed.), *UBISWRA: research bulletin, 1966*, Birmingham 1966, 37–40

—— 'The Balsall Heath survey: a report', in J. G. Davies (ed.), *UBISWRA: research bulletin, 1967*, Birmingham 1967, 56–72

Hirst, R., 'Social networks and personal beliefs: an example from modern Britain', in G. Davie, P. Heelas and L. Woodhead (eds), *Predicting religion: Christian, secular and alternative futures*, Aldershot 2003, 86–94

Hocken, P., *Streams of renewal: the origins and early development of the Charismatic movement in Great Britain*, Carlisle 1997 edn

Hoggart, R., *The uses of literacy*, London 1957

Hopewell, J. F. (ed. B. G. Wheeler), *Congregation: stories and structures*, Philadelphia 1987

Hopkins, E., *The rise and decline of the English working classes, 1918–1990: a social history*, London 1991

Hopkins, F. E., 'Cotteridge and its churches' (Kings Norton Historical Society), Birmingham 1986

Hornsby-Smith, M., *Roman Catholics in England: studies in social structure since the Second World War*, Cambridge 1987

—— *The changing parish: a study of parishes, priests and parishioners after Vatican II*, London 1989

—— (ed.), *Catholics in England, 1950–2000*, London 1999

Howker, E. and S. Malik, *Jilted generation: how Britain has bankrupted its youth*, London 2010

Hull, J. M., *What prevents Christian adults from learning?*, London 1985

Hunt, S., *The Alpha enterprise: evangelism in a post-Christian era*, Aldershot 2004

Hurst, J., 'Religious requirement: the case for Roman Catholic schools in the 1940s and Muslim schools in the 1990s', *Journal of Beliefs and Values* xxi (2000), 87–98

Inglis, K. S., *Churches and the working classes in Victorian England*, London 1963

Jaeger, H., 'Generations in history: reflections on a controversial concept', *History and Theory* xxiv (1985), 273–92

Jarvis, P. and A. G. Fielding, 'The church, clergy and community relations', in Bryman, *Religion in the Birmingham area*, 85–98

Jasper, R. C. D., *Worship and the child*, London 1975

Jasper, T., *Jesus and the Christian in a pop culture*, London 1984

Jenkins, T., *Religion in English everyday life: an ethnographical approach*, New York–Oxford 1999

Jeremy, D. J., 'Businessmen in interdenominational activity: Birmingham youth for Christ in the 1940s–1950s', *Baptist Quarterly* xxxiii/7 (1990), 336–43

Jewell, A. (ed.), *Older people and the Church*, Peterborough 2001

Jones, I., '"More desperate than any other diocese in England"? Christianity in modern Birmingham', in N. G. Holm (ed.), *Christianity and Islam in school religious education*, Åbo 2000, 137–66

—— 'The clergy, the Cold War and the mission of the local church: England, c. 1945–60', in D. Kirby (ed.), *Religion and the Cold War*, Basingstoke 2003, 188–99

—— 'Daily life and worship: introduction', in Dyas, *The English parish church*, section 6: Churches to the present day

—— and P. Webster, 'Anglican "establishment" reactions to "pop" church music in England, c. 1956–1990', in K. Cooper and J. Gregory (eds), *Elite and popular religion* (SCH xlii, 2006), 429–41

—— with P. Webster, 'Expressions of authenticity: music for worship', in Garnett, Harris, Grimley, Whyte and Williams, *Redefining Christian Britain*, 50–62

—— and P. Webster, 'Church music', in Dyas, *The English parish church*, section 6: Churches to the present day: daily life and worship

——and P. Webster, 'The theological problem of popular music for worship in contemporary Christianity', *Crucible* (July–Aug. 2006), 9–16

Jones, N., *The English Reformation: religion and cultural adaptation*, Oxford 2002

Kay, W. K. and L. J. Francis, *Drift from the Churches: attitude towards Christianity during childhood and adolescence*, Cardiff 1996

Keating, J., 'Faith and community threatened? Roman Catholic responses to the welfare state, materialism and social welfare, 1945–62', *TCBH* ix (1998), 86–108

Kirby, D., 'The archbishop of York and Anglo-American relations during the Second World War and early Cold War, 1942–1955', *JRH* xxiii (Oct. 1999), 327–45

Lambert, Y., *Dieu change en Bretagne: la réligion à Limerzel de 1900 à nos jours*, Paris 1985

Langley, A. S., *Birmingham Baptists, past and present*, London 1939

Laqueur, T. W., *Religion and respectability: Sunday schools and working class culture, 1780–1850*, New Haven–London 1976

Levin, B., *The pendulum years: Britain and the Sixties*, London 1970

Levitt, M., 'Where are the men and boys? The gender imbalance in the Church of England', *Journal of Contemporary Religion* xviii (2003), 61–75

Lloyd, R., *The Church of England in the twentieth century*, II: *1919–1939*, London 1950

Loukes, H., *Teenage religion: an enquiry into the attitudes and possibilities among British boys and girls in secondary modern schools*, London 1961

Lynch, G., *After religion: 'Generation X' and the search for meaning*, London 2002
—— '"Generation X" religion: a critical evaluation', in Collins-Mayo and Dandelion, *Religion and youth*, 33–8
McKay, R., *John Leonard Wilson: confessor for the faith*, London 1973
McKibbin, R., *Classes and cultures: England, 1918–1951*, Oxford 1998
McLeod, H., *Class and religion in the late Victorian city*, London 1974
—— 'The privatisation of religion in modern England', in F. Young (ed.), *Dare we speak of God in public?*, London 1995, 4–21
—— *Religion and society in England, 1850–1914*, Basingstoke 1996
—— 'Protestantism and British national identity, 1815–1945', in P. van der Veer and H. Lehmann (eds), *Nation and religion: perspectives on Europe and Asia*, Princeton, NJ 1999, 44–65
—— *Secularisation in western Europe, 1848–1914*, Basingstoke 2000
—— 'Being a Christian at the end of the twentieth century', in McLeod, *Cambridge history of Christianity*, ix. 636–47
—— 'The crisis of Christianity in the west: entering a post-Christian era?', in McLeod, *Cambridge history of Christianity*, ix. 323–47
——'The religious crisis of the 1960s', *Journal of Modern European History* iii (2005), 205–29
—— 'Why were the 1960s so religiously explosive?', *Nederlands Tijdscrift voor Teologie* lx/2 (2006), 109–30
—— *The religious crisis of the 1960s*, Oxford 2007
___ (ed.), *The Cambridge History of Christianity*, IX: *World Christianities*, Cambridge 2005
—— and W. Ustorf (eds), *The decline of Christendom in western Europe, 1750–2000*, Cambridge 2003
Machin, I., 'British Churches and moral change in the 1960s', in W. M. Jacob and N. Yates (eds), *Crown and mitre: religion and society in northern Europe since the Reformation*, Woodbridge 1993, 223–41
—— *The Church and social issues in twentieth century Britain*, Oxford 1998
Mandler, P., 'Two cultures – one – or many?', in Burk, *British Isles*, 127–55
Mannheim, K., *Ideology and utopia: an introduction to the sociology of knowledge*, London 1952
—— 'The problem of generations', in his *Essays on the sociology of knowledge* (1927), London 1952, 276–322
Marler, P. Long, 'Lost in the fifties: the changing family and the nostalgic Church', in Ammerman and Clark Roof, *Work, family and religion*, 23–60
Martin, D., *A sociology of English religion*, London 1967
—— *The religious and the secular: studies in secularisation*, London 1969
—— *A general theory of secularisation*, Oxford 1978
Marwick, A., *British society since 1945*, 3rd edn, London 1996
—— *The Sixties: cultural revolution in Britain, France, Italy and the United States, c. 1958–1974*, Oxford 1998
Mead, M., *Culture and commitment: a study of the generation gap*, London 1970
Moller, H., 'Youth as a force in the modern world', *Comparative Studies in Society and History* x (1967–8), 237–60
Morgan, K. O., *The people's peace: British history since 1945*, 2nd edn, Oxford 1999
Morgan, S., 'Knights of God: Ellice Hopkins and the White Cross Army, 1883–

95', in R. N. Swanson (ed.), *Gender and Christian religion* (SCH xlii, 1998), 431–45

Morris, J., *Religion and urban change: Croydon, 1840–1914*, Woodbridge 1992

—— 'The strange death of Christian Britain: another look at the secularisation debate', *HJ* xlvi (2003), 963–76

Mort, F., 'Social and symbolic fathers and sons in post-war Britain', *JBS* xxxviii (1999), 353–84

Moseley, R. M., D. Jarvis and J. W. Fowler, 'Stages of faith', in Astley and Francis, *Christian perspectives*, 29–58

Moyser, G., 'In Caesar's service? Religion and political involvement in Britain', in Badham, *Religion, state and society*, 344–73

Munsey Turner, J., *Modern Methodism in England, 1932–1998*, Peterborough 1998

Nelsen, H. M., 'Life without afterlife: toward congruency of belief across generations', *JSSR* xx/2 (1981), 109–18

Nelson, C. E., 'Does faith develop? An evaluation of Fowler's position', in Astley and Francis, *Christian perspectives*, 62–76

Nelson, G. K., 'Religious groups in a changing social environment', in Bryman, *Religion in the Birmingham area*, 45–59

Norman, E., *Church and society in England, 1770–1970: a historical study*, Oxford 1976

Nuttall, G. F., 'Dissent in Birmingham: the first two centuries', in Nuttall and Briggs *Dissent in Birmingham*, 1–9

—— and J. H. Y. Briggs, *Dissent in Birmingham, 1689–1989*, Birmingham 1989

Osgerby, B., *Youth in Britain since 1945*, Oxford 1998

Osmond, R., *Changing perspectives: Christian culture and morals in England today*, London 1993

Page R. J., *New directions in Anglican theology: a survey from Temple to Robinson*, London 1965

Parker, S., *Faith on the home front: aspects of church and popular religion in Birmingham, 1939–45*, Bern–Oxford 2005

Parks, S., 'Young adult faith development: teaching in the context of theological education', in Astley and. Francis, *Christian perspectives*, 201–14

Parsons, G., 'The rise of religious pluralism in the Church of England', in Badham, *Religion, state and society*, 1–20

—— 'Between law and licence: Christianity, morality and permissiveness', in Parsons, *Growth of religious diversity*, ii. 231–66

—— 'Contrasts and continuities: the traditional Christian Churches in Britain since 1945', in Parsons, *Growth of religious diversity*, i. 23–94

—— 'From consensus to confrontation: religion and politics in Britain since 1945', in Parsons, *Growth of religious diversity*, ii. 123–60

—— 'Introduction: deciding how far you can go', in Parsons, *Growth of religious diversity*, ii. 5–22

—— 'Introduction: persistence, pluralism and perplexity', in Parsons, *Growth of religious diversity*, i. 5–22

—— 'There and back again? Religion and the 1944 and 1988 Education Acts', in Parsons, *Growth of religious diversity*, ii. 161–98

—— 'How the times they were a-changing: exploring the context of religious transformation in Britain in the 1960s', in J. Wolffe (ed.), *Religion in history: conflict, conversion and co-existence*, Manchester 2004, 161–89

—— (ed.), *The growth of religious diversity: Britain from 1945*, I: *Traditions*; II: *Issues*, London 1993

Peacock, R., 'The 1892 Birmingham religious census', in Bryman, *Religion in the Birmingham area*, 12–25

Perkins, E. Benson, *With Christ in the Bull-Ring*, London 1935

—— *So appointed: an autobiography*, London 1964

Perman, D., *Change and the Churches: an anatomy of religion in Britain*, London 1977

Peterson, R. A., 'Why 1955? Explaining the advent of rock music', *Popular Music* ix/1 (1990), 97–116

Pickering, W. S. F., 'The secularised Sabbath: formerly Sunday, now the weekend', *Sociological Yearbook of Religion in Britain* v (1972), 33–47

Pilcher, J., *Age and generation in modern Britain*, Oxford 1995

Power, N. S., *The forgotten people: a challenge to a caring community*, Evesham 1965

Pratt, M. W., B. Hunsberger, S. M. Pancer and D. Roth, 'Aging, belief, orthodoxy and interpersonal conflict in the complexity of adult thinking about religious issues', *JSSR* xxxi (1992), 514–22

Prochaska, F., *Christianity and social service in modern Britain*, Oxford 2006

Reed, B., *80,000 adolescents: a study of young people in the city of Birmingham, by staff and students of Westhill Training College, for the Edward Cadbury Charitable Trust*, London 1950

Rex, J. and R. Moore, *Race, community and conflict: a study of Sparkbrook*, London 1967

Reynolds, S., 'Roman Catholicism', in Stephens, *The city of Birmingham*, 397–410

Richter, P. and L. J. Francis, *Gone but not forgotten: church leaving and returning*, London 1998

Robbins, K., 'Britain, 1940 and "Christian civilisation"', in K. Robbins (ed.), *History, religion and identity in modern Britain*, London 1993, 195–213

Roberts, E., *Women and families: an oral history, 1940–1970*, Oxford 1995

Roberts, P., *Alternative worship in the Church of England*, Cambridge 1999

Robinson, J. A. T., 'The house church and the parish church', *Theology* liii (Aug. 1950), 283–9

—— *Honest to God*, London 1963

—— and D. L Edwards (eds), *The Honest to God debate*, London 1963

Robson, G., *Dark satanic mills? Religion and irreligion in Birmingham and the Black Country*, Carlisle 2002

Rodd, C. S., 'Religiosity and its correlates: Hall Green, Birmingham', in Bryman, *Religion in the Birmingham area*, 99–110

Roodhouse, M., 'Lady Chatterley and the monk: Anglican radicals and the Lady Chatterley trial of the 1960s', *JEH* lix (2008), 475–500

Roof, W. Clark, *A generation of seekers: the spiritual journeys of the baby-boom generation*, San Francisco 1993

—— *Spiritual marketplace: baby-boomers and the remaking of American religion*, Princeton, NJ 1999

—— J. W. Carroll and D. A. Roozen (eds), *The post-war generation and establishment religion: cross-cultural perspectives*, Boulder, Co 1995

—— and L. Gesch, 'Boomers and the culture of choice: changing patterns of work, family and religion', in Ammerman and Clark Roof, *Work, family and religion*, 61–80

Rose, R. B., 'Protestant non-conformity', in Stephens, *County of Warwick: Birmingham*, 411–34

Rosman, D., *Evangelicals and culture*, London 1984

—— *The evolution of the English Churches, 1500–2000*, Cambridge 2003

Routley, E., *Church music and the Christian faith*, London 1978 edn (first publ. in 1959 as *Church music and theology*)

Rumsby, D. (ed.), *Carrs Lane Church* (rev. edn of *Carrs Lane Church*, 1970), Birmingham n.d. [1990?]

Russell, A., *The clerical profession*, London 1984

Ryan, D., *The Catholic parish: institutional discipline, tribal identity and religious development in the English Church*, London 1996

Ryder, J. and H. Silver, *Modern English society*, 2nd edn, London 1970

Sandbrook, D., *Never had it so good: a history of Britain from Suez to the Beatles*, London 2005

—— *White heat: a history of Britain in the swinging sixties*, London 2006

Sanderson, M., 'Education and social mobility', in P. Johnson (ed.), *Twentieth century Britain: economic, social and cultural change*, London–New York 1994, 375–91

Schuman, H. and J. Scott, 'Generations and collective memories', *ASR* liv (1989), 359–81

Shaw, R. and G. Shaw, 'The cultural and social setting', in B. Ford (ed.), *Modern Britain*, Cambridge 1992, 2–44

Shils, E. and M. Young, 'The meaning of the coronation', *Sociological Review* i (1953), 63–81

Shulik, R. N., 'Faith development in older adults', in Astley and Francis, *Christian perspectives*, 305–15

Slater, T., *A century of celebrating Christ: the diocese of Birmingham, 1905–2005*, Chichester 2005

Smail, T., A, Walker and N. Wright, *Charismatic renewal*, 2nd edn, London 1995

Smith, G., 'The unsecular city: the revival of religion in East London', in M. Northcott (ed.), *Urban theology: a reader*, London 1998, 329–38

Smith, J. Scott, 'The strange history of the decade: modernity, nostalgia and the perils of periodisation', *Journal of Social History* xxxii (1998), 263–86

Smith, Malcolm, 'The changing nature of the British state, 1929–1959: the historiography of consensus', in Brivati and Jones, *What difference did the war make?*, 37–47

Smith, Mark, *Religion and industrial society: Oldham and Saddleworth, 1740–1865*, Oxford 1994

—— 'The roots of resurgence: Evangelical parish ministry in the mid-twentieth century', in K. Cooper and J. Gregory (eds), *Revival and resurgence in Christian history* (SCH xliv, 2008), 318–28

Snape, M. and S. Parker, 'Keeping faith and coping: popular religiosity and the British people', in P. Liddle, J. Bourne and I. Whitehead (eds), *The Great World War, 1914–45*, II: *The people's experience*, London 2001, 397–42

Snell, K. D. M. and P. S. Ell, *Rival Jerusalems: the geography of Victorian religion*, Cambridge 2000

Southcott, E. W., 'The house church', *Theology* lvi (May 1953), 167–71

Spitzer, A. B., 'The historical problem of generations', *American Historical Review* lxxviii (1973), 1353–85

Springhall, J. O., *Youth, empire and society: British youth movements, 1883–1940*, London 1977

—— *Youth, popular culture and moral panics: penny gaffes to gangsta-rap*, Basingstoke 1998

Stacey, N., 'The parish newspaper', *Theology* lix (Dec. 1956), 487–91

Starkey, M., *God, sex and Generation X*, London 1997

Stephens, W. B. (ed.), *A history of the county of Warwick*, VIII: *The city of Birmingham*, London 1964

Stevenson, K., 'Gathering threads', in R. Cotton and K. Stevenson (eds), *On the receiving end: how people experience what we do in church*, London 1996, 5–12

Street, J., 'Shock waves: the authoritative response to popular music', in D. Strinati and S. Wagg (eds), *Come on down? Popular media culture in post-war Britain*, London–New York 1992, 302–24

Stringer, M. D., *On the perception of worship: the ethnography of worship in four Christian congregations in Manchester*, Birmingham 1999

—— *A sociological history of Christian worship*, Cambridge 2005

Summerfield, P., 'Approaches to women and social change in the Second World War', in Brivati and Jones, *What difference did the war make?*, 63–79

—— *Reconstructing women's wartime lives: discourse and subjectivity in oral histories of the Second World War*, Manchester 1998

Sutcliffe, A. and R. Smith, *History of Birmingham*, III: *Birmingham, 1939–1970*, London 1974

Sykes, R., 'Popular religion in decline: a study from the Black Country', *JEH* lvi (2005), 287–307

Szreter, S. and K. Fisher, *Sex before the sexual revolution: intimate life in England, 1918–1963*, Cambridge 2010

Tamke, S. S., *Make a joyful noise unto the Lord: hymns as a reflection of Victorian social attitudes*, Athens, OH 1978

Taylor, C., *The ethics of authenticity*, Cambridge, MA 1991

Taylor, S., *A land of dreams: a study of Jewish and Caribbean migrant communities in England*, London 1993

Tebbutt, M., *Women's talk? A social history of 'gossip' in working class neighbourhoods*, Aldershot 1995

Temple, W., *Christianity and social order*, London 1942 edn

Thomas, K., 'The double standard', *JHI* xx (1959), 195–216

Thomas, T. (ed.), *The British: their religious beliefs and practices, 1800–1986*, London–New York 1988

Thompson, D. M., 'The older free churches', in Davies, *Testing*, 87–115

Thompson, E. P., *The making of the English working class*, London 1963

Thompson, K., 'How religious are the British?', in Thomas, *The British*, 211–36

Thompson, P., 'Imagination and passivity in leisure: Coventry car workers and their families from the 1920s to the 1970s', in D. Thomas, L. Holden and T. Claydon (eds), *The motor car and popular culture in the twentieth century*, Aldershot 1998, 244–74

Thompson, R. H. T., *The Church's understanding of itself: a study of four Birmingham parishes*, London 1957

Thomson, A., M. Frisch and P. Hamilton, 'The memory and history debates: some international perspectives', *OH* xxii/2 (1994), 33–43

Thomson, D. W., 'A lifetime of privilege? Aging and generations at century's end', in Bengtson and Achenbaum, *Changing contract*, 215–38

Thornton, M., *English spirituality: an outline of ascetical theology according to the English pastoral tradition*, London 1963

Thurman, J. V., *New wineskins: a study of the house church movement*, Frankfurt-am-Main 1982

Tilley, J. R., 'Secularisation and ageing in Britain: does family formation cause greater religiosity?', *JSSR* xlii (2003), 269–78

Tiptaft, N. (ed.), *Religion in Birmingham*, Warley 1972

Todd, S., 'Young women, work and leisure in inter-war England', *HJ* xlviii (2005), 789–809

Tomlinson, D., *The post-Evangelical*, London 1995

Tomlinson, J., *The politics of decline: understanding post-war Britain*, Harlow 2000 edn

——'Economic growth, economic decline', in Burk, *British Isles*, 63–89

Toulis, N., *Believing identity: Pentecostalism and the mediation of Jamaican ethnicity and gender in England*, Oxford–New York 1997

Towler, R., 'The social status of the Anglican minister', in R. Robertson (ed.), *Sociology of religion*, London 1969, 443–50

—— *The need for certainty: a sociological study of conventional religion*, London 1984

—— and A. Chamberlain, 'Common religion', *Sociological Yearbook of Religion in Britain* viii (1973), 1–25

Tudur Jones, R., *Congregationalism in England, 1662–1962*, London 1962

Turner, B. and T. Rennell, *When Daddy came home: how family life changed for ever in 1945*, London 1995

Upton, C., *A history of Birmingham*, Chichester 1993

Village, A. and L. J. Francis, 'An anatomy of change: profiling cohort differences in beliefs and attitudes amongst Anglicans in England', *Journal of Anglican Studies* viii (2009), 59–81

Voas, D., 'Explaining change over time in religious involvement', in Collins–Mayo and Dandelion, *Religion and youth*, 26–32

—— and A. Crockett, 'Religion in Britain: neither believing nor belonging', *Sociology* xxxix (2005), 11–28

Wadsworth, M. E. J. and S. R. Freeman, 'Generation differences in beliefs: a cohort study of stability and change in religious beliefs', *BJS* xxxiv (1983), 416–37

Walford, R., *The growth of 'New London' in suburban Middlesex (1918–1945) and the response of the Church of England*, Lampeter 2007

Walker, A., *Restoring the kingdom: the radical Christianity of the house church movement*, Guildford 1998

Walker, M. J., 'Baptist worship in the twentieth century', in Clements, *Baptists in the twentieth century*, 21–30

Walter, T. and G. Davie, 'The religiosity of women in the modern west', *BJS* xix (1998), 640–60

Walvin, J., *A child's world: a social history of English childhood, 1800–1914*, London 1982

—— *Victorian values*, London 1987

Ward, P., *Growing up Evangelical: youth work and the making of a subculture*, London 1996

—— 'The tribes of Evangelicalism', in G. Cray and others, *The post-Evangelical debate*, London 1997, 19–34

—— *Liquid Church*, Carlisle 2002

—— (ed.), *The Church and youth ministry*, Oxford 1995

Warren, H. A., 'The shift from character to personality in mainline Protestant thought, 1935–1945', *Church History* xlvii (1998), 537–55

Watson, J. R., *The English hymn: a critical and historical study*, Oxford 1999

Webster, A., 'Parish magazines', *Theology* xlvii (July 1943), 156–9

Webster, P. and I. Jones, 'New music and the "Evangelical style" in the Church of England, c. 1956–1991', in M. Smith (ed.), *British Evangelical identities*, i, Milton Keynes 2008, 167–79

Weeks, J., *Sex, politics and society: the regulation of sexuality since 1800*, 2nd edn, London 1989

Welsby, P. A., *A history of the Church of England, 1945–1980*, Oxford 1984

White, H., *Metahistory: historical imagination in nineteenth century Europe*, Baltimore 1975

White, J. W, *Intergenerational religious education: models, theory and prescription for interage life and learning in the faith community*, Birmingham, AL 1988

Whitfield, S. J., *The culture of the Cold War*, Baltimore 1991

Whyte, W., 'The *Jackie* generation: girls' magazines, pop music and the discourse revolution', in Garnett, Harris, Grimley, Whyte and Williams, *Redefining Christian Britain*, 128–37

Wickham, E. R., *Church and people in an industrial city*, Cambridge 1957

Wiebe, H., 'Benjamin Britten, the "national faith" and the animation of history in 1950s England', *Representations* xciii (Winter 2006), 76–105

Wilkinson, A., *Dissent or conform? War, peace and the English Churches, 1900–1945*, London 1986

Wilkinson, J. L., *Church in black and white: the Black Christian tradition in 'mainstream' Churches in England: a white response and testimony*, Edinburgh 1993

—— R. Wilkinson and J. H. Evans, Jr, *Inheritors together: Black people in the Church of England*, London 1985

Williams, J. G., *Worship and the modern child: a book for parents, clergy and teachers*, London 1957

Williams, R., *Keywords: a vocabulary of culture and society*, London 1984

Williams, S. C., 'The problem of belief: the place of oral history in the study of popular religion', *OH* xxiv/2 (1996), 27–34

—— *Religious belief and popular culture in Southwark, c. 1880–1939*, Oxford 1999

Wills, A., 'Delinquency, masculinity and citizenship in England, 1950–1970', *P&P* clxxxvii (May 2005), 157–85

Wilmott, P., *The evolution of a community: a study of Dagenham after forty years*, London 1963

Wilson, B., 'Time, generations and sectarianism', in B. Wilson (ed.), *The social impact of new religious movements*, New York 1981, 217–34

Wilson, D. Smith, 'A new look at the affluent worker: the good working mother in post-war Britain', *TCBH* xvii (2006), 206–29

Wilson, E., *Only half way to paradise: women in post-war Britain, 1945–68*, London 1980

Wimber, J. with K. Springer, *Power evangelism: signs and wonders today*, London 1985

Wolffe, J., '"And there's another country ...": religion, the state and British identities', in Parsons, *Growth of religious diversity*, ii. 85–122

—— 'The religions of the silent majority', in Parsons, *Growth of religious diversity*, i. 305–46

——'Religion and secularization', in P. Johnson (ed.), *Twentieth century Britain: economic, social and cultural change*, London–New York 1994, 427–41

—— '"Praise to the holiest in the height": hymns and church music', in J. Wolffe (ed.), *Religion in Victorian Britain, V: Culture and empire*, Manchester 1997, 59–100

—— (ed.), *Evangelical faith and public zeal: Evangelicals and society in Britain, 1780–1980*, London 1995

Wuthnow, R., 'Recent pattern of secularisation: a problem of generations?', ASR xli (1976), 850–67

Yates, N., *Love now, pay later? Sex and religion in the fifties and sixties*, London 2010

Yeo, S., *Religious and voluntary organisations in crisis*, London 1976

Young, M. and P. Wilmott, *Family and kinship in east London*, London 1957

—— and P. Wilmott, *Family and class in a London suburb*, London 1960

—— and P. Wilmott, *The symmetrical family: a study of work and leisure in the London region*, London 1973

Unpublished papers and dissertations

Brown, C. G., 'The secularisation decade: the haemorrhage of the British Churches in the 1960s', 'Decline of Christendom in Western Europe' conference, Paris 1997

—— 'Secularisation in the 1960s', University of Birmingham secularisation seminar, Feb. 1998

Brown, W. and M. Brown, 'The hidden poor: a report to consider the needs of peoples living in the large outer-ring council estates of the Birmingham diocese', Birmingham 1995

Bussell, I., 'Church placement: semester paper' [on Cotteridge Church], unpubl. paper, Queens Foundation for Ecumenical Theological Education, Birmingham 1997

Collins, S., 'Young people's faith in late modernity', PhD, Surrey 1997

Harris, A., 'Transformations in English Catholic spirituality and popular religion, 1945–1980', DPhil. Oxford 2008

Hill, C., 'Living in two worlds: a study of the variety and characteristics of church life and policies in selected Church of England parishes', PhD, Open University 1988

Hill, M. J., 'Churchgoing as a social process: a study of three Methodist churches in the Edinburgh and Forth circuit', PhD, Glasgow 1989

Parker, S., 'Faith on the home front: aspects of church life and popular religion in Birmingham, 1939–1945', PhD, Birmingham 2003

Perry, A., 'Anglican Christianity in Birmingham, 1945–1975', MPhil. Birmingham 2010

Sykes, R. P. M., 'Popular religion in Dudley and the Gornals, c. 1914–1965', PhD, Wolverhampton 1999

Taylor, C., 'British churches and Jamaican migration: a study of religion and identities, 1948–65', PhD, Anglia 2002

Walford, R., 'As by magic: the growth of the diocese of London north of the Thames, 1920–1939', PhD, Anglia 2003

Index

adolescence: as life stage, 19, 60, 68, 74, 90, 179, 186; as metaphor for cultural change 163, 174, 189; patterns of belief and practice in, 59–61, 65–6, 68, 87, 103, 136, 170, 182, 186. *See also* young people; youth clubs and organisations.

affluence 10, 12, 77, 83, 89, 91, 150, 141, 167, 184

African-Caribbean Christianity, 33–4, 35–6, 37–40, 45, 46, 111, 132–6, 136

age: age, denomination/churchmanship and religious affiliation, 36–7, 58–61, 65–8, 96; age, ethnicity and religious affiliation, 33–4, 135–6; age, gender and church affiliation, 34–6, 82, 185; age-related patterns as a factor in secularisation, 11, 13, 17, 96, 176, 181, 185–6; and attitudes to changing community life, 146; and attitudes to evangelism and faith-sharing, 169–71, 185; and attitudes to moral/ethical issues, 156, 163–6; and attitudes to worship, 106, 109, 110, 114, 117, 120–2; and church health, 41, 43, 45, 47, 50, 69, 71, 176; and church-leaving/returning, 68–9; as component of personal or collective identity, 1, 3, 12, 18–22, 89–92, 178–9, 188–9; distribution within case-study churches, 39, 41, 43, 44–5, 46, 48, 49, 51, 55; as metaphor for cultural change, 162–3, 174, 189. *See also* children; generation; middle-age; old age; worship.

Aitken, Revd Robert (Baptist minister), 75 n. 17, 88, 93, 130, 159

All Saints', Kings Heath (Anglican), 43

Alpha Course, 45, 131

'alternative worship', *see* worship

Alum Rock, 45, 128, 132. *See also* Grenfell Baptist Church, Alum Rock; Thornton Road Fellowship (Baptist).

Ammerman, Nancy, 126

Andrew, Fr Agnellus (Roman Catholic priest), 161

Appleford, Revd Patrick (Anglican clergyman and hymn writer), 112

Aston, Birmingham, 29, 32

Aston Parish Church (St Peter and St Paul), 25

Attlee, Clement, 152

baby-boom, 16

'baby-boomers', *see* generation

'baby-busters', *see* generation

Balsall Heath (Birmingham), 13, 38–9, 102, 132, 145. *See also* Moseley Road Methodist Church, Balsall Heath.

Barnes, Rt Revd E. W. (Anglican bishop of Birmingham), 137

Beaumont, Revd Geoffrey (Anglican clergyman and composer), 112

Berry, Revd Sidney M. (Congregationalist minister), 47

Bible, 11, 38, 48, 71, 101, 131, 185; bible-reading habits of churchgoers, 44, 46; traditional and contemporary language translations, 105–6

Bird, Matt, 17–18

Birmingham: civic pride, 26, 30; culture, heritage, tourism, 30; industry, 13, 25, 29, 30, 50, 125, 151, 163; 'inner ring' areas, 13, 27–8, 30, 33–4, 38, 45, 73, 125, 134, 138, 153; 'outer ring' areas, 13, 27–8, 33, 57, 66, 124–5, 132, 136–43; politics, 26, 150–1; population, 25–9, 31–3, 36–7. *See also* Alum Rock; Aston; Balsall Heath; Bournville; Brandwood; Castle Bromwich; Cotteridge; Fox Hollies; Handsworth; Kingstanding; Lozells; Nechells; 'Pitt Heath'; Selly Oak; Sparkbrook; Sparkhill; Sutton Coldfield; and individual churches.

Birmingham cathedrals: St Chad's (Roman Catholic), 50; St Philip's (Anglican), 25